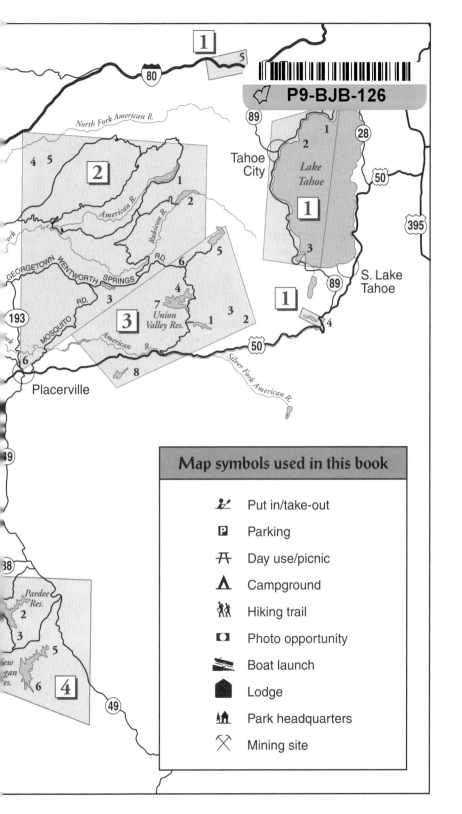

P9-BJB-126

North Fork American R.

1

5

89

80

1

2

Tahoe City

28

Lake Tahoe

50

395

2

4 5

American R.

Rubicon R.

1

2

89

1

GEORGETOWN

WENTWORTH

SPRINGS

RD.

6

5

S. Lake Tahoe

193

RD.

3

4

7

Union Valley Res.

3

3

2

1

4

MOSQUITO

3

50

6

American R.

1

Silver Fork American R.

Placerville

8

49

38

Pardee Res.

2

3

5

ew gan es.

6

4

49

Map symbols used in this book

🚶	Put in/take-out
🅿	Parking
⊓	Day use/picnic
△	Campground
🚶	Hiking trail
▭	Photo opportunity
🛶	Boat launch
🏠	Lodge
🏚	Park headquarters
⚒	Mining site

DEDICATION

To the Memory of John Stoffle
—June 6, 1953-June 19, 1999—

Fellow paddler, friend and mentor who died
while boating the South Yuba River. His presence continues
to be missed by many in the Sacramento paddling community.

Up the Lake
with a Paddle

Canoe and Kayak Guide
Volume 2

Tahoe Region, Crystal Basin, and Foothill Reservoirs

BY WILLIAM VAN DER VEN

FineEdge.com

IMPORTANT LEGAL NOTICE AND DISCLAIMER
Outdoor activities are an assumed risk sport. This book cannot take the place of appropriate instruction for paddling, swimming, or lifesaving techniques. Bodies of water, by nature, contain hazards and they change with time and conditions. Every effort has been made to make this guide as accurate as possible, but it is the ultimate responsibility of the paddler to judge his or her ability and act accordingly.

The editors, author, publishers, and distributors accept no liability for any errors or omissions in this book or for any injuries or losses incurred from using this book.

Credits
Cover Photos: William Van der Ven
Author Photo: By Suzanne M. Johnson
Photographs within text: William Van der Ven
Book Design: Sue Athmann and Elayne Wallis
Maps and Diagrams: Suzanne Athmann
Editor: Réanne Douglass

Library of Congress Cataloging-in-Publication Data

Van der Ven, William, 1949—
    Up the lake with a paddle: canoe and kayak guide / by William Van der Ven. — 1st ed.
        p. cm.
        Contents: v.   1. Sierra Foothills and Sacramento Region
        ISBN 0-938665-54-5 (v.1)
        1. Canoes and canoeing—California, Northern—Guidebooks.
2. Kayaking—California, Northern—Guidebooks.   3. California, Northern—Guidebooks.   I. Title.
GV776.C2V36 1998   98-16844
917.94—dc21   CIP

Address requests for permission to:
FineEdge.com, 13589 Clayton Lane, Anacortes, WA 98221
www.FineEdge.com
Printed in the United States of America
First Edition

CONTENTS

CONTENTS

Acknowledgments

Without the support of Louise, my wife and friend, none of these volumes would have been possible. She kept the wolf away from the door and every once in a while I fed her some ammunition. To my parents, Peter and Lydia, I owe a deep gratitude; they stoked the fires of learning by introducing us to the world of books and museums.

To the special folks at Kinko's on Madison—Douglas, Crystal and Lillian. Your professional demeanor and cheerful assistance are gratefully appreciated—get ready for Volume III!

Within the paddling community, I am indebted to Dan Crandle, owner of Current Adventures, for accepting me into the Current Adventure Family, and trusting me to take on new "Adventures." Thanks, Dan, for the time and paychecks—both necessary for writing my book! John Seals and Lisa Ross, former Dagger Reps: Many, many thanks for your support and friendship; your move to South Carolina, while understandable, closed a fond chapter and you will be missed. Colleen, your organizational skills have not gone unnoticed; I could plan my research around your scheduling. To Kurt Renner: The years you spent instructing me have come home to roost; I could not have written the section on boats without your foundation—however, any mistakes or errors are mine! John Weed: By training me as a respectable guide, you allowed me to re-think ways of presenting information in this book—but I still can't carry a note to save my soul! It's always a pleasure, Dr. Mark, to bounce ideas and concepts off you. And finally, Adam Scherer; your "kick in the butt" brought me around and I never looked back. Thanks, hombre!

I want to thank Don and Réanne Douglass for taking a chance on me the first time around and for having the patience to walk me through this business. Within the Fine Edge "family," thanks to Cindy Kamler for her suggestions in the initial manuscript and to Sue Athmann and Elayne Wallis for their ability to produce a book under a tight time-frame.

And, to Gale E. Stockdale, "the Mogul," an officer and a gentleman of the old school who hired a paddler to do a sailor's job: thanks for the flexibility and patience as I worked in your chandlery!

Lastly, to publishers Henry Holt & Company for permission to reprint excerpts from *All Colts Are Crazy in the Spring* from <u>The Old Man and the Boy</u> by Robert Ruark, ©1953,1954,1955,1956,1957 by Robert C. Ruark, and to Houghton Mifflin, to reprint excerpts from <u>The Wilderness World of John Muir</u>, edited by Edwin Way Teale, ©1954 by Edwin Way Teal. Copyright renewed 1982 by Nellie D. Teal.

Introduction

The publication of my first volume of *Up the Lake with a Paddle* brought a response that caught me off guard, mainly requests for more historical background and other "interesting trivia" on the lakes and rivers of California. As a result, in Volume II I have provided more information than "just the facts, ma'am." I have included some of my own experiences, as well as information on the geology, plants, animals, and human history of the areas.

Whether paddling past the intermixed layers of dark rock confining the waters of little Oxbow Lake, enjoying a foothill reservoir surrounded by rolling hills of chaparral and oak, or gliding past an expanse of sparkling granite near a high Sierra lake, you may wonder how the layers were formed, what kind of oaks those are, or what makes the granite sparkle. You'll find the answers to your questions in the text.

The waters of the foothill reservoirs almost always cover former Native American sites, Gold Rush communities, mines, or other places of historical interest. You'll find written sketches describing the places over which you are paddling. The feature called In the Eddy furnishes more detailed information on places, names and events, and there is a definitive, bibliography in the Appendix to guide you to other sources, as well as books, articles, and videos that cover the sport of paddling.

In a new section, I have provided information on choosing boats and the gear necessary to paddle these beautiful places. For those of you interested in the background history of traditional paddle designs you will find Some Thoughts On Boats an interesting read.

Why have I chosen some places and not others? In general, each destination or paddle area came under the following considerations:

Driving time and accessibility: Is the driving time from Sacramento to the location between two to six hours? Would local paddlers and their families be willing to make the drive for a day or weekend at this body of water? If yes, what are the access roads like? If a shuttle is necessary, how long and difficult is it? Are there amenities here for the family? (In some places where accessibility is fine, the scenery too good to miss, but the comfort margin slim, I have included the area anyway.) Would kids be safe and have fun, too? What are the put-ins/ take-outs like? Is there a launch fee? If so, how much?

Paddle difficulty: Does the place meet the definition of quiet water, wind and boat wakes aside? How many miles is the paddle? Can a part of the area be paddled and still provide the paddler with a sense of accomplishment and fulfillment? Is the paddle area for novices and families, or is a higher skill level necessary to ensure safety? Are there portages? How many, how hard, and how far? Are there hazards such as submerged rocks, tree stumps, sweepers, or man-made obstacles. Will wind and weather be a factor? **Will the paddler want to return?** Is there more to explore than can be done in one day or one weekend? What other activities are available? Are there nearby hiking, walking, or biking trails? Are there interpretive trails or historical sites to visit? If you want to spend the night, are developed campsites available? If so, how many and what is the cost? What condition are these sites in and what facilities do they provide? Also included is information on undeveloped camping sites—the old fashioned kind—that may or may not have toilets, fire rings, or other amenities.

Note: Families interested in overnight paddle adventures in non-established camping areas should invest in some sort of portable toilet system. This is not only a health issue, but sensitivity to the pressures being placed by Man on the environment.

With this guide book in hand, you'll have all the information you need for a fun-filled and safe family-adventure.

May all your paddles bring health to the body, joy to the heart, and peace to the spirit!

Wilderness Ethics

With the increased pressure on our forests, lakes, rivers and backcountry in general, the need for a philosophy of use followed by comon sense guidelines has become mandatory.

It is not just the careless, casual camper who needs to be educated on wilderness preservation, but the experiencd outdoors person who thinks he is following correct skills when today, they are not.

One such concept that has evolved recently to address the heavy impact on our landscape is based on the principle of "going light." Originally directed toward the backpacker, it has now taken over as the ethos of all participants in wilderness activities. The idea behind this practice is to:

"...spare the land and the sensibilities of other people. You choose your gear, your route" [or paddle] and your schedule with the welfare of the wilderness in mind."*

For an in-depth understanding of going light by using low-impact skills, and the eduational program of leave No Trace Camping, read John Hart's: *Walking Softly in the Wilderness* or contact the National Outdoor Leadership School whose internet addres is: www.Int.org

So, as you enjoy the paddles and journeys that your canoe or kayak may bring, remember to tread lightly on the land, and leave behind only the boat wake of your passing.

*Excerpt taken from *Walking Softly in the Wilderness,* by John Hart. Published by Sierra Club Books, San Francisco, CA, 3rd ed., 1998, Pg. 7.

Using This Guide

Up the Lake with a Paddle, Volume II, has four chapters divided into paddling areas. For example, Chapter 1 covers Lake Tahoe and Tahoe Basin Lakes; on the North Shore, Paddling Area 1 describes Agatam County Beach from Crystal Bay or Flick Point. In Chapter 2, Tahoe National Forest Lakes, French Meadows and Hell Hole reservoirs are among the paddle areas described. Information on each body of water is given below each chapter title and includes the county and national forest as well as its size and elevation.

Trip Length lets you know whether the place can be paddled in an afternoon, a full day, or whether an overnight stay makes more sense.

Paddling Distances: Unless otherwise specified, all distances are taken from a 1:24,000, 7.5-minute USGS topographical map. The distances were obtained by using either a topographic map measurer from American Map Corporation or an official USGS 1:24,000-scale ruler made by Mansfield-Sterling.

Difficulty pertains to the effects of wind and weather, obstacles in the water, and other conditions that may affect paddling.

Season: Lets you know the best time of the year to paddle the body of water. Although some reservoirs, such as the ones in the foothills, are open to boating all year, spring or fall may be a better time in which to appreciate their natural beauty.

Maps: The list includes the pertinent USGS topographical map sheets and, because the majority of these do not reflect current conditions, secondary sources. Area/Road Maps show the best routes to the region and paddle area.

Access: Directions for driving to the paddle area are given. While generally these are either the most direct or the only way to get there, I sometimes include a "meander route" that highlights scenic, as well as historic, places of interest along the way.

Highlights includes good and bad points, parking and camping information, bear warnings, nearby attractions and more.

Description: This is the heart of the book. I give you the "nuts & bolts," of each body of water to give you a feel for the paddle.

Quiet Water

In a canoe you slip through the landscape without disturbing it. You make no noise. You advance with a 'silken silence' through the water. You see more. You approach wild creatures more closely, see the wildlife of remote swamps and stretches of streams not visited by any other craft ... You can enter the "in-between land"–too wet to approach on foot, too shallow to reach in a larger maneuverable craft.

–Ann Zwinger and Edwin Way Teale, *A Conscious Stillness: Two Naturalists on Thoreau's Rivers*[1]

Just what is "quiet water" boating and is quiet water really "quiet?"

Quiet water boating is canoeing or kayaking on open bodies of water such as lakes or rivers. Quiet or flat water is found in bodies of water with little or no current where the main source of surface activity is wind or boat wakes.

Wind is the primary culprit in turning quiet water rough. Wind can bring rapid changes in the weather and is an indicator of unstable air that can create potentially dangerous summer storms. The wind and lightning accompanying sudden thunder storms are the primary hazards of open-water boating on lakes, bays and reservoirs.

The direction of the wind can make or break a paddler's day. Paddling into a continuous headwind blowing 10 to 15 miles per hour can become physically grueling and mentally draining, with the added worry of capsizing.

Watch for information on wind and weather in the description of each paddle. Choose those conditions that help ensure a quiet-water paddle.

[1]Zwinger, Ann, *A Conscious Stillness: Two Naturalists on Thoreau's Rivers*, HarperCollins Publishers, ©1982 by Ann Zwinger and the Estate of Edwin Way Teale

Some Thoughts On Canoes and Kayaks

The timeless question . . . canoe or kayak or maybe both?

The answer may revolve around your style of paddling and the other priorities you place on a boat. Let's look at the advantages and disadvantages of canoes and kayaks. Bear in mind, however, that your choice should "start the juices flowing" and put a BIG smile on your face when you think about your next paddling adventure in *that* boat! That should be the bottom line when you make your final decision.

> "The movement of a canoe is like a reed in the wind. Silence is part of it. It is part of the medium through which it floats, the sky, the water, the shores. A man is part of his canoe and therefore part of all it knows."
>
> *—Sigurd F. Olsen*

A Canoe for You?

The mystique of the canoe and its use by Native Americans, voyageurs, trappers and guides has become an integral part of American and Canadian frontier lore. Use of the birch bark canoe in opening the West has never been fully documented, but whenever its use was mentioned the craft's versatility, load capacity and ease of repair were always praised.

Indeed, the canoe continues to be the boat of choice offered to legions of scouts, campers and weekend boaters who visit the many lodges, camps and retreats throughout the United States and Canada.

Many people first use canoes at either a scout or summer camp. Subsequently, upon retirement or when broadening their sports interests, they return to that first love affair—the canoe.

It has always been a joy for me to watch a retiree kneel in a canoe and catch the twinkle in his or her eye as the years drop off and childhood memories return, to witness proud parents brag about canoe journeys past, or to see boys and girls running their hands over the gunwales, climbing in and out of the boat and pleading with their parents to take them canoeing.

Canoe Basics

Remember! Most reputable dealers either provide a demo program or are willing to let you try out their boats prior to purchase. Check with your dealer about his demo program. Furthermore, only by paddling the canoe or kayak will you be certain if it is the right model for your needs.

The canoe is your friend.

There is no such thing as the perfect canoe . . . or kayak, for that matter. What there is depends on what compromises you are willing to make in the design of the boat to achieve your paddling needs. The design features of a canoe dictate its use. Certain features—shortness in length, round bottoms and sharp upturn in their ends (called rocker)—allow maximum mobility and the opportunity to enjoy the adrenaline rush of white water. On the other hand, canoes built for cruising long distances and carrying lots of gear are longer in length, may have a shallow arch or a shallow-V bottom, and provide ample room for gear. Here, the longer length is important for speed and storage, and the two styles of hull will allow for easier tracking toward a given reference point. Both styles of design, whether for white water or touring, have similarities that make the craft identifiable as a canoe.

First, to make the best decision, you must make an honest evaluation of how you will use that canoe. The dream of paddling the Yukon for the summer may be, in reality, weekend paddles on local lakes and slow rivers. It's okay to accept that and choose a boat for weekend paddling rather than high adventure. If your adventurous dream becomes a reality, you can always rent the proper canoe.

If you are thinking of a good all-around boat for the quiet waters of a lake or slow river, then five design elements should be considered: length, width, depth, rocker and bottom shape.

Length

Longer canoes *track* (move in a straight line) better, therefore are usually faster and easier to paddle. Their length provides some degree of stability missing in a shorter boat, if width is not a factor. Length also allows you to carry heavier loads without compromising on the speed of the canoe. As you increase your paddle strokes, the canoe's length provides a longer glide with each stroke, allowing for a more efficient paddling experience.

These attributes are important when paddling on quiet water where distances are more important than negotiating obstacles or tight turns. Too much length, however, may work against you. Usually, the longer the canoe, the more weight it will have and the less maneuverability. This is where the second design element comes into play.

Width

A boat's width is related to a concern for stability. You need to have enough width to offset the narrowness of a long canoe built primarily for speed. The width of a canoe is measured at two points—the boat's beam and its waterline. *Beam* is the distance between the two wide ends on top of the boat. *Waterline width* refers to the widest point of the boat as it rests in the water. Too much beam width and paddling efficiency is lost because you cannot bring your forward stroke close to the centerline of the boat, thereby losing forward momentum. A broad waterline width increases carrying capacity and provides more stability, but you have to paddle harder because the hull pushes more water. As a rule of thumb, the wider the boat, the more stable; however, you sacrifice boat handling characteristics with increased width. The end result is a canoe that is ". . . stable as a bathtub . . . but paddles like a barge."

Again, it becomes a tradeoff that you will have to consider prior to purchase.

Depth

The depth of a canoe is measured at the centerline from the top edge (called a *gunwale*; but pronounced "gunnel") of the boat to the floor. Obviously, the greater the depth, the more load the canoe will carry. The high waterline will keep the boat dry from spray, but it may become susceptible to winds. A high freeboard acts as a sail, allowing the wind to push one end of the canoe away from your direction of travel, called *side slipping* or *weather cocking*.

Rocker

I've mentioned the importance of rocker in whitewater canoes. *Rocker* is the amount of curvature beginning at the center and running to the ends on the bottom of a canoe or kayak. Rocker should also be considered when purchasing a touring canoe. With the exception of the design of the *stem* (the rake of a boat's hull at the bow and stern), rocker is one of the most distinctive design elements of a canoe. Therefore, its influence is felt almost immediately upon paddling the canoe.

Extreme rocker allows for high maneuverability, just what you need in a whitewater environment. Conversely, no rocker increases tracking ability at the expense of maneuvering—great for racing or beating the squall to your campsite. A moderate rocker gives you a little of both.

If you are going to paddle primarily on lakes or use your craft as a workout boat, then a *straight keel line* with no rocker is the way to go. If you want to use your canoe in lakes and slow rivers, some rocker would be advisable. How much rocker? Again, this is where taking a demo paddle in a variety of canoes will help you answer that question.

Bottom Shape

To understand the differences in design of a canoe hull's bottom, line up several canoes and look down their ends. There are primarily three main shapes of hull: flat-bottom, rounded and V-shaped. From there come variations to suit different paddling conditions. The edge of a hull where an abrupt change or transition occurs is called its *chine*. A *soft chine* means a gentle rounding or "softening" of the bottom as it transitions into the side of the canoe, whereas a *hard chine* means an extreme or abrupt edge delineating the hull from the side of the canoe.

A *flat bottomed canoe* has *primary (initial) stability*, but upon encountering rough water—chop from wind or boat wake—the canoe's stability is lost if the craft's leaning exceeds its critical angle. A slightly *rounded boat* appears more tipsy when you first get in, but given the same rough conditions as above, it has more *reserve* or *secondary stability* because you can lean the boat toward the gunwales and feel the critical angle before all stability is lost. However, a more rounded boat will not stop at its critical angle but keep on rolling until it is completely over. Not much help to you there!

To combine the initial stability of a flat bottomed hull with the rounded bottom hull's more secondary stability in rough water, the shallow arched canoe hull was developed. This design is not new. It was built into some of the birch bark canoes of Native Americans and later into the large load-bearing canoes of the voyageurs.

A *V-shaped hull* is designed to maintain tracking and therefore increase speed on flat water. The deeper the V, the more pronounced straight-line direction a canoe will sustain, but the trade-off is that it will have less stability. To off-set the deep V-shaped hull's instability, some canoes are built with a shallow V configuration.

One canoe manufacturer specializes in canoes with hulls configured into a shallow arch. A slight V at the bow, to initiate tracking, then a subtle arching outward along the length of the hull gives these canoes great stability, speed and overall versatility.

Note on carrying capacity: Most canoe manufacturers avoid listing the weight a canoe can carry. There is a sound reason for this. Too many times novice paddlers read those numbers as gospel and proceed to load their canoes right down to the last ounce . . . no matter the weather or water conditions to be paddled. The best answer to "How much can I carry in this size canoe?" is: "It depends on the conditions under which it is paddled and how much gear you must take." In general, a good touring canoe is 17 or 18 feet long with volume enough to carry your gear safely.

The Innards of a Canoe

Although you may order a canoe with a variety of options and custom fittings, most canoes arrive from the manufacturer with these items:

Bow caps and stern caps: Used to help stiffen the ends of the canoe.

Gunwales: The top edges of a canoe running the length of the boat. These rails may be made of either wood, aluminum or vinyl. Wooden gunwales are more traditional, but require extra attention; aluminum and vinyl cost less but are less aesthetic. Wooden rails are sometimes split down the center into an inwale facing the inside of the boat and an outwale running the outside length of the canoe. Some wooden gunwales have slots or holes in them. These slotted rails are tie-down points for lashing down gear. The purpose of gunwales is to provide stiffness and form to the design of the hull.

Thwarts: Made traditionally of wood, many canoes now come with aluminum thwarts. Their primary purpose is to provide structural support to the hull.

Seats: Besides providing a comfortable placement for paddling, seats also help stiffen the hull of the canoe. The common materials in most canoe seats are wood and cane. Synthetic straps, aluminum framework, fiberglass and kevlar are also utilized. Most canoe manufacturers provide fixed seats as standard but as an extra, will build a sliding seat that allows you to trim the boat by sliding the seat forward or backward.

Flotation: Aluminum canoes did not float high enough to clear obstacles, so some means of flotation became necessary. Traditionally, vinyl bags filled with air were lashed (part of the outfitting on a whitewater canoe) either to the bow or stern ends or in the center of the canoe. Modern canoes are manufactured with the choice (primarily as a weight consideration) of having a sealed compartment built into the boat. These air tanks keep the canoe afloat when the boat is filled with water. Whitewater canoes and canoes used on expeditions where rivers are to be run, commonly add additional flotation for safety.

Protection: Some boaters, especially those who paddle more moving water, add kevlar strips to the bottom of the bow and stern of their canoe. This protects the canoes bottom ends from abrasion and impact. You may do the job yourself with the purchase of a skid-plate kit, or special order a set to be placed on your canoe at the factory. One manufacturer even molds the skid plates into the hull during construction, eliminating the drag and maintaining the appearance of the craft.

To put the whole thing into perspective, a good cruising doubles (as opposed to a solo) canoe should, at a minimum, be 17 feet in length, have enough depth and volume to carry the combined weights of the paddlers and their gear without sacrificing seaworthiness and safety. It should be designed with the proper strength to withstand abuse, yet be light enough to portage. Finally, you should have complete trust that you can paddle the boat in a variety of conditions. These conditions may include still waters, where distances are measured in days traveled, to the choppy swells of a wind-blown reservoir.

What About Canoe Paddles?

A Bit 'O Tradition
Part of the initiation into the realms of "master canoeist" was the ability to carve your own personal paddle. This blade had to show the "right stuff" in its design as well as its aesthetic appearance. The end product was a functional tool with a blade that was able to withstand long-

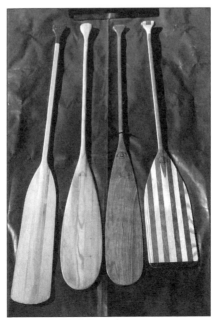

Figure A: Paddle styles

17

term abuse on rocks and gravel. The shaft was strong enough to take the torque of positioning a fully-laden canoe exactly, and subsequently, to a constant cadence. At the same time, the shaft could not be so rigid as to lose the flex needed for absorbing shocks produced during the paddling cycle.

The finished product was carved out of either maple, ash, birch or even spruce. These paddles averaged 60 inches in length, had a blade width between 7 or 8 inches and a blade length ranging between 26 to 30 inches. They followed three basic styles: *The Ottertail* (sloping shoulders, straight sides & flat tip); *Beavertail* (oval); and the *Sugar Island* (a racing paddle developed from an earlier native design, then modified by Canadians for racing purposes).

Because the majority of the paddling took place either in a sitting-kneeling and even standing position, the old paddles had to be long to provide " . . . more leverage and a deeper, fuller sweep with the blade."

Although there are still individuals who can carve a paddle that fits the above requirements, the majority of us have to depend on a manufacturer's end product. Luckily, there are some excellent companies making superior paddles, even better crafted, I dare say, than some of the early wooden blades.

In fact, the issue is not just the quality of the paddle, but a combination of an individual's skill level, *together with* the correct paddle, that allows one to confidently maneuver a canoe in any type of water.

Paddles are like the boats they propel—certain ones are better suited for distances, others for speed in racing, and some are designed for precision blade placement in white water. These attributes can be broken down into five design elements: grip, length, blade style, weight, and material.

The Grip

Grips can be broken down into four styles.

Pear grip: A rounded shape that is comfortable when grasped from almost any angle. Usually the choice of most recreational and touring boaters.

Flared grip: Characteristic of the NorthWoods Guide Paddle, the end is flat-topped, then flares as it descends into the shaft. The flared portion is thinned considerably to provide additional "spring" upon recovery of the paddle cycle. (Not pictured.)

T-grip: The grip of choice by most whitewater boaters, free-style paddlers and racers. These paddlers do a lot of turning and therefore need a grip that will provide a constant reading on the angle of the blade in the water.

Figure B: Canoe grips

Offset Grip: Best on bent-shaft paddles because it positions your hand forward where the primary force of the forward stroke becomes the most effective. [See Fig. B.]

Paddle Length

As I mentioned earlier, traditional paddle length was anywhere from 48 to 60 inches, with lengths of 84 inches not unheard of. These lengths were necessary because of the varied paddling positions—sitting, kneeling and standing—common to old time canoeists.

The archaic method of determining proper length is best described by Bill Riviere in his book, *The L. L. Bean Guide to the Outdoors*, page 233: "The old time formula for length called for a paddle that reached from your toes to your chin for the bow, or from toes to eyes for the stern."

Modern paddlers require shorter paddles because they do not use the same recovery strokes as the early canoeists, and standing is not an option for the majority of today's paddlers.

To determine the correct paddle length for a canoeist, the most common method is to sit in a canoe while it is on the water. Place the paddle blade into the water until the blade's throat is deep in the water. The paddle's grip should be at your shoulder. A less reliable method, but one that provides a close general fit, is to place a paddle vertically on the floor, then place the grip into your armpit; all things being equal, a snug fit suggests the proper length of paddle for basic recreational paddling.

Note: These guidelines are primarily for the straight-shaft paddle; the proper length of a bent-shaft blade is usually approximately 2 inches shorter than a corresponding straight-shafted paddle.

The Bent-Shaft Paddle

To further complicate the waters, the recent innovation of an angled shaft or bent-shaft paddle provides an additional dimension to the quest for the perfect paddle.

The story behind the origin of the bent-shaft design has two versions. The first suggests that a paddle manufacturer was paddling with a friend who developed a sore wrist and could not maintain a vertical position of the blade through the power stroke. No matter how he tried to position his wrist, the angle continued to aggravate the tendons and increase the pain. By positioning the shaft vertically on the blade of a paddle, the paddlemaker's partner could keep the blade reasonably vertical throughout the majority of the power phase of the stroke and therefore reduce the pain to his wrist.

The second, and more technical, version is based on the fact that the bent-shaft paddle increases the efficiency of a racing canoe's forward movement. When propelling a canoe with a standard paddle, the forward motion of the power stroke forces a canoe downward; the secondary phase, or release point, reduces the downward pull of the canoe causing the boat to "bob" upward. This up and down movement reduces the speed of the canoe. With a bent shaft, the forward part of the power stroke is maintained as a longer part of the cycle, thus reducing the bobbing effect. It's the short, quick strokes of a racing paddler that the bent-shaft blade attains peak efficiency.

Both versions are correct in describing the usefulness of the bent-shaft paddle. Modern bent-shaft paddles come in a variety of angles and lengths. Today's best bet on a bent-shaft would be a paddle approximately 2 inches shorter than your straight shaft, that maintains some flex in the shaft and contains a 12° bend. Finally, the blade itself should be symmetrical.

"The subject of blade-width has kept many a campfire discussion going far into the night."

—Bill Riviere

Blade Style

Three primary blade shapes found on canoe paddles [see Paddles, Fig. A].

Beavertail: The traditional and most recognizable of all canoe paddles, 24" to 26" in length by 6"-7" in width. The beavertail has its origins in an earlier design called the Malecite, no doubt named after the Indian tribe that lived in the woodlands of New Brunswick and Maine. A long, narrow blade with its oval shape creates a paddle that is difficult to break and is silent on the water. All things considered, the length is usually a bit longer than on a modern paddle. A version of the beavertail, modified particularly at the grip, became known as the

Northwoods Guide paddle. This was the style of paddle preferred by guides and other Northwoods canoeists. With practice, a quiet, subtle paddle stroke, along with a J-stroke, is mastered.

Cruising Blade: The cruising blade which has straight sides, a square tip and noticeably tapered shoulders, is approximately 22"-27" long and 7-1/2" or 8" wide. The blade's width provides plenty of control in churning water and enough surface area to maintain a comfortable stroke for many miles on flat water. Use a paddle with a longer blade on deep lakes, and a shorter blade for shallow rivers. Aspects of this design may be seen in the paddles of the early French Voyageurs. The *Ottertail* blade design is probably the ancestor of today's cruising styles.

Racing Blade: The width of the blade provides the racer with plenty of surface area to work with in pulling the canoe through the water. It is approximately 20"-22" in length by 8"-9" in width. The narrow sloping shoulders of the shaft are designed to allow the canoeist to bring the paddle blade as close to the canoe as possible, thereby providing maximum power, less side-to-side movement, and more directional control. Racing blades are typically shorter and lighter than cruising blades, allowing for quicker recovery during the paddling cycle. This style of blade design probably was used by the early inhabitants of present-day Sugar Island, located on the St. Lawrence River just inside Canada. In modern times, Sugar Island became the property of the American Canoe Association. Today, it is the site of many international canoe races.

Weight
In the words of Cliff Jacobson: "The lighter the paddle, the better. Period!" Amen!

Materials Used
Wood is the traditional material of choice. It is light and easy to work with yet provides the right amount of tensile strength to withstand abuse from rocks, gravel, sand and mishandling by careless paddlers. Nevertheless, wood is still "springy" enough to act as a natural shock absorber for the hands, arms and shoulders as they maintain a steady paddling cycle. If you have shopped at many paddle sports stores, you have seen the other reason wooden paddles continue to have a loyal following: you can't substitute the inherent beauty of a well-made wooden paddle with the cold efficiency of a high-tech synthetic product.

Subjective reasoning and personal bias aside, today's paddles are well-made be they wooden or synthetic. Don't be misled by the cost of any of these paddles either. A well-crafted, all-handmade wooden paddle will price out at $200+, a cost compatible with any exotic composite paddle of similar design.

Non-wooden paddles may be constructed of exotic materials such as fiberglass, kevlar, carbon-fiber, or a mixture of those called composites, along with more pedestrian components combining aluminum and high-density plastics. When it comes to your final choice, the weight and "feel" of the paddle in your hands should be the final factor in making the purchase.

Given all the variables described above, proper stroke technique is what ultimately determines how well a paddle functions in the water. So, no matter what "stick" you choose, be sure to take a lesson or two in paddling techniques.

And Now, The Kayak!

"The kayak is perhaps the most efficient example of a primitive hunting boat; it can be propelled at high speed by its paddler and maneuvered with ease . . . The kayak, remarkable for its seaworthiness, lightness and strength, has been perhaps one of the most important tools in the Eskimo fight for existence."

—Adney, Edwin, Tappan & Howard I. Chapple,
The Bark Canoes and Skinboats of North America

Kayaks are divided primarily into four categories: *recreational kayaks, touring kayaks* (sea kayaks are a specialized version of a touring kayak), *whitewater kayaks,* and *down-river racing kayaks.* An additional style, usually lumped into the recreational and touring category, but that deserves a place of its own, is the highly-popular *sit-on-top* or *open cockpit kayak.*

An additional category is growing in popularity; namely, the *inflatable kayak* or *IK.* Due to the increase in technology, improved fabrics and other materials that go into their manufacture, these inflatable kayaks have become more rugged and, therefore, durable. New IKs show a creative and sophisticated design that maintains rigidity, allowing increased maneuverability and greater stability.

Comparing inflatables against hard-shell boats, the IK is rather sluggish, particularly on flat water. However, its popularity on moving water in general, and white water in particular, has increased. Its buoyancy and more-forgiving nature has made the inflatable kayak the growing choice of many beginning and part-time boaters.

A sub-category that has been around for many years, but enjoys a greater following in Europe, is the *folding kayak.* This craft is made of coated fabric or canvas stretched around a take-apart yet rigid wood or light metal (usually aluminum) frame. Some models even contain baffled chambers of coated fabric. Upon inflation, these chambers provide increased floatation to the kayak. When taken apart a folding kayak fits into one or two duffel-style bags.

There is nothing flimsy about this type of craft. Take-apart kayaks which have been used to cross the Atlantic and paddled on white water continue to perform on many high-risk expeditions. They are light, easy to paddle (but less responsive than hard-shell kayaks) and may be transported as luggage in aircraft. Many are still hand-made and

Figure C: Touring kayak
without rudder

use sophisticated structural materials; they can be very expensive. Because the subject of this book pertains to quiet waters and lakes, I describe only the touring, recreational and open cockpit categories.

The Touring Kayak

Two popular misconceptions exist about kayaking and kayaks: all kayaks are used only to run white water, and a kayak paddler needs to be proficient in an Eskimo roll before he can enjoy paddling his boat. As a matter of fact, the primary use of the small one-man skin boat—called a *ikyax* by the Aleuts and later anglicized to *kayak* [see *In the Eddy*] was used for hunting, and not for white water. The craft's remarkable buoyancy, stability and maneuvering capabilities were applied to recreation at a later date, and by White Man, not the Eskimo. [See Fig. C.]

The primary difference between the canoe and the kayak is one of height. A canoe, by its inherent design, sets the paddler higher in the water—either kneeling or sitting—than in a kayak. The kayaker, because his center of gravity is so much lower, has greater stability.

The old saying, "You paddle a canoe, but you wear a kayak," has merit when you observe how one enters a kayak. First, you step into a skirt-like item of clothing called aptly, the *spray-skirt*. Then you slide into a small (by canoe standards) open cockpit and adjust your spray-skirt over the curved lip of the cockpit called the *coaming*. Your legs lie along the inside hull of the boat and your feet adjust to the pegs that provide a bracing point for paddling the kayak.

Once you initiate the paddle stroke, the response from the boat differentiates a true touring kayak from a whitewater or recreational kayak. A well-built touring kayak is designed to track well, be comfortable when paddling long distances and have ample storage capacity for gear. In certain designs it includes a rudder to help in tracking.

As in choosing a canoe, picking out the correct type of touring kayak ultimately depends on how and where you will use it the majority of time. If want to spend the day slowly exploring a favorite small lake or lazy river, then a general-purpose recreational kayak will do the job.

What to Look For
As with a canoe, length and width are important features. We already know that length equals speed, so touring kayaks are usually longer than any other style of kayak (flatwater racing kayaks are the exception). Single-seat touring kayaks are between 16' to 19' in length, with doubles reaching lengths of up to 23'. Their widths are relatively narrow (between 21" to 24") and they possess a straight keel line with either a rounded bottom, flat bottom, shallow-V, or rounded-V hull.

Some manufacturers have been experimenting with the use of well-defined *chine lines* (called *hard chines* or, when the chines are spaced close together, *double chines*))to further delineate the hull shape of their designs and thereby provide more secondary stability during a lean. These design features are not new; certain early Eskimo tribes integrated hard chines into their own design.

The Concept of Shape (Symmetry)
The shape of the kayak has a direct relationship on how functional it is when paddled. All kayaks are designed along some form of preconceived symmetrical lines. In a truly *symmetrical boat*, the front half is the same shape as the back half. This is not true of an *asymmetrical boat*. The symmetrical boat is easier to maneuver than an asymmetrical boat, although the longer, more streamlined bow of an asymmetrical boat allows for a more efficient glide through the water; however, the price you pay is a decrease in maneuverability.

Asymmetrical boats are designed around two shapes: the *Fish form* and the *Swede form*. The *Fish form* has more beam or mass built in the front of the cockpit, with a more slender stern area. This feature allows better tracking and stability under more varied conditions.

The *Swede form* has less body in the front area of the boat but increases in mass behind the cockpit. This more slender bow feature increases the kayak's speed and turning abilities.

Figure D: Top: integrated rudder; bottom: stern-mounted rudder with flip-top blade

Some Other Design Features

The deck of a touring kayak will be relatively flat to prevent side-slipping in the wind. Again, the deck cannot be too flat or it allows water to spill over the deck and capsize it. To prevent this, a well-constructed touring kayak will have *bulkheads* (water-tight walls separating the different compartments of a boat). These bulkheads also provide additional strength and support to the design of the kayak, somewhat like thwarts on a canoe. These separated chambers act as combination storage compartments for gear and as sealed floatation for the kayak. Kayaks without sealed compartments have to add air bags (called *float bags*) that are inflated upon insertion into the bow and/or stern of the kayak. Access to these storage compartments is gained by first removing either a rim-sealed outer hard cover (*deck hatch*), followed by "popping" off a soft inner cover usually made of neoprene.

Some American designers are following the European (British) concept of using an all rubber gasket as a one-piece water-tight outer cover. The feature built on most, but not all, touring kayaks is the

Figure E: Bottom, Retractable skeg

exposed, *stern-mounted rudder* [see Fig. D] lowered and raised by pulling on a cord attached to the stern deck of the kayak or by a handle recessed in a designated well near the cockpit of the boat. When the rudder blade is in the down position, directional control or tracking may be aided by the use of foot pedals inside the kayak.

Some kayaks have a feature similar to a skeg mounted underneath the bottom of the kayak as part of the built-in design feature of the stern. This device is called an *integrated rudder* [see Fig. D]. The system operates by foot control, like the traditional rudder but, unlike the exposed system, there is no blade to catch the wind, bend or get in the way.

A feature that is being re-introduced into some of the newer kayaks is the *retractable skeg* [see Fig. E]. A skeg is a fin-shaped blade similar in appearance and function to the fin on a surfboard. It is positioned in the stern area underneath the hull. The skeg's purpose is to aid in tracking when paddling long distances under adverse conditions. With this type of setup, there is no directional control as there is with a more traditional foot-operated rudder system. The skeg remains "fixed" when engaged and unlike a traditional, exposed, rear-mounted rudder system, the skeg will not catch the wind as the traditional rudder blade does in an arrested position; it is also lighter.

The down side of both "newer" systems is that the shallow depth of the blade prevents a firm tracking guide when the rudder or skeg is engaged. In addition, with the skeg you must remember its presence when paddling in shallow waters or beaching the boat. Running over a shallow rock or other obstruction can tear the skeg assembly off the boat, creating a day of no joy.

Some touring kayaks without rudders or skegs have design features that preclude the use of a rudder; instead, they are paddled with the understanding that all directional control will come from the paddler's skills.

Recreational Kayaks

Recreation: Refreshment of one's mind or body after labor through diverting activity; play.
—American Heritage Dictionary of the English Language

Playing is what recreational kayaks do best. This category of kayak seems to be undergoing a transformation with the increase of paddling as an alternative sport, and a family endeavor.

In the recent past, these small, beamy and all-round fun boats were tolerated and put down as not "real" kayaks. What prompted a change in the industry was the "discovery" of kayaking by the general public, which created a dramatic rise in sales and consequently, forced a rise in technology to maintain a competitive edge among boat manufacturers.

The result is an astounding variety of recreational kayaks that are relatively inexpensive and fun to paddle.

So What is a Recreational Kayak?

The big distinction between a touring kayak and one for general recreational use may be seen in its length and hull design. The main emphasis of the recreational boat is fun—the fun of spontaneous play. The recreational kayak user is more apt to want a boat for casual use and therefore it is far shorter than a kayak designed for serious touring. The length of recreational kayaks run anywhere from 8' to 15' for singles and up to 17' for a double. Since use of these boats is usually unplanned and by non-boaters, stability becomes a key design factor. Many recreational kayaks are recognizable by their width or beam. In the past, this extreme width-to-length ratio has kept the designs of these boats to a bland "pumpkin seed" look. As casual enthusiasts become more proficient and adept in paddling, their demand for more sophisticated designs have sparked ongoing changes that continue to alter the initial reaction to this category of kayak.

Today's recreational boats are still designed for casual all-around use, but their designs are becoming more sleek (some recreational models come with rudders or drop skegs), sacrificing initial stability (the pumpkin seed shape) for easier paddling on small lakes. Others are being designed with slight rocker for casual river paddling or use in mild whitewater.

Figure F: Kris Johnson demonstrates the open-deck kayak.

Bells and Whistles

In the past, the majority of recreational boats had a basic shape, and if you were lucky, maybe a small, very small, storage compartment where you could cram your gear. NOT ANYMORE! Storage compartments similar in size and construction those found on any touring kayak may be ordered on some recreational kayaks. In addition to the installation of rudders and skegs, some of the newer recreational kayaks come with decks covered with "stuff"—everything from fishing rod holders to bait buckets. Even compasses and GPS (Global Positioning System) units may be seen on the decks of certain models.

Deck rigging in the form of shock cord (similar to the material making up elastic tie-downs) crisscross the decks as standard features. A paddler may attach water bottles or other gear to the rigging or place items underneath this taut line of cordage.

Open Cockpit Kayaks (The Sit-On-Top)

As kayaking increases in popularity, more and more beginners get their first introduction to the sport by paddling a sit-on-top kayak, usually from a kayak livery when they are on vacation. [see Fig. F] These easy-to-handle, fun boats have captured the imagination of many who have recently joined the ranks of paddling enthusiasts. From humble beginnings as dive boats, new designs, better building materials, and a growing list of accessories have ensured a permanent category for these multi-use kayaks.

As the name implies, to paddle one of these boats you sit on top of the deck in a seat molded as part of the kayak's design. A series of wells provide bracing for your feet. If the kayak is equipped with a rudder, the steering is done with the feet, using pads connected by cables running to the rudder-assembly attached to the stern. This same style of rudder-assemblage is found on a standard sit-in kayak. Some models are equipped with either a skeg or an integrated rudder similar in operation to a sit-in kayak.

Because of the style of seating—on top rather than within—the range of use is greater than that of a conventional kayak. Divers who were the first to exploit these boats used them to paddle past the surf zone and provide a relatively stable diving platform that provided rest and storage of gear. Outfitters and rental agencies purchased many of them for tourists wishing to enjoy an alternative sport but who had no experience in a conventional kayak or who felt uncomfortable in an enclosed cockpit.

As the popularity of these boats increased, newer and better designs were incorporated. Today's open-cockpit kayaks are designed for touring, racing, surfing, and whitewater action.

Besides the different steering systems, sit-on-tops also may be purchased with a wide variety of accessories.

Materials
As with touring kayaks, you can find recreational and open-decked kayaks manufactured out of polyethylene plastic, the least expensive and most conventional material for the majority of different boats. Other materials used include composites such as fiberglass, kevlar and, recently, graphite. Some manufacturers offer touring and recreational kayaks made from wood that come in a kit with instructions for building the kayak yourself.

Kayak Paddles
Choosing the correct kayak paddle will pay off in comfort and efficiency. Making the right choice, however, takes a little time and forethought. Remember, once your homework is done and all the advice given, pick the paddle that you feel most comfortable with that is within *your* budget.

There are obvious differences between touring paddles and white water paddles. There are also subtle but important differences between the various styles of touring paddles. First, the length of a touring paddle is longer than a whitewater paddle. The length should be determined, in part, by your height, the type and amount of paddling you do, and the design of your boat.

The design features of the paddle's blades and its *swing weight* (a paddle's balance, how it feels as you move the paddle through your paddling cycle) should also be considered prior to your selection. Finally, what material should it be for the material determines a paddle's weight, durability and price.

Paddle Length

Length distinguishes a touring paddle because a comfortable touring stroke is more horizontal than the aggressive vertical stroke that denotes a whitewater paddler. In touring, distance is more important than speed and maneuvering; hence, a steady and slower stroke rate is sought.

Shaft lengths of 230 cm (kayak paddle length is in centimeters) and longer support a more relaxed style of stroke because you hold the paddle at a lower angle. An average-sized person should consider a paddle length anywhere between 210 cm and 230 cm. The disparities have to do with personal stroke comfort as well as the types of boats being paddled. The shorter lengths (from 210 cm to 220 cm) allow a paddler to hold the paddle-shaft in a more vertical position, providing a more aggressive stroke. This style of paddling is important for racing or exercise. If purchasing a sporty, but not beamy recreational kayak, or one for children, the shorter-shafted paddle may prove to be a better choice.

With the increase of families, and particularly women and children, into kayaking, paddle manufacturers are designing paddle shafts with a smaller diameter, allowing for a more comfortable grip around the shaft. If storage is important, either at home, on the vehicle, or in the boat, then you may want to consider a *take-apart* (break-down) paddle to your list. Take-aparts may be purchased either as a two-piece or up to a four-piece for ease of stowage.

The *crank shaft*, or *ergonomic bent shaft paddle* (it resembles a weight lifter's curling bar) was designed for the same reasons as the canoe bent shaft paddle—to relieve the stress on the wrist as you bend or twist it to catch a stroke.

Because this design style adapts well to the aggressive strokes needed for kayak racing and whitewater paddling, the crank shaft is fitted on the lighter and more expensive paddles. If the design catches on with the general public, the crank shaft will become incorporated into paddles whose cost fits a family budget.

Until recently, the only way a paddler could try out one of the "original" native kayak paddles was to carve one from a design. With the interest in ALL aspects of the sport and the growing awareness of the sport's history, some paddle manufacturers have heeded the requests by paddlers and produced several hybrid designs based on the Greenland-Style paddle. These designs incorporate Greenland features with modern concepts to fit the paddling styles of most contemporary paddlers. (For a review of these unique paddles, read David Anderson's "Greenland-Style Paddles," *Sea Kayaker Magazine*, June 1999.)

The Blade: A Different Angle:

In addition to the shaft length, the shape and angle of a paddle's blade will determine how that paddle will perform in the water. All paddle blades are divided into a *back face* and a *power face*. It is the power face along with its shape that propels a paddler and his boat through the water. Of secondary importance is a concept called *feathering*, where the blades are offset to a particular angle; this in turn forces paddlers to rotate their wrists to "set" the paddle blade at the correct angle before placing it into the water.

The difference in paddling techniques incorporating a feathered or unfeathered style is summed up best in an article written by Tony Jones for October 1997 issue of *Outfitter Magazine*. In it, he interviews Bruce Furrer, president of Werner Paddles, on the dynamics between paddling with a feathered or unfeathered blade:

"Unfeathered is probably the easiest to learn, and that's what you see most of the time when you go out to a resort . . .[feathering assists with the natural body rotation of the torso when a paddle stroke is employed.] . . . If you rotate with a proper stroke . . . the shaft automatically rotates in your hands.

Having a paddle with a feathered or offset blades is advantageous when you start using proper technique." The key phrase here is: "when you start using proper technique."

Unfortunately, many beginners purchase kayak paddles without proper guidance in their correct usage. It has been medically proven that over a long period of time, paddling with a feathered paddle held incorrectly will increase the chance of tenosynovitis. Personally, although I paddle with a feathered blade, when exploring a coast or shoreline to obtain photographs, I prefer an unfeathered paddle.

Getting back to the shape and angle of a paddle's blade, the traditional shape found in many rental shops is flat and oval (in paddle jargon an oval blade is said to be symmetrical). These paddles are inexpensive to make and allow the novice paddler to "push and pull" through the water without too much trouble. But are they efficient? The answer is, no, just inexpensive.

Another common blade, but not practical for common touring, is a design called the *spoon-blade*. As the name suggests, the power face is concave as on a spoon. As the blade enters the water, the concave face creates friction, thereby scooping water into the concave face, forcing it backward in order to propel forward.

The large amounts of water backed up by the "scooping effects" of the power face as it is pushed through the water builds pressure around the edges of the blade, causing it to "flutter," or move from side to side while still in the water.

Some paddle manufacturers attempt to solve this flutter by designing a paddle blade with a *dihedral* powerface. The dihedral angle gives "direction" to the water as it flows off the blade during a forward stroke, subsequently reducing the force of the water that creates the pressure that causes that irritating flutter. To further test this blade design, ask your paddle sports dealer to demo a paddle built with this feature.

As Furrer explained, "If a paddle flutters, no matter what paddlesport you're in, you have to grip the shaft a little bit tighter in order to overcome fluttering action, which can lead to fatigue and potentially tendonitis."

A modified modern version of the spoon-blade called the *wing paddle* is utilized primarily by racers who have the strength and are willing to sacrifice moving large amounts of water for maximum speed.

For practical touring, the first sign of an efficient blade design is the angled end on the tip of the power face. This degree of angle creates an *asymmetric* shape that allows for a cleaner bite as the angled edge enters the water. The second sign of a well-designed paddle is how easily the blade passes through the water, allowing the paddler to maintain a light enough stroke to propel the boat with the least amount of strain.

To gain an understanding of these dynamics, the best method is to demo as many paddle types as possible. Again, as with canoes and kayaks, a reputable paddle sports dealer will provide the customer with the opportunity to gain this knowledge.

Thus the Birch Canoe was builded
In the valley, by the river,
In the bosom of the forest;
    And the forest's life was in it,
    All its mystery and its magic,
    All the lightness of the birch-tree,
    All the toughness of the cedar,
    All the larch's supple sinews;
    And it floated on the river
    Like a yellow leaf in Autumn,
    like a yellow water-lily."
        –Henry Wadsworth Longfellow

IN THE EDDY

Umiak, Kayak & Baidarka

The terms *kayak, umiak,* and *baidarka* are often encountered in the literature of the Arctic skin boat. The word kayak, from the Aleutian Eskimo word *ikyax* or *qayaq* (loosely translated as "hunter's boat"), slowly evolved into our anglicized word, kayak.

An umiak, or *oomiak,* is an open boat with a flat bottom, ranging from 15 to 60 feet in length, with a beam of up to 8 feet. The umiak was propelled either by oars, paddles, a sail, or sometimes it was even towed. Those umiaks used in the early 20th century were powered by small outboard gasoline engines.

The purpose of the umiak is a bit sketchy. Its primary use was probably to haul family along with household gear and food during a migration; this was especially true of the Eskimo in the eastern Arctic. The men paddled alongside the family kayaks in separate kayaks to take advantage of hunting opportunities.

The umiak of the western Arctic, built of sturdier materials, was used to hunt walrus and whale. The Greenland Eskimo, however, referred to the umiak as a "women's boat," to be used exclusively for hauling household gear.

Upon the arrival of the Russians, their first encounter with the umiak and kayak brought about a natural comparison with boats of similar use on the lakes and rivers of Russia. The larger boat or umiak called *bidara(baidara)* or *bidarke* (plural) by the Russians used a sealskin outer covering on a wooden or bone frame. The craft looked similar to the Russian craft used on the Dnieper River (located in present day Ukraine). The smaller kayak was called a *baidarka*. The diminutive suffix *-ka* emphasized the differences in size. The plural ending *-ke* or *-ki* also referred to the number of holes or cockpits in the kayak.

Today, the baidarka refers primarily to a particular type of skin boat that incorporates features of an Aleutian Eskimo kayak used for long-distance hunting expeditions. These features were in danger of dying out until George Dyson and later, other enthusiasts of Arctic skin boats, began to reconstruct the Eskimo kayak using designs saved by Howard I. Chappelle and earlier explorers of the Arctic.

These days you can attend a workshop on traditional skin boat construction, or purchase a ready-made replica, constructed of a combination of traditional and modern materials or all high-tech components.

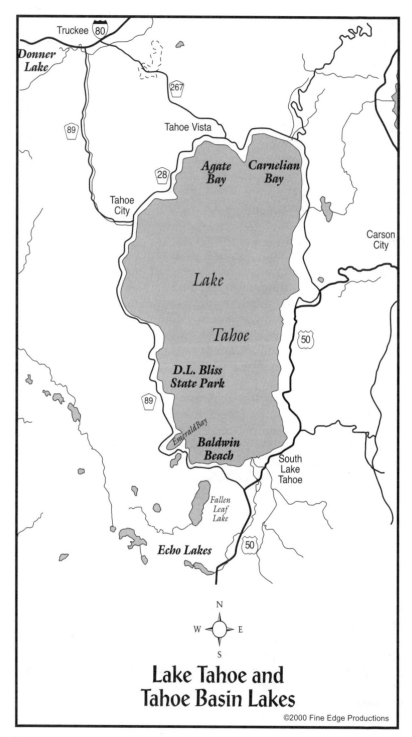

Lake Tahoe and Tahoe Basin Lakes

©2000 Fine Edge Productions

Lake Tahoe & Lake Tahoe Basin Lakes
(Lake Tahoe Basin Management Unit, U.S. Forest Service)

> ... Suddenly, after having covered peak and slope, meadow and shore, with snow to a depth of six, eight, ten or more feet, the Storm King retires and Solus again reigns supreme. And then! Ah, then is the time to see Lake Tahoe...
> —George Wharton James, *Lake Tahoe: Lake of the Sky*

Introduction

Considered the "gem" of the Sierras—Lake Tahoe—has drawn multitudes of admirers to its shores. With the recent growth of canoe and kayak touring, it is only natural that Lake Tahoe has become a favorite destination for the paddler. Unlike many other lakes, however, paddling the waters of Tahoe requires basic boating skills. The miles of shoreline are exposed to wind, chop and rapid weather changes.

The Tahoe paddling areas described below were chosen for their scenic appeal, their protection from the elements, and their proximity to other localities around the lake. (For example, the put-in at D. L. Bliss State Park is within paddling distance of Sugar Pine Point.)

The lakes in the Tahoe Basin, especially the Echo Lakes, bring you into intimate contact with the majestic beauty of the Sierra Nevada high country. The rugged grandeur of the glaciated granite, viewed from the deck of a kayak or the seat of a canoe, humbles our egos so that we can truly understand the words of John Muir:

> Wilderness is a necessity. Mountain peaks and reservations are useful, not only as fountains of time and irrigating rivers, but as fountains of life!

Paddling Donner Lake is akin to traveling into a slice of history. Not only are you reminded of the Donner Party disaster that occurred during the winter of 1846-47, but other less-documented evidence of Man's attempt to master Nature is on display. Slicing across the glaciated walls of granite, tracks of the Western Pacific Railroad were laid down by the unappreciated toil of thousands of Chinese. When floating on the water, the entire China Wall—a huge ridge of granite where progress was measured by inches blasted in a day—is clearly revealed to the paddler.

Twisting and turning as they follow the passes, old Highway 40 and the modern Interstate 80 can be seen by the paddler cruising the surface of the lake.

But all of these intrusions by Man are dwarfed by the visible evidence of Nature's handiwork. The bare granite polished to a mirror-like finish, along with twin moraine fields rising to 800 feet of rubble, culminates in Donner Lake itself, providing graphic testimony to the work of ice and water on the landscape.

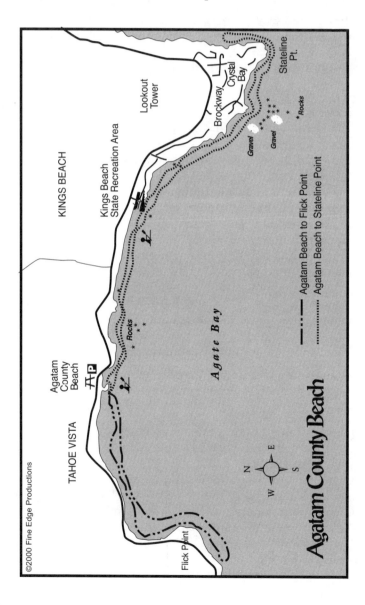

Agatam County Beach

- - - Agatam Beach to Flick Point
.... Agatam Beach to Stateline Point

PADDLING AREA 1

Agatam County Beach, North Shore, Lake Tahoe

The north shore of Lake Tahoe is in Placer and Washoe counties.

Elevation: 6,225 feet
Maximum depth: 1,590 feet (1998 USGS study)
Shoreline: 71 miles long; the lake itself is 21 miles long, 12 miles wide.
Surface temperatures: from 68°F (maximum) to 41°F (minimum).

Trip Length: Each paddle, in a leisurely fashion, will take 2.5 to 3 hours.
Difficulty: The waters of Lake Tahoe are very deceiving. Unless you have experience on rough, choppy water, the best time to paddle the lake is either early in the morning or late in the afternoon.

If the wind comes up suddenly, as it does, immediately head for shore before the chop and wind shear broaches your boat. Caution: Because the waters of the lake are cold enough to produce hypothermia, a good idea to know how to execute an Eskimo Roll or be accomplished in other self-rescue techniques.

In addition to the wind, during the summer months thunder showers may occur suddenly and with very little warning. If you suspect a change in the weather, do not hesitate to paddle shoreward before you hear thunder or spot the flash of lightning. Be wary of speeding motor boats and other water craft that do not always pay attention to objects in their path.

A well-written handout offered free courtesy of the California Department of Boating and Waterways—Safe Boating Hints for Lake Tahoe— may be picked up at almost any marina or phone (916) 445-2616.
Season: Depending on your endurance, Lake Tahoe may be paddled year-round. However, the official boating season begins sometime in late spring and lasts until the first snowfall in late October or early November.
Maps: There is a plethora of maps covering Lake Tahoe. The USGS topographical sections for the lake are best for reading the terrain features around the lake, but marginal for helping the paddler recognize the many cultural or historical features around the lake.

USGS, 7.5 minute series (North Shore): *Kings Beach; Marlette Lake* (Nevada);*Tahoe City* (optional). (South Shore: *Meeks Bay ; Emerald Bay; South Lake Tahoe; Homewood* (optional); *Glenbrook* (Nevada).

USFS: *Lake Tahoe Basin Management Unit* (foldout map); NOAA: *Lake Tahoe* (metric), #18665

Area/Road Maps: Compass Maps, Inc.: *Lake Tahoe*; Benchmark Maps: *California Road & Recreation Atlas*; Family Fun Maps: *Lake Tahoe*
Access: Take Interstate 80 East to Highway 89 North/267 exit (the exit past Donner Pass Rd. turnoff) for Old Town,Truckee (Commercial Row). Take 267 exit and loop back to the four-way intersection on Commercial Way/Donner Pass Road. Make a left turn just before the Union 76 gas station. Cross the Southern Pacific Railroad tracks, go over the Truckee River Bridge and follow the highway (Brockway Rd./ North Shore Blvd.) south for approximately 10 miles (driving over Brockway Summit, elev. 7,199) into the town of Kings Beach.

At the T-intersection of Highway 267 (North Shore Boulevard) and Highway 28 (North Lake Boulevard), make a right turn onto North Shore Boulevard. Drive past the Safeway store on your right and the entrance to North Tahoe Beach Center on your left. Approximately one mile from your turnoff, look for the small roadway sign on the right with a directional arrow to the small parking lot of Agatam Beach. The beach parking lot is directly across from the Old Range Steakhouse Restaurant.

Highlights:
• From Agatam Beach, one may paddle Carnelian Bay, Agate Bay or into Crystal Bay.
• Exceptional views of the peaks bordering South Shore. This range is part of the Desolation Wilderness Area.
• Public access is free, but parking is limited. The park contains shaded picnic tables, restroom and a small sandy beach.
• Additional public access to beaches is available, but little or no directions make them hard to find.
• No dogs are allowed on the beach.
• Weather: For Lake Tahoe's North Shore, phone: (530)546-7251, then enter the 4-digit code: 5050.
• Lodging, restaurants, shopping and two paddle sports retailers/ outfitters are conveniently located in the community of Kings Beach.
• Kayak Cafe, a new, open-decked kayak, canoe & mountain bike rental, has opened at Carnelian Bay next to Sierra Boat Company. (530)546-9337.
• North Lake Tahoe Chamber of Commerce Visitors Information (530)581-6900.

Description: A beach located on the North Shore of the lake that contains a sandy beach, shade for the afternoon, no crowds and free parking is a deal hard to pass up. Agatam County Beach, in the small community of Tahoe Vista on the western limits of King City, is such a spot. It meets and surpasses the requirements for a "choice" day on the beach. From here, you can take a paddle craft and explore the sheltered cove near the beach, practice paddle strokes, teach the kids basic boat-handling skills, or venture out and view the greater expanse of either Carnelian Bay or Agate Bay.

Two paddles from this beach highlight the primary points of interest near Carnelian Bay and the shoreline of Agate Bay, including Stateline Point where it borders the tip of Crystal Bay.
Note: Both paddles are best done in the early morning when the lake's surface is calm, before the wind and power boats churn the water into unmanageable chop. Sometimes by late afternoon, usually after 4:00 PM, the wind dies down, allowing a comfortable paddle into the open bay.

Agate Bay to Crystal Bay

Upon launching from Agatam Beach, paddle left past the small boat jetty, around the point with the glass windbreak and the site of the La Petite Pier Restaurant (considered one of the best French restaurants on the West Coast). The two other restaurants are Captain Jon's and Shoreline.

Weave through the moored and berthed boats belonging to Tahoe Vista Marina. (The large L-shaped pier that is part of the marina was built in the early 1900s to allow the docking of the steamer Tahoe when it arrived on its daily mail run.) Either follow the shoreline, or if the bay is calm, aim the bow into the open lake.

Before passing the marina, however, take note of how the many smaller boats are stacked for storage. When an owner wishes to use his craft, giant forklifts ease the boat out of its slot and drive it to an open berth on the marina's shore.

Paddling among the boulders

Once past the clutter of moored boats, take a breather and enjoy the panorama of water, mountains and sky. The bay you are paddling on was named for the agate and crystals (possibly quartz) found on the shore by members of the 1856 Marlette and Day's California Wagon Road and Boundary Survey Party. Prior to that, it was called "Little Carnelian" when it was used to supply trout and hay to the miners of the "great silver strike" on the north side of Brockway Summit in present-day Martis Valley.[1]

The community of Tahoe Vista has a colorful story pertaining to its origins. Just when the new subdivision of Tahoe Vista (named after the Tahoe Vista Hotel, an 80 by 30 foot lodge built on a bluff overlooking the water) was heralded as the next "summer family retreat," the first lot was purchased on July 18, 1911 by Cherry de St. Maurice, notorious madam from Sacramento and owner of the finest 'parlor house' on the Pacific Coast, whose "'Goddam it, Sam, we got the lot!' [reached]

First settlers saw these forests much as we enjoy them today.

clearly to the ears of the startled watchers who froze in shocked amazement."[2] Needless to say, this real-estate venture collapsed before it could, well . . . develop.

As you gaze outward over the green carpet of conifers spreading over the slopes of the tall peaks, remember that, had you been on the water at this same spot in the early 1900s, the peaks would have been denuded of many of the trees that now surround "Big Blue."

The first settlers in the Tahoe Basin saw the forests as a "wilderness" to be exploited for personal wealth and progress. Consequently, logging on a massive scale prevailed throughout the Tahoe Basin. The logging done was not the typical felling of trees that were dragged by oxen or short-line flatcars. Although those methods were used, timbering in the high country revolved around a unique concept known as the "gravitation chute."

Once a tree was cut and trimmed, it was ready for its journey down the mountainside and into a staging area. This was accomplished by hoisting the log into a single or double dry-log chute and letting gravity do the rest. An excellent description of this operation is quoted in Edward B. Scott's *The Saga of Lake Tahoe:* "Tons of sugar pine move faster and faster, forty - fifty - sixty - then seventy miles an hour, now leaving a rocket's trail as sparks and clouds of smoke fan out behind the hurtling missiles, caused by the frictional heat generated as they plunder down the greased runway. Often the ground on which the log chutes lie is irregular, and the whistling projectiles make gigantic leaps into the air, sometimes even jumping the track, to pinwheel over and over down the mountainside. Ahead is the deep-water pool at the bottom of the canyon, and the screaming logs careen off into space . . . cracking into the water barrier with an ear-splitting report heard over a mile distant. An arching sheet of spray is driven into the air to a height of nearly 100 feet . . ."

One can imagine that within a short period of time the forests around Lake Tahoe were denuded except for small patches centered around steep and inaccessible terrain. Owners and operators of future resorts, hotels and subdivisions had to replant trees around their establishments to give the place a proper atmosphere. Consequently, the present-day forest seen from the waters of the lake is second-growth—or even third, planted after the large-scale, clear-cut logging operations ceased.

Back to the present. As you continue your paddle, note the narrow, vacant lots with small beaches nestled between houses or commercial establishments. These are public beaches that may or may not be advertised to the public, but are known to locals or long-time seasonal visitors. One way of recognizing these small "oases" is to look for the ubiquitous cinderblock restroom or equally common Port-a-Potty. Nearby should be a lone picnic table and a metal 5-gallon trash can.

Two such beaches sandwiched between resorts and the Kings Beach Recreation Area are Moondunes Beach (closest to Tahoe Vista Marina) and Seacline Beach (just south of North Tahoe Beach Center).

A short distance down from the marina, you will spot a beach with a boathouse full of assorted canoes and kayaks. Above is a pleasing wooden building where natural hot springs flow out of the ground above the lake. The early resort drew vacationers to the site to "partake of the waters" Today, these luxury condos, some privately owned and others available for rent, all have natural hot water courtesy of Mother Nature.

As you paddle around the point, notice the many rock formations and vegetation-covered slope that comprise Stateline Point. If you enter some of the hidden coves nestled along the rocky point, you may spot mergansers, Canada geese, and other waterfowl using the coves as shelter.

When you reach the entrance of Crystal Bay, you pass from California into Nevada. The handsome wooden houses perched on the top of the ridge are older summer homes, some of them boarded up or vacant.

Contrary to the popular belief that Crystal Bay was named for the clarity of its water, the bay was named for George Iweis Crystal, a lumberman from Douglas County, Nevada, who laid claim to the timber sections around the bay in the late 1860s.

Paddling down the Nevada side of the point, you enter a small cove with a dilapidated boat pier where you can take a break and admire the view before you turn around and return to Agatam Beach.

[1,2] Scott, Edward B., *The Saga of Lake Tahoe.*

 ## PADDLING AREA 2

Agatam Beach to Flick Point
(Carnelian Bay)

Departing from the shores of Agatam Beach, follow the right-hand shoreline past the small rocky point that borders the upper boundary of the park. This short paddle will introduce you to some of the lakefront houses built on the cliffs off Flick Point and give you a panoramic view of the peaks that border this end of the lake.

By taking this paddle in the late afternoon, you will be able to view the tree-covered slopes of Martis Peak (8,656 feet) which flank the north shore of the lake. In the early 1920s, the fire lookout and ranger station on the peak was the home of a local character by the name of Frank Maher, known as "Waddles" for his rolling gate. For 30 summer seasons, he lived on top of Martis Peak in a building he called "Hotel de Chipmunk" because of the swarms of chipmunks that "came a-runnin'" whenever he whistled. His dress was described as: ". . . rather limp shirt, immediately followed by a pair of tattered trousers, hanging from his barrel-like form on wide suspenders, with chipmunks for accessories."[1]

The high peak behind Flick Point that sets off the outline of Carnelian Bay is Mount Pluto, an extinct volcano (8,617 feet) named after the Roman god of the dead and ruler of the underworld. Ancient lava flows from this volcano fanned out and covered the lake floor south of Dollar Point, the southern boundary of Carnelian Bay. When the flows cooled they created underwater plateaus with deep fissures. Some of the lava has eroded into strange patterns and shapes, and may be seen as you paddle off Dollar Point.

Note: You can access Dollar Point, the southern part of Carnelian Bay, and the area of Lake Forest via Carnelian Bay Beach, from Hwy. 28 (North Lake Boulevard) between the Sierra Boat Co. & Gar Woods Grill & Pier in Carnelian Bay.

Flick Point
The point was named after the three Flick brothers, Joseph, Nicholas and William, who purchased the land fronting Carnelian Bay. Their primary occupation was commercial fishing until they made their fortune selling off the land around 1909-1910. Their historical, if dubious, distinction was that all three were bachelors, all were born on Christmas Day—William in 1841, Joseph in 1847 and Nicholas in 1851––and all died in the month of April. William died first in April of 1929, followed by Joseph and Nicholas on April 9 and 19, nine years later.

Caution: When paddling away from the shoreline toward Flick Point or on the open waters of Carnelian Bay, be wary of the winds. If, late on a calm afternoon, you observe an agitated or fuzzy look marring the lake's surface, it means the tranquillity of the bay will be gone within minutes. The blow may last a few short minutes or continue to intensify. No matter how long the wind lasts, once it arrives, the surface instantly becomes a broiling mess of agitated chop. If you are on a tack between the beach and the point, chances are that your boat will come under the pounding of irregular choppy waves breaking over the beam (side) of your boat. The irregular wave pattern completely takes the fun out of the paddle. You are either attempting to paddle, bracing, or getting ready to brace, and swearing—all at the same time, if you have enough air left in your lungs to swear. You can continue on, hoping to reach Agatam Beach before your strength gives out or the boat swamps, but a better choice would be to turn the boat and allow the wind to "push" you toward shore. Near the shoreline, the effects of the wind and waves are reduced, allowing you the chance to paddle back to Agatam Beach.

[1] Scott, Edward B., *The Saga of Lake Tahoe.*

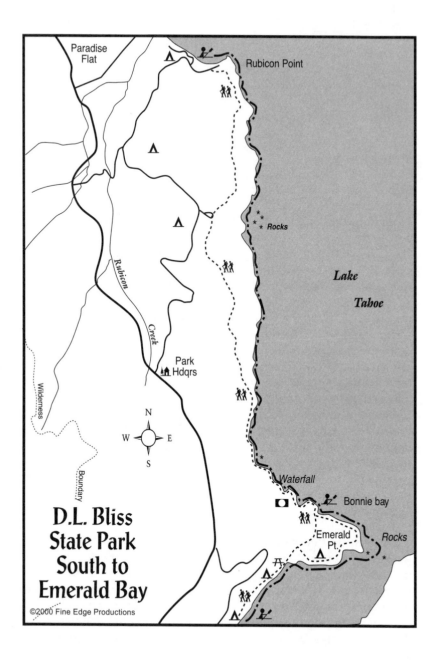

Paradise Flat

Rubicon Point

Rocks

Lake

Tahoe

Rubicon

Creek

Park Hdqrs

Wilderness

Boundary

N
W · E
S

Waterfall

Bonnie bay

Emerald Pt.

Rocks

**D.L. Bliss
State Park
South to
Emerald Bay**

©2000 Fine Edge Productions

PADDLING AREA 3

South Shore, Lake Tahoe:
D.L. Bliss State Park South to Emerald Bay

Trip Length: Give yourself at least a half-day to complete the round trip between D.L. Bliss Beach and Emerald Bay. A sound alternative would be to camp at the Emerald Bay Boat Camp and explore the Bay at your leisure.

Paddling Distances (one way):
From Rubicon Point to Bonnie Bay: 2.0 mi.
From Rubicon Point to tip of Emerald Point: 2.5 mi.
From Rubicon Point to Emerald Bay Boat-in Campground: 3.5 mi.
From Rubicon Point to boat dock at Vikingsholm: 4.0 mi.

Difficulty: Because of the distances and sudden water and weather changes involved, this paddle should be undertaken only by boaters possessing intermediate boating skills and having the proper gear.

The early morning glassy surface of the lake is deceiving. By 10:30 AM, the combination of a freshening breeze and increased power-boat traffic changes the calm surface into a choppy wake-filled mess. Paddling next to the shoreline also brings you into contact with the refractive waves bouncing off the rocks. These non-directional wave conditions force you to brace constantly against their surprise pummeling of your boat.

If you paddle further out, away from the shoreline, you miss the beauty of the area and are exposed to speeding power boats as well as the force of the wind.

To further add to the equation, afternoon thunderstorms, particularly in the late summer, arrive suddenly and with powerful fury. *Note:* Because the waters of the lake are cold enough to produce hypothermia, it is prudent to either be able to conduct an Eskimo Roll or be accomplished in other self-rescue techniques.

A well-written handout offered free courtesy of the California Department of Boating and Waterways entitled Safe Boating Hints for Lake Tahoe can be picked up at almost any marina or ordered by phone at (916)445-2616.

Season: Technically, you can paddle Lake Tahoe year round, weather, gear and skills permitting but the best time to paddle this area is late spring through fall.

Maps:
USGS 7.5 minute series: *Meeks Bay*, CA-NV (optional); Emerald Bay, CA-NV

National Oceanic and Atmospheric Administration (NOAA): *Lake Tahoe Official Navigation Chart* (metric) # 18665.
USFS: *Lake Tahoe Basin Management Unit*
Area/Road Maps:
  Compass Maps Inc.: *Tahoe-Carson*
  Family Fun Maps: *Lake Tahoe*

Access: You may reach the South Shore of Lake Tahoe either by way of US Interstate 80 East or US Highway 50 East.

From US 80: Exit onto State Highway 89 South at Truckee, CA toward Tahoe City. You will follow the Truckee River past Squaw Valley and Alpine Meadows Ski Resorts before arriving at the crossroads called "the Y," in Tahoe City. To continue on 89 South, look for a right bend as you arrive at the beginning of the Y immediately upon entering the city limits. The road bends past the bronze statue honoring the famed Mackinaw Trout before crossing the Truckee River over Fanny Bridge (so named because of the "hanging fannies" of the onlookers viewing and feeding the Rainbow Trout swimming below), and continuing along the lake toward Emerald Bay and South Shore. The entrance to DL Bliss State Park is located on your left just past One Ring Road, approximately 14 miles from Tahoe City.

From Highway 50: Take Highway 50 East into South Lake Tahoe. At the Y intersection, merge left to continue on State Highway 89 North (locally named Emerald Bay Road). The entrance to DL Bliss State Park will be on your right, approximately 9 miles north of South Lake Tahoe.

Highlights:
- You will paddle on one of the world's most majestic lakes.
- Lake Tahoe is the second deepest lake in America; Oregon's Crater Lake is deeper at 1,932 feet.
- The lake itself was formed as a result of fault slippage, not volcanic action.
- Although Lake Tahoe itself is too large to freeze over, Emerald Bay has been coated over with a layer of ice.
- 63 streams flow into the lake, but only one, the Truckee River, flows out. The outflow is at North Shore's Tahoe City. The river flows past Truckee, CA and Reno, NV before emptying into Pyramid Lake.
- In addition to the paddling, the park is known for its two spectacular beaches—Calawee Cove Beach and Lester Beach.
- If planning to stay for the day only, arrive early. There are only 25 parking permits sold each day and they're gone by 10 AM.
- Camping: You can camp at the nearby campground and paddle the lake at your leisure. D. L. Bliss Campground contains 168

campsites. Information: (530) 525-7277; Camping reservations: (800) 444-7275.

The Boat-in campground sites—20 sites for tents only—on the north end of Emerald Bay Point are on a first-come, first-served basis. Piped water, chemical toilets. Leashed pets are permitted. Closed in winter. 1999 price $10/night. Contact Emerald Bay State Park (530) 525-7277.

• Weather: Plan your paddle around the weather. If thunder storms are predicted, you should be on your return leg by the middle of the afternoon. (The shoreline between Rubicon Point and Emerald Bay contains few, if any, coves to seek shelter in.)

To obtain current weather for Lake Tahoe's South Shore, call (530)541-0200, then enter the 4-digit code: 5050.

If the weather does not cooperate, you may view the same area you would have paddled by taking a day hike along the 4.5 mile Rubicon Trail. The first half of the trail (3.1 miles) leads to Rubicon Point, then continues on to terminate at Vikingsholm Castle at the adjoining Emerald Bay State Park.

Caution: Be alert rounding Rubicon Point, the point's deep blue waters brings power boats from all directions of Lake Tahoe. Because the water depths allow boaters to literally "touch the rocks," the combination of numbers of boats and their wakes may provide a recipe for an accident waiting to happen.

Small boat launch, Emerald Bay Boat Camp

Description: The secret to a successful paddle on Lake Tahoe starts with an early put-in somewhere around "0 dark thirty". . .say 6 or 7 in the AM! The rosy tint on the mountains created by the rising sun, along with the glassy, oil-smooth surface of the lake, will provide all the impetus needed to undertake such an early start. As I mentioned earlier in the chapter, the longer the lake's surface stays smooth, the easier and, subsequently, more enjoyable your paddle will be.

Upon launching from the beach, head for the rocky tip of Rubicon Point jutting southeasterly into the lake. With the water calm and the rising sun illuminating the depths, you may spot boulders and fish 80 or more feet below. During the last half of the 19th century, captains of steamships carrying tourists used to enjoy the anguished, not to mention frightened looks of the passengers as they headed directly for the towering cliffs of the point, only to come about within touching distance at the very last second.

Rounding the point, the jumble of domed granitic rock leaps to eye-stretching heights and a carpet of green-hued conifers covers the rocky surface. Across the expanse of the lake, stretching from north to south, the Carson Range stands silhouetted before the rising sun.

Continuing your paddle, the length of the ridge that borders the lake here seems to stretch on forever. Resist the urge to paddle away from the shoreline and aim from one point to another. Instead, embrace the coast and study the inlets for birds, animals and plants that you may spot if you take the time to do so. Not long into your paddle, keep an eye out for a bare rock with a light-colored top. The light color is guano and marks the location where families of mergansers gather. Their buff and rust markings blend into the rock surface, enabling these shy birds to drop into the water and fly off before you are aware of them. If you can spot the rock they use repeatedly for drying their feathers, chances are you will be able to spot their shape and make a silent approach.

Looking high into the tree line bordering the lake's edge, study the tops of lone snags standing apart from the living trees. On some, ospreys build their nests and their young may be seen well into August. The birds' distinctive, high-pitched whistle—kyew kyew kyew kyew— should alert you to their presence. *Caution:* Do not disturb these birds! If you spot a nesting pair, stay clear of the snag holding the nest, use binoculars or paddle to an adjacent inlet to observe the birds.

If the surface of the lake is still glassy, you might have the good fortune to watch the ospreys hover over the water, then dive feet first and snatch their prey. If the birds are successful, they will fly to a nearby limb, often one that is part of the nesting tree, where they will feed on the fish. If there are young still in the nest, the parent bird will fly up to the nest, flaring its wings before settling to feed the nestlings.

It is easy to lose track of time watching the birds. Give yourself a time period and stick to it; otherwise you will have to start your return

Rugged Rubicon Point

before you reach Emerald Bay.

As you continue, notice the many shapes and sizes of the boulders lying near the water. These differences provide the photographer with many interesting compositions for that "special photo."

At the mid-point of the paddle, if you are close to the shoreline, listen for the distinct sound of rushing water. Partially hidden by a small thicket of brush and trees, the only waterfall on this paddle cascades down from the heights above. To the immediate left, as your bow faces the falls, a towering face of granitic rock stands sentinel over this tiny covelet. During the course of the day, many hikers negotiating this portion of the Rubicon Trail stop to view the lake from the high level clearing.

The cliff face and waterfall also act as reference points to your approach into the small cove of Bonnie Bay, the first and only cove with a beach suitable for landing your boat. Given the amount of time you have been in your boat, there are several good reasons to stop here for a break. This early in the morning chances are good that you will have the popular cove to yourself. On your return, remember that this bay will be the last possible stop before your take-out at DL Bliss. If the paddle made you sweaty, or just for the thrill of it all, you will find a short swim to be brisk but refreshing.

If this cove is occupied, just around the small point is another smaller cove with a picturesque sandy beach.

An osprey nest found along the shore.

Paddling the shoreline between the two coves, look carefully for freshly gnawed trunks and limbs with the bark removed. These are sure signs that the industrial engineer of the animal kingdom, the beaver, is residing nearby. In addition to the fallen tree and stripped limbs, many of the small alders growing near the banks of the ridge you paddled past may show signs of having been gnawed. Here at Lake Tahoe, the beaver either dig their homes into the muddy banks, then cover the burrow with limbs and brush, or construct a lodge on shore, near the water.

Emerald Bay
As you approach the point that marks the entrance into Emerald Bay, look across the mouth of the bay to the opposite point. That is Eagle Point; a sure sign of its location is the lone snag with a magnificent osprey nest at the very tip of the point. Both points are remnants of past glacial activity that occurred repeatedly in the area. These piled mass of rock and debris, called lateral moraines, were created as the ice, pushing down slope from the canyon above, carved out the bay, scooping the debris into the piles on either side of present-day Emerald Bay. These ancient glaciers were at least as tall as the moraine piles, somewhere around 1000 feet in height. If the glaciers had moved a

few hundred yards farther beyond the mouth, Emerald Bay would not be part of Lake Tahoe; instead, it would resemble nearby Cascade Lake or Fallen Leaf Lake.

Caution: Be careful rounding Emerald Point, it is deceitfully shallow and contains many rocks. By late summer or in dry years, you may actually be able to rock hop beyond the point where you are paddling and view the inside of the bay. There is a reason why clusters of brush are growing so well, standing in water!

Hopefully, your first view of Emerald Bay will be one to remember. By mid-morning, the sun's rays should highlight the outline of the bay and spotlight Fannette Island (sometimes called Emerald Isle), along with the small teahouse perched on the island's crest before delineating all the rocks, fissures and crevices of the bare rock canyon above the bay.

If you continue to paddle into the bay, following the moraine pile of Emerald Point, you will notice several choice clearings, each complete with a private sandy beach, a sheltering canopy of conifers, and a clear view of the bay. You are paddling past one of the best deals for camping on the lake. Above Parson Rock to the tip of Emerald Point lies Emerald Point Boat-in Campground (hikers are welcome too). The official site for the campground is at the small pier jutting out into the bay a few hundred yards past Emerald Bay Point. Look for the wooden sign welcoming boaters; then pay your fee and register your site.

The campground has piped water and toilets, so even if you are not planning on camping overnight, these facilities are a welcome sight.

If you are planning to visit Fannette Island, then paddle there before beaching the boat at Vikingsholm Beach. Emerald Bay draws boaters from the entire lake, so if you want a tranquil paddle across and a choice take-out at the island, arrive early.

Fannette Island

Although the chemical composition of the rock is similar to volcanic rock, the island itself is not a volcano. This resistant pile of granitic bedrock escaped the repeated onslaught by glacial ice that leveled the remainder of the terrain; it is a proud survivor of two opposing forces—gravity-induced movement of ice sheets and the continuous actions of weathering agents.

I have found that there is no easy take-out spot in which to secure your boat for the exploration of the island. If you paddle into the semi-sheltered area on the northwest end of the island, you may wedge your boat, then carefully use your paddle to brace against the motion of the water, and slide slowly out of the craft. Once out and on land, slide the boat up onto the shore as much as possible. As the power boats arrive, their wakes will pound your boat against the granite bank, scratching and gouging it, or pulling the boat out into the lake.

When your boat is secure, proceed along the bank following the well-established trail through the brush and onto the granite steps leading upward to the teahouse. When you reach the level spot containing the granite structure, the view of the bay and surrounding mountains will literally take your breath away.

The teahouse was built by Mrs. Lora Josephine Moore Knight, owner and builder of the famed Vikingsholm. She first purchased the property bordering the southwest end of the bay; subsequently, along with the property, came possession of the island then known as "Emerald Isle." In the spring of 1928, the purchase price for the entire property was a reputed $250,000 cash! The property was described as:

> [A] *safe harbor, beautiful white sand beach, wild flowers, pure, ice-cold water, matchless cliffs (later known as the 'back fence'), mammoth pine and cedar, waterfalls and an exquisite island.*[1]

During construction of Mrs. Knight's main castle, she also oversaw construction of her "teahouse" upon the island's rocky summit. The finished cottage was a one-room stone hut complete with a miniature fireplace and four windows overlooking Emerald Bay. Inside, the only furnishings were a table and four wooden chairs.[2]

Today, only a granite shell remains. The glass is long gone and the remaining wooden window frames have been vandalized with the names of countless thoughtless visitors. Although the miniature fireplace is still here, its charm may only be imagined. But the view remains. . . and what a view it is! To the east, the moraine-flanked bay extends outward, merging into the darker-hued water of Lake Tahoe. Turning west, the rounded end of the bay frames a rising forest of evergreens that are dissected by the thin road cut of Highway 89. To your left, the clear scar of a 1955 rock slide stands out well at the "cleavage" of Maggies Peaks. Shift your eyes to the center of the view; the tumble of partially-obscured Eagle Falls cascades downward and disappears into the forest. Rising above the falls are the bare, sunlit granite walls of the former cirque that once harbored the glaciers responsible for this scenery.

Before construction of the teahouse, with its subsequent attraction, the same site harbored an earlier tourist draw. During the late 1800s, when this part of the lake was still a wilderness, the property, along with the island, belonged to the famous stagecoach magnate, Ben Holladay. Holladay's caretaker was Captain Richard Barter, better known as the "Hermit of Emerald Bay." The hermit became known ". . . as a salty, seafaring character, who combined a prodigious alcoholic intake with an enviable capacity."[3]

After several mishaps and near drownings, he had a premonition of his death. This feeling caused him to construct a cottage on the south side of the island, the present level area where everybody gathers before making the climb to the summit. He then went on and excavated a solid rock tomb on the summit where today's teahouse stands. Over the tomb, he built a wooden Gothic chapel complete with a wooden cross at the apex of the roof.

The captain's sudden demise by drowning in a gale off Rubicon Point in 1873 was further complicated when his body was never recovered. Because of Barter's notoriety, for several decades the now-defunct "Hermit's Tomb" became a prime tourist attraction until it was replaced by the teahouse.

As the morning progresses, you will begin to feel traces of the breeze that will eventually intensify, turning the tranquil waters of the lake into agitated motion. But before you turn back, or if you are planning to camp at the boat-in campground, don't end your paddle without a visit to the sandy white beach marking the site of Mrs. Knight's former home, Vikingsholm.

Vikingsholm

After carefully entering your boat, the short paddle to the beach allows you to study Eagle Falls and appreciate Mrs. Knight's aesthetics in the placement of her home. Small groups of Canada geese begin to appear as you paddle closer to the beach. These unofficial greeters have been pampered and spoiled by countless visitors so that they have no fear of humans. Even before you reach the shore, the geese will swim up to your boat demanding food. Between dodging geese, other boats and swimmers, you must attempt to find a clear spot to land and beach your boat.

Once that task has been accomplished, leave your gear in the boat and follow the path up beyond the sand into the tall conifers and gaze in awe at this handsome stone structure. The house is an exact replica of a Scandinavian country house, albeit built to grander specifications than those of typical Scandinavian country folk. It contains 38 rooms; upon completion in September of 1929, "Vikingsholm was judged to be the finest example of Scandinavian architecture in North America." [4]

In his excellent book, *The Saga of Lake Tahoe*, E. B. Scott eloquently describes the house on page 133: "The mansion was built in the shape of a horseshoe with its northeast and southwest wings facing away from the bay . . . Hand-hewn timbers, intricate carvings, turrets and towers were carefully coordinated. The stone foundation and walls, formed of granite boulders, followed the exact construction pattern used in early Viking churches and palaces and many of the heavy exterior beam supports were joined without the use of nails or wooden pegs . . . Sod-covered lead sheathing topped the wings of the castle, upon which a carpet of grasses and native wild flowers grew, maintained a glistening green by sprinklers built into the roof. Nordic fireplaces, within the structure, terminated in brick "Crown chimneys," topped by weather vanes."

Be sure to take one of the tours that are run during the summer months. In 1999, the cost of a tour was $3 for adults and $2 for children. You will leave impressed! Note: The house is open every day for tours during the peak summer months from July 1st through Labor Day, after which the house is open only on weekends.

Many people who come to visit the house spend a little time on the beach but do not venture past the immediate house site. Leave some time to hike up the trail above Vikingsholm to view Eagle Falls.

Once that hike is accomplished, your senses should be completely saturated with many sights and scenes to think about on your return to the campsite at Emerald Bay or above the beach at DL Bliss State Park in a couple of hours.

[1-4] Scott, E. B., *The Saga of Lake Tahoe.*

Charles Goodwin, in his Comstock Club, placed these words in the twinkle of an Irishman's brogue when he spoke of the Big Blue:

'Her natural face is bluer than that of a stock sharp in a falling market, but when the wind comes a-wooin' and she dons her foamy lace, powders her face with spray, and fastens upon her swellin' breast a thousand diamonds of sunlight, O but she is a winsome looking beauty to be sure!'

—Edward B. Scott, The Saga of Lake Tahoe

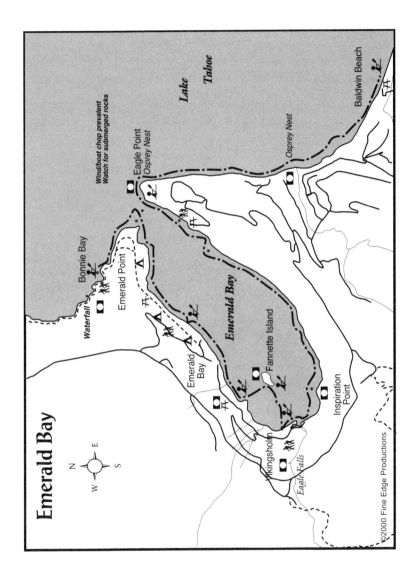

Emerald Bay

≈ PADDLING AREA 4

Lake Tahoe, South Shore:
Baldwin Beach to Emerald Bay

Trip Length: Plan on at least a full morning if you paddle from Baldwin Beach to Eagle Point. A full day would be the norm for paddling into Emerald Bay, exploring Fannette Island and the Vikingsholm.
Paddling Distances (one way):
Baldwin Beach to first osprey nest at mouth of Cascade Creek: 0.5 mi.
Baldwin Beach to osprey nest at entrance to Emerald Point: 1.5 mi.
Baldwin Beach to Vikingsholm Beach: 3.5 mi.
Emerald Point entrance to Vikingsholm Beach (following south shoreline): 1.75 mi.
Emerald Point to Boat Camp dock (following north shoreline): 0.75 mi.
Eagle Point to Emerald Point: 0.2 mi.
To D.L. Bliss State Park beach from Baldwin Beach: 5 mi.
Difficulty: Never underestimate the rapid changes that may occur in the weather when paddling Lake Tahoe. If you are comfortable paddling distances and handling the cross wakes produced by motorized craft or wind, and refracted off rock walls, then this paddle will not present any undue hardships.
Caution: Any paddle on Lake Tahoe that involves prolonged time on the water is not suited for beginners.
Season: Although it is feasible to paddle Lake Tahoe year round, the popular time for kayakers is late spring through fall.
Maps:
USGS 7.5 minute section: *Emerald Bay*, CA-NV
USFS: *Lake Tahoe Basin Management Unit*

Access: You may reach the South Shore of lake Tahoe by way of either US Interstate 80 East or US Highway 50 East.
From US 80: Exit onto State Highway 89 South at Truckee toward Tahoe City. You will follow the Truckee River past Squaw Valley and Alpine Meadows Ski Resorts before arriving at the crossroads called the "Y," in Tahoe City. To continue on 89 South, look for a right bend as you arrive at the beginning of the Y immediately upon entering the city limits. The road bends past the bronze statue honoring the famed Mackinaw Trout before crossing the Truckee River over Fanny Bridge (so named because of the "hanging fannies" of the onlookers viewing and feeding the Rainbow Trout swimming below). Continue along the lake toward Emerald Bay and South Shore. Stay on Highway 89 South for approximately 25 miles. The turn-off will be on your left.

The entrance to DL Bliss State Park will be on your right, approximately 9 miles north of South Lake Tahoe.

From Highway 50 (South Shore): Take Highway 50 East into South Lake Tahoe. At the Y intersection, merge left to continue on State Highway 89 North (locally named Emerald Bay Road). Continue for 4 miles, passing the small resort communities of Tallac Village and Camp Richardson. The entrance will be on your right, 1.5 miles past Camp Richardson.

Drive to the kiosk and either pay the person at the window, or if the kiosk is closed, insert your payment into the bill machine in front of the ticket booth. Drive through the electronic gate, and proceed for a short distance until you come to a Y intersection. Take the left fork and drive down to the parking area fronting the beach and lake.

Highlights:

- One of the best public beaches on the lake, the beach itself is a long sandy strip, with a picturesque pond nearby.
- The paddle along Eagle Point Ridge is wind protected and there are at least 6 osprey nests to view alongside the ridge.
- Outstanding views of Mt. Tallac and Maggies Peaks.
- Baldwin Beach is named after Elias J. "Lucky" Baldwin, a 19th Century Tahoe entrepreneur. The remnant of his resort, Baldwin Estate, contains the Tallac Museum. The museum is free and contains exhibits on the Washoe Indian Culture and the history of the Baldwin Resort.
- Baldwin Beach is for day-use only. Tap water is available and there are public restrooms, phone, picnic tables, fire pits and barbecue stands.
- The portage from car to lake is extremely short, but come early for a parking space closest to the water.
- The best beach for launching and the best parking is at the smaller beach to the left (north) of the Y intersection located near the public phone.
- Be sure to bring dollar bills for the "iron ranger" if planning on an early paddle. The entry fee with boat was $3 in the spring and summer of 1999. For current information, call the U. S. Forest Service Visitor's Center at (530) 573-2674.
- Camping: Eagle Point (California State Parks) (530) 525-7277; Bayview (USFS) operated by California Land Mgmt. Inc. (530) 544-5994; Camp Richardson (operated through a Special Use Permit), (800) 769-2746 or (530) 541-1801; Fallen Leaf (USFS) operated by California Land Mgmt. Inc., (530) 544-0426.

The Boat-in campgrounds on the north end of Emerald Bay Point are on a first-come, first-served basis. Fee (1999) was $10 per night. Contact Emerald Bay State Park (530) 525-7277. There are 20 sites for tents only. Piped water, chemical toilets. Leashed pets are permitted. Closed in winter.

• Weather: To obtain current weather for Lake Tahoe's South Shore. phone: (530) 541-0200, then enter the 4-digit code: 5050.

Description: The round-trip paddle from Baldwin Beach, alongside the forested slopes of Eagle Point, into Emerald Bay, is the best day paddle on the lake. While there are other paddles that are equally scenic, the combination of location, terrain, and distance provide the paddler with just the right amount of time to fully enjoy the day without compromising safety or time on the water. Just the ability to launch from a beautiful sandy beach located within sight of your vehicle should start your day off with a smile. An end to a perfect day would be to have a picnic or barbecue at the beach when you return from your paddle.

If you are not in a hurry, the marshy area located on both sides of the road leading into the beach area is definitely worth exploring. The larger marsh visible from the parking lot nearest your beach is fed by

Emerald Bay from Eagle Point Ridge

the waters of Tallac Creek. The smaller marsh paralleling the lake is maintained by Taylor Creek, whose origin is Fallen Leaf Lake.

Once you have launched from the beach, take a moment to soak in the view of the glaciated terrain bordering the sculpted flanks of Mt. Tallac (elev: 9,735 feet). To your right (facing west) are the twin summits of Maggies Peaks (left to right: 8,699 feet and 8,499 feet).

As you continue your paddle, the small beach to the right of Tallac Creek is part of the Baldwin Beach Recreation Site, although few visitors are aware of this. Just a stone's throw to the north, however, is private land. On my last paddle, a new cabin was being constructed in the tree-covered glen.

Part of this area was in private hands until the forest service obtained the land. You can still see the rusting barbed wire fence line as it disappears into the water near the edge of the beach. Paddling a little further past the beach, you come upon the first of the older cabins that mark the transition from public to private land.

Dodging the variety of private piers that extend outward from the cluster of homes, you eventually reach the mouth of Cascade Creek and the beginning of State Park lands. Coincidentally, the first osprey nest is also located only a few feet past the north shore of Cascade Creek. Do not approach too closely or disturb the birds or their nest.

High on the tip of a long dead standing pine, the bundle of sticks appears rather small, particularly from the deck of a bobbing kayak. Don't make the mistake of thinking the nest is empty, especially if paddling here in summer through early fall. In a short time, you will spot one of the parent birds soaring overhead before making the sudden approach into the nest. Look for fish in the parent bird's talons. They will sometimes carry it into the nest if the young are old enough to feed by themselves, especially true during the end of the nesting season. Sometimes the parent bird lands on a nearby limb close to the nest and proceeds to tear apart and consume the fish. As the young grow older, both birds leave the nest to hunt for food to feed the ever-hungry nestlings.

I have found that if you are not in a hurry, you can paddle to shore and beach the boat amongst the brush and observe the birds without stressing them. If the first nest is vacant or you need to proceed, you will encounter at least five additional nest trees before you round the point into Emerald Bay. The last time I paddled this route in late August, every nesting tree contained families of ospreys.

In addition to the ospreys, families of mergansers (diving ducks) may be spotted sunning themselves on the boulders near the shore. They are not always easy to locate because their coloration blends well into the colors of the surrounding granite. You will become aware of their presence when what at first appears to be the top of a granite boulder suddenly rises up and "plops" into the water. Often there may be as many as six or more birds resting on the boulder before your arrival. Once the mergansers have dropped into the water, they dive and reappear several yards from your boat, quickly form into a group, and paddle away in formation. In addition to the mergansers, kingfishers dart from tree limb to tree limb, staying ahead as you progress to the point.

As you approach the point, pay close attention to the increased boat traffic that becomes more pronounced near the entrance to the

M.S. Dixie II cruises out of Emerald Bay.

bay. Many of the power boats speeding toward the bay are busy observing the scenery and not always aware of an oncoming canoe or kayak.

Emerald Bay (The Entrance)

One of the attractions that distracts many approaching boaters is the famous huge osprey nest that resides at the tip of Eagle Point and acts as a landmark into Emerald Bay. Rounding the tip of Eagle Point, you will have not only boats to deal with, but many sharp rocks in the shallow edge of the point. Due to the many boat wakes, the water stays pretty agitated and the location of these rocks becomes difficult to spot.

Immediately after rounding the point, you will not yet see the famous view of the bay and island. Instead, you enter a small cove bordered by brush, where you can take a break before entering the main body of Emerald Bay. Just inside the brush cover is a small inlet where families of mergansers and Canada geese hide. Located above the cove is a tall standing snag. The nest within the top branches of this snag is usually used by a family of ospreys. From the protected shelter of the small cove, you can observe the boat traffic and wind conditions at the mouth of the bay. If you are planning to camp overnight at the Emerald Bay Boat Camp, you can orient yourself toward the location of the campground, and plan on your approach. *Note:* For paddlers wishing to spend the night at the boat camp, I strongly advise an early put-in. Once you reach the entrance into Emerald Bay, paddle to the camp and secure a camp site before exploring the bay.

If you are only paddling for the day and returning to Baldwin Beach, this small cove provides a secure spot in which to plan and make a decision as to which side of Emerald Bay you want to paddle first. If a crossing is called for, you will be in a good position to time your crossing before large groups of power boats or one of two tourist stern-wheelers—the *Tahoe Queen* or the *M. S. Dixie*—appears.

Emerald Bay (Southern Shoreline)
For a complete description of Emerald Bay see the previous paddle, Lake Tahoe, South Shore: D.L. Bliss State Park to Emerald Bay.

When you reach the inner tip of the small cove and paddle past the line of brush that obscured your initial view, the panorama of Emerald Bay is finally revealed. The twin peaks with the deforested scar of a massive rock slide below their saddle are Maggies Peaks (the politically correct name for the former 19th century anatomically explicit sobriquet). The southernmost peak is the tallest (elevation 8,699 feet) and the right peak is 8,499 feet. From Maggies Peaks, your eyes are drawn to the barren granite slopes of the former cirque, home to the ancient glaciers that carved the bay. Not readily visible to the naked

Yes, there are beaver in Lake Tahoe!

eye, a thin silvery ribbon of water glistens as it tumbles down the face of the granite. Eagle Creek drains Eagle Lake, carves its way through the weak zones in the rock, slides down the first slopes of granite, and rushes through the man-made culvert underneath Highway 89 before cascading down in the showy finale of Eagle Falls. Beneath the falls, the creek quietly gathers itself into a less-demonstrative form and quietly enters the bay.

Cutting a diagonal slash across the flanks of the exposed granite and following the outline of the bay is State Highway 89, Emerald Bay Road. Following the line of the highway as it climbs north past the cirque, the road cuts shortly through the waste rock of the former moraine field before disappearing around the lower flank of Jakes Peak (9,187 feet).

Standing in a dignity all its own, the lone conifer-topped island, known by a variety of names (Fannette and Emerald are the two most common), rises to its haughty height of 80 feet above the surface of the bay. With binoculars, you can make out the shape of the small former teahouse built by the last private owner of the island, Mrs. Lora Josephine Moore Knight.

Leaving their evidence on the surface of the bay are the wakes of countless models of boats buzzing around the island. Their coming and going reminds me of the worker bees that service the needs of their queen.

Putting your paddle to the task at hand, steer your boat toward the second and larger cove appearing to your left. As your approach brings you closer to the shore, you can make out the tree-sheltered beach with its quiet pool sitting serenely amongst the busy outer waters of the bay. The trail leading away from the beach and up to the heights of the forested ridge comes out at the Eagle Point Campground situated on the top of Eagle Point Ridge. This small pocket of serenity is the only decent take-out on this side of Emerald Bay. The other beaches with treeless sandy shores and safe swimming areas begin north of the mouth of Eagle Creek. Due to its afternoon exposure, I usually stop at this beach for a swim on the return leg of the paddle.

By now you may have noticed the difference between the terrain bordering the two shorelines of the bay. Although both sides of the bay have steep forest-covered slopes leading down to the water's edge, this southern shore is steeper and contains a denser forest. There are no trails readily visible snaking their way alongside the ridge line. Few if any hikers are present; those that are stay close to the water's edge.

Where the brush and trees do not cover the ground, boulders of various shapes and sizes litter the sloping sides of the ridge. At one time, before the arrival of vegetation, this pile of rocky debris was the lateral moraine field that flanked the southern edge of the last glacier that carved its way down to the lake. The northern twin to this moraine field is the elongated ridge of Emerald Point.

If you drive to any of the scenic stops off Highway 89 overlooking Emerald Bay, you will have an excellent perspective on the course that the glacier took on its way to the lake. The layout of the two moraine fields resembles the twin tusks of an elephant; where they curve into each other was the snout or end of the glacier.

Because this southern end of the bay is so inaccessible, you will have an excellent chance to view the varied birds that make their home in the dense forest as you paddle close to the shore. In addition to osprey, bald eagles are apt to perch here rather then on the northern shore. Colorful yellow and red western tanagers, and the bright yellow evening grosbeaks all pass through here. At the waters edge, the American dipper or water ouzel may be spotted sitting on a low branch overlooking the water or emerging from the shallow bottom where it hunts for insects. Throughout the forest, the scolding cry of the Steller's jay is heard. Eventually, its bright-blue plumage may be spotted as the jay flies from the limb of one tree into the boughs of another.

Just past the mid-point of the bay, you pass the closest approach to Fannette/Emerald Island. From here you can alter course and either paddle to the island or continue following the shoreline. If you wish to explore the island and learn its history, see Fannette Island in the previous paddle.

As you round the inner bay, if you continue along the shore you will pass the area of the slide scar you saw separating Maggies Peaks. The slide occurred on December 26, 1955 as a result of construction of Highway 89. Gliding by the area, you can spot a large number of boulders that came down from the unstable slope. Further down the end of the bay, the dense conifers give way to deciduous trees that outline the location of Eagle Creek. A short paddle brings you to the first sandy beach and the take-out for Vikingsholm and the beaches of the northern shoreline [see previous paddle, Bliss State Park to Emerald Bay.]

From here, you can explore further options such as touring Vikingsholm, hiking to Eagle Falls or just lying on the beach.

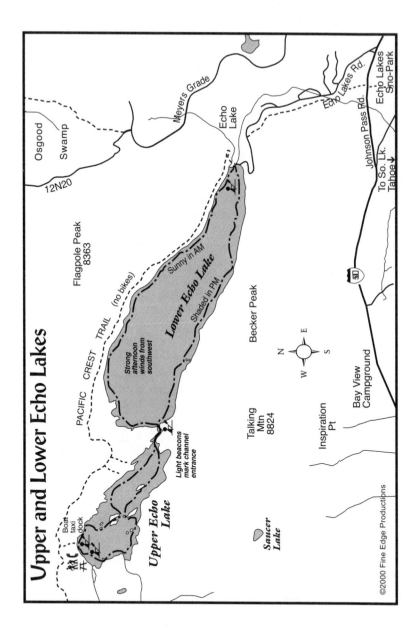

Upper and Lower Echo Lakes

Osgood Swamp

12N20

Meyers Grade

Echo Lake

Echo Lakes Rd.

Echo Lakes Sno-Park

Johnson Pass Rd.

To So. Lk. Tahoe

Flagpole Peak 8363

PACIFIC CREST TRAIL (no bikes)

Sunny in AM

Shaded in PM

Lower Echo Lake

Strong afternoon winds from southwest

Becker Peak

N E S W

Light beacons mark channel entrance

Talking Mtn 8824

Inspiration Pt

Bay View Campground

Saucer Lake

Upper Echo Lake

Boat taxi dock

©2000 Fine Edge Productions

PADDLING AREA 5

Tahoe Basin Lakes
(Eldorado National Forest)
Upper and Lower Echo Lakes

Echo Lakes
Echo Lakes lie in El Dorado County at an elevation of 7,414 feet above sea level. Lower Echo Lake is 1.5 miles long and 0.5 mile wide, while the upper lake is 0.75 miles long and 0.38 mile wide. The combined surface is 300 acres.

Trip Length: A full day on the water will allow you to paddle the entire shorelines of both lakes.

Paddling Distances (one way):
Boat ramp to the inlet of the channel into upper lake: 1.75 mi.
Boat ramp to the water taxi dock on upper lake: 2 mi.
From the channel inlet of lower lake to the water taxi dock: 0.75 mi.

Difficulty: Lower Echo is known for its strong afternoon winds. By timing your departures and arrivals to the early morning and late afternoon, you stand a good chance of missing the worst effects of the wind. In addition to the wind, Lower Echo also receives power boats and water skiers.

Upper Echo is protected by the steep walls of the cirque and the trees growing along the shoreline. The shallowness and a mandatory speed limit on Upper Echo makes it more conducive to car-top boating.

Season: Spring through fall. By September, the water level is too low for paddling through the channel between the lakes and portaging is necessary.

Maps:
USGS 7.5 minute series: *Echo Lake*
USFS: *Eldorado National Forest*
Area/Road Maps:
Compass Maps Inc.: *Lake Tahoe*

Access: From Highway 50 East approximately 50 miles, access is just before the top of Echo Summit. Look for a sign indicating exit for Echo Lakes, Berkeley Camp and Atwood Tract. Exit left onto Johnson Pass Road. Drive for 0.6 miles and turn left onto Echo Lakes Road. (If you miss the Echo Lakes road turnoff and continue on Johnson Pass Road, you will loop down onto Hwy. 50. Just turn right and follow Highway 50 back to the turnoff.) Continue on Echo Lakes Road to the boat ramp located below the large parking area just above Echo Lakes Chalet.

Lower Echo Lake Marina near the dam

Highlights:
- Echo Lakes Road is a two-lane asphalt road built for one standard vehicle. It is not suitable for large RVs and trailers.
- If planning a day paddle, arrive early to obtain a parking space near the launch ramp. Otherwise you will need to drive your vehicle back up the hill to the boat trailer parking area and walk down. Having a parking area near the ramp insures a hassle-free time period for loading and unloading of boats and gear.

Day use only (unless you are either staying at the chalet or have access to a lake shore cabin). Day use on the lakes is free.
- There is a $6 launch fee for car-top boats
- Be sure to fill-out the Visitor's Permit even for a day.
- A water-taxi to outlying areas is available for $6 per person each way.
- The chalet has a small store for any last-minute items.
- Public restrooms are located opposite the boat ramp and to the right of the chalet.
- Be sure to fill all water bottles before you arrive. I saw no water faucets or other means to fill containers. If the store is open, you can purchase bottled water.
- Overnight accommodations may be booked at Echo Chalet, 9900 Echo Lakes Road, Twin Bridges, CA 95735. Phone (916) 659-7207.
- Camping: For overnight camping within Desolation Wilderness, you need to pay a Reservation Fee and Camping Permit Fee. Phone reservations: (530) 644-6048. To reserve by fax: (530) 295-5624.

- Lower Echo Lake is subject to strong afternoon winds; water skiing is allowed.
- Plan on an early start for Upper Echo Lake. There is no water skiing, it is protected from wind, and it's warm enough for swimming.

Description: In the month of May, 1866, Ramsdale Buoy, a well-known Lake Tahoe promoter, was "talking up a storm" to several prospects along the shoreline of what was then Osgood Lake.

"Raise the Dead!" he bellowed. His friends repeated the cry and a resounding chorus of echoes followed. The clamorous sound bounced against the mountains, grew fainter and finally died away.

"Just like a pack of lovesick coyotes howling at the moon," Buoy grunted. "But if that's the best you can do, boys, I still give you Echo Lake."[1]

The former Osgood's Lake had been renamed.

Originally the lakes were divided by a narrow strip of land. In 1876, a tunnel was bored from the present spill site of the lower lake to dump water into the South Fork of the American River. The small dam built adjacent to the spillway raised the water level of Lower Echo and connected the two lakes.

Today, Echo Lakes is a photographer's dream—a deep blue alpine lake set within a bowl of towering ice-carved granite. You know that the sight of this lake will be special because of the scenery that captivates you driving the last mile of the road into the lake. Where you bottomed your car on the unseen "dip" passing Berkeley Camp, the forest begins to thin and a hazy view slowly emerges. Rounding the turn past a group of ancient cabins, the haze gives way to a breathtaking view of the Lake Tahoe Basin. If the conditions are right, you can clearly sight Washoe Meadows, small Angora Lakes, the larger expanse of Fallen Leaf Lake, and the majesty of Lake Tahoe.

Although the view is nothing short of spectacular, give some attention to the cabins built along the roadside. The owners certainly have taken pride in their property as evidenced by the cared-for but "rustic" look that seems to blend well into the overall scenery.

Once past the group of cabins, you arrive at the upper parking area. This lot is for vehicles towing trailers, backpackers on multi-day treks, and overflow parking from below. It is from here that you obtain your first view of Lower Echo Lake.

Follow the road down to the lodge, marina and boat ramp. This is the central hub at which residents, lodge visitors, backpackers and boaters co-mingle as they arrive or depart from the lake or backcountry surrounding the lakes. If you are not pressed for time, take a minute and enjoy this ebb and flow of humanity. All the noise and confusion, the pitch of emotion from voices that greet, bid good-by, or sound confused, just adds to the drama of the scene.

This thoroughly modern theater, however, is not without roots. If you let your imagination go for a moment, this same scene undoubtedly was played out a century ago by the miners and loggers, hunters and fishermen, farmers and other visitors to the lakes, all standing around waiting or readying their means of transportation before departing.

Back to the present. Hopefully you have found a parking spot near the ramp. If not, I suggest that you unload quickly the boats and gear, then drive up to the overflow lot before your vehicle gets blocked in by other arrivals.

If the small marina office located just to the left of the boat ramp is closed, you may pay the launch fee either at the store or the lodge, or wait until you return at the end of your paddle. To the right of the ramp is the information sign on backcountry rules and regulations. It also contains the storage box with the Visitor's Permits for all day use. You only need to fill one permit for the entire party; be sure to keep the green copy with you as you explore the lakes and/or hike the surrounding trails.

Lower Echo Lake

If you are starting out in the morning and will return that same afternoon, I suggest a counter-clockwise paddle route. You will start your paddle in the warmth of the morning sun; subsequently, your paddle back will be in the coolness of the shade on the opposite shore. In addition, the slope of the ridge on the west shore, with its thick growth of conifers, provides protection against the strong afternoon winds.

Upon leaving the buoy line located just past the marina, stay close to the shore, turn your boat around and note the boardwalk on top of the dam, with the sluice hugging the far left shoreline. Pacific Gas and Electric (PG&E) built the current dam, thus owning twelve feet of lake water. When the company uses this amount, usually by early fall, the lakes are once again separated at the small channel where boaters paddled through prior to the drop in lake levels.

Turning around, you see a huge mass of granite (7,758 feet) on your right, part of a roche moutonnee, an abrasion-resistant rock partially sculpted by glacial action. If you look on the down slope side of this rock mass, toward the chalet, you may spot hikers either climbing up or working their way downward from the slope. The trail that follows the lakes before winding its way into the Desolation Wilderness Area is a portion of the Pacific Crest Trail that extends from the Canadian border to Mexico.

Once you have paddled around the first mass of granitic rock, the imposing wall of Flagpole Peak (8,363 feet) looms even higher. Yes, there is a flagpole on top! Across the lake, the jumbled pile of rock with the short steep saddle is Becker Peak (8,320 feet).

An early-mormng start means calm water.

On some occasions, you may spot rock climbers working their way along a fracture or joint on the exposed face of one of these granite walls.

Paddling up the lake following the eastern shoreline, you will notice some of the cabins that are part of the lake's scenery. I have to admit that many of these structures are well maintained. and some are down right picturesque. My favorites are the two-story log cabin with a window-encased dining area that sits on a dimpled bench of granite surrounded by pines at the upper northeast end of lower lake and the stone cabin located on Upper Lake. The latter has a very solid permanent look to it, not unlike the ones I have seen in Germany.

Looking beyond the architectural styles, note that there are no roads or presence of vehicles near these cabins. The only access is by means of private boat or boat-taxi; consequently, you will see boats piled high with lumber and other building materials criss-crossing the lakes. Additionally, the only power for the cabins comes from either a generator, solar panels, batteries or old-fashioned candles.

All this mention of cabins, which may seem to digress from the description of the lake, does contain some important information. Although the lakes are open to the public, some of the land, particularly near these same cabins, is private and not for public use. Before attempting to beach your boat in proximity to a cabin, look around for any signs indicating private land. This is more of an issue on the eastern shore and the area near the channel connecting the two lakes

About mid-section of Lower Echo, along the eastern shoreline, you will pass a weathered slab of granitic rock that descends down into the water. On the face of the rock are small pinnacles of rock that do not resemble the granite. Running in a diagonal line between these pebbled pediments is a weathered ridge of mineral that resembles a tiny tunnel. Interspersed around the whole scene are shiny facets on the rock surface that reflect sunlight, not unlike miniature mirrors. The raised bits of foreign rock are called inclusions and are bits of older surface rock that came into contact with the rising molten mass that cooled and formed into granite. As the surrounding granitic rock weathered away, the inclusive bits of foreign rock were revealed. Eventually, these pieces of rock will fall away from their granitic matrix and join the other rocks along the shoreline.

The raised tunnel-like ridge was formed when molten matter penetrated a former crack or fissure in the existing rock. As this intrusive molten material cooled, it crystallized. This belt of crystals, being more resistant to weathering then the surrounding rock, was left exposed on the surface of the decomposing granite. The shiny polished surfaces that reflect sunlight were created by the abrasive scouring of former glaciers.

It was these same glaciers that formed the original lakes and surrounding topography. As you take in the view to the northwest, the steep bowl-shaped canyon bordering Upper Echo from the Desolation Wilderness Region is known as a cirque. A cirque is the exposed headwall of a former glacier that has melted away. In addition to the semicircular shape of cirques, their steep cliffs bind a rock basin that may contain a small lake or pond.[2] In this case, the cirque surrounding us also contains the waters of Echo Lakes.

The short trees with reddish bark that shreds when pulled off are Western junipers. Some have lived to be 2,000 years old. The taller pines are a mixture of Jeffrey (the bark gives off a vanilla or pineapple-like scent) and lodgepole.

Eventually you reach the end of Lower Echo Lake and, by following the downward slope of barren granite, the narrow nondescript opening leading to Upper Echo Lake. The entrance is rather deceiving. Unless you spot the two light bars, or see a boat emerging from the channel; you may paddle past the channel mouth.

Upper Echo Lake

Because the entire channel is extremely narrow and contains tight bends, listen for any approaching motor boats before paddling into the entrance. Although the majority of residents are cautious when motoring through, visitors—and especially the boat-taxi—have a tendency to "push" the 5-mph speed limit.

The nice part about paddling through is that there are small shallow coves that you may dart into if a motor boat approaches. These same coves are perfect for sitting in and observing the variety of boat traffic entering and departing the channel.

Some islands resemble bonzai planters.

As you cool off in the shade of the pines, take note of the different species of plants and animals that live here. Because the soil base is richer, with the tall pines providing shade and shelter from the wind, other types of plants not seen on the barren granite have found a home here. Alders form a dense thicket near the base of granite boulders to the left of the first cove upon entering the channel. Striking a handsome pose against the green background are stalks of scarlet or red columbines. The plants have large red flowers with yellow stamens that hang down.

Making your way through the channel, you make the left bend and pass through the twin beacons that mark the channel entrance at night, and suddenly your boat crosses over into the upper lake. The first thing you notice are the number of islands in the center of the lake. There are at least twelve islands of various sizes scattered throughout the upper lake.

From your boat, you can make out more detail on the granite walls of the cirque. The top of the ridge line marks the boundary of Desolation Wilderness. The high mountain on your right is Echo Peak (8,895 feet). At the same time, the noise from high speed motor boats and water skiers has ceased, replaced by wind through the pines and water lapping on the shore.

Within this lake area, no high-speed boating or water skiing are allowed. As you begin your meander through the islands, be sure to keep an eye out for the families of ducks and geese that use the many islands as nest sites. When you reach the group of islands located more or less in the center of the lake, take note of some of the smaller rocky knolls. With their lichen-covered boulders, and pines and junipers growing at odd angles, they resemble large bonsai planters. Chances

71

are, that you will meet other fellow paddlers enjoying the natural beauty of these many rocky isles.

On some of the islands, cabins have been constructed. On others, remnants of former cabins can be seen. Passing through a channel between two such islands, you can spot the remains of a chimney on one island and a cabin on the other.

The boat dock located at the far northern end of the lake is where the water taxi docks when it either drops off or picks up backpackers and day visitors exploring the backcountry. Just inside the grove of pines at the shoreline is a wooden hut with a pay phone. Because the location receives so much traffic, paddle a short distance southwest of the dock before beaching your boat. The spot I recommend contains two picnic tables, a wooden platform at cockpit level, and a nice grassy strip. Here you can enjoy a nice break, go for a swim, or hike out into the areas behind the lake.

At one time this area contained Camp Harvey West, a former boy scout camp; consequently, there are trails leading off from the lake in many directions. If you just want a small taste of the area, I suggest hiking south along the shoreline trail until you reach the creek bed. Follow the creek back for as long as you like. You will pass through forest, meadow and glaciated granite within an hour of hiking. If you continue to follow the stream bed, you will reach the spot where it splits into a Y. The southern stream flows out of Cagwin Lake, while the larger stream has Tamarack Lake as its source.

In hiking around the area, you will notice many meadows. Some are small and some as large as several acres. In the 19th century, hay was grown and baled here, then transported to Virginia City where it sold for as much as $90 to $100 a ton.

Evidence of former cabins and other sites can also be seen. Just above the stream where it flows past an outcrop of granite is a former garbage dump. In the afternoon sunlight, you will observe the sparkle of broken glass, the sheen of crockery shards, and see rusted metal and chunks of fired brick. Lying in a bed of alders is a large iron boiler rusted to a deep orange-brown.

On your return paddle, when re-entering the lower lake, follow the west shoreline. Not only will you be protected from wind, but the shade will feel refreshing after being in the sun all day. This side is also more forested then the eastern shore and you will pass impressive stands of pine and occasional fir. When you reach the marina, the concrete boat ramp will be on your left to the right of the dam and boardwalk.

[1]E. B. Scott, *The Saga of Lake Tahoe.*
[2]Gilluly, Waters, and Woodford, *Principles of Geology.*

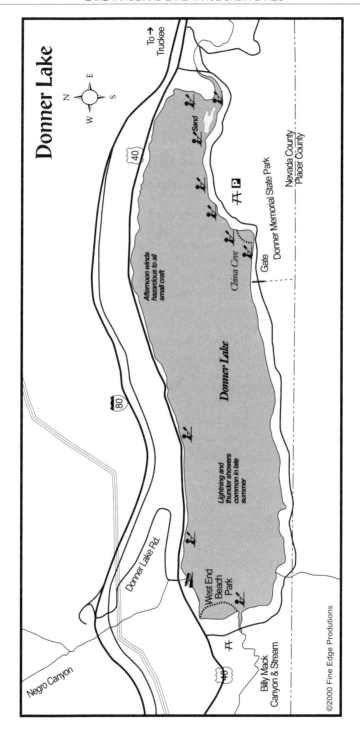

Donner Lake

To → Truckee

40

80

Sand

Donner Lake

China Cove

P

Gate

Donner Memorial State Park

Nevada County
Placer County

Afternoon winds hazardous to all small craft

Lightning and thunder showers common in late summer

Donner Lake Rd.

West End Beach Park

Negro Canyon

Billy Mack Canyon & Stream

40

©2000 Fine Edge Produtions

PADDLING AREA 6

Tahoe Basin Lakes: Donner Lake

Size: 3 miles long/0.75 miles wide; 840 surface acres; 7.5 miles shoreline
Elevation: 5,963 feet
County: Nevada

Trip Length: Paddling the area of West End Beach falls primarily into the day-paddle category. This area is a multiple-use family beach and paddling is just one of the many activities available. Time on the water is governed by your interest in exploring the shoreline.

If you choose to launch from Donner Memorial Park near China Cove and spend the day exploring the shoreline around the east end of the lake, this would be considered a full-day activity.

Launching from any of the public piers, or from the north side in general, means adding approximately 30 minutes of travel time to reach either end of the lake.

Paddling Distances (one way):
China Cove picnic area (Donner Memorial Pk.) to West End Beach: 2 mi.
China Cove picnic area to swimming lagoon: 0.5 mi.
Donner Lake Launching Facility to China Cove picnic area: 1.75 mi.
Donner Lake Launching Facility to West End Beach: 0.33 mi.
Shoreline Park to West End Beach: 1.25 mi.
Shoreline Park to China Cove: 0.75 mi.
Shoreline Park to Donner Creek Dam: 1.5 mi.

Difficulty: Either end of the lake makes a great day-paddle for paddlers of all skill levels. Venturing out for an extended paddle, be prepared for boat wakes, wind and chop, and rapid changes in the weather.

Season: The best time for paddlers on the lake is either in early spring or fall when the crowds are gone and so are the majority of power boats.

Maps:
USGS 7.5 minute series: *Norden; Truckee*
USFS: *Lake Tahoe National Forest*
Area/Road Maps:
Compass Maps, Inc.: *Nevada & Sierra counties*

Access: To West End: Take Interstate 80 East to the Donner Lake Road exit, immediately past the Donner Lake Vista exit. Follow the road to the intersection of Donner Pass Road. For West End Beach Area, turn right, and drive through Donner Lake Village. Turn left onto South Shore Drive. (West End Park stretches from the corner of Donner Pass Roard along the lakeside edge of South Shore Drive). Turn into the first left driveway and park. For official boat launch or public piers, turn left onto Donner Pass Road from Donner Lake Road. The boat ramp and launch facility is located approximately 500 feet from the intersection and across from the fire department. Take the second exit, drive past the parking area for vehicles with trailers and park in one of the spots adjacent to the restrooms.

If launching from either one of the piers or the small public park and fishing access, note the small white sign on the right immediately past the boat launch facility which marks the beginning of the public piers. Any pier from this sign (unless posted) to the Donner Tract housing area may be used as your put-in/take-out. Shoreline Park is down the road, about 1 mile past the official launch facility.

To East End (Donner Memorial State Park): Continue on Interstate 80 East past the Donner Road turnoff; turn off at the next exit. Turn right onto Donner Pass Road and follow the signs to the park entrance. Upon entering the park, stay to the right and follow the road to the turnaround and China Cove Swimming and Picnic Area. *Note:* You may launch from either side (but not within the swimming area).

Highlights:
- Donner Lake is a natural alpine lake, created initially through glacial scouring of the basin floor, then the filling of the basin by the melting glacier. Present lake levels are maintained by snow melt and runoff.
- The natural water level of the lake is 5,924 feet. With the construction of the dam at the lake's outlet, the man-made lake level of 5,936 feet is 12 feet higher.
- If you are eastbound on Interstate 80, don't miss the chance to view Donner Lake from the Vista Exit, 4 miles into your descent down Donner Summit.
- With the exception of the south shore (private homes with no lake access), there are numerous launch sites on the remaining three areas of shoreline. Some of them are free.
- The best day paddle on the lake is located within the vicinity of the shoreline bordering Donner Memorial State Park.
- Although not mandatory for paddle craft, there is a counterclockwise direction of travel for all power boats towing skiers. If you are planning a paddle during summer, following this rotation is advisable.
- The Donner Lake Launching Facility located off Donner Pass Road does not charge launch fees after the summer season, usually by mid-September. Otherwise, a $5-10 launch fee for non-California residents is required. Immediately east of the launch facility, on the same road, are numerous public piers. These are free and require no fees. Some have better lake access than others.

Looking across a sandbar toward Donner Lake.

Approximately 1 mile from the official launching facility on Donner Pass Road is a small park and fishing access—Shoreline Park. Boat launching, swimming and fishing are allowed with no charge; there are picnic tables. (For those of you who wish to paddle the entire lake, this spot, approximately mid-lake, makes an ideal put-in/take-out.)

Caution: Due in part to the natural setting of the lake in a basin, afternoon winds are strong enough to be considered hazardous. In addition to the winds, thunder showers, accompanied by intense lightning activity, may occur by the afternoon particularly in late summer (usually from August through the fall).

•Phone numbers for additional information: Truckee-Donner Chamber of Commerce (530) 587-2757; Donner Memorial State Park (530) 582-7894.

Description: The first glance, its difficult to imagine that Donner Lake, this large, oval, open body of water, can offer a paddler much enjoyment. However, if you divide the lake into paddling sections, it becomes easier to appreciate Donner Lake and all its charm.

West End Beach
This large family complex contains a playground, beach, swimming area, boat rentals, picnic tables and grills. Upon payment of a minimal entry fee, all the facilities are available for your use. For anyone wishing to use the West End Area as their base from which to paddle, I recommend the picnic site at the mouth of the small creek south of the main beach. Located just inside the creek mouth is a small former boat ramp ideal for a take-out or a put-in. You are far enough from the

swimming area that your boat will not be considered hazardous to unwary swimmers.

Once on the water, one of the first places to explore is the creek you launched your boat in. Paddling upstream past the small bridge, you leave the lake behind and enter another environment. The creek narrows and makes a bend to the right. By late summer, when the lake water drops, a sand bar appears mid stream. Houses, some used as summer cabins while others are year-round homes, are located on both sides of the creek. Small craft of all types and lengths are moored or stored nearby. Looking high above the homes, you have a clear view of the snow sheds that protect the trains crossing on the flank of Donner Peak.

Steller's jays hunt for food along the muddy banks while the American dipper or water ouzel dives into the creek to hunt for insects living on the bottom. Several bends up from the bridge, you come upon large earth rafts created by the spring runoff. As the melt water cascaded down from the upper canyon (known as Billy Mack), it tore into the brushy banks, tearing out huge pieces of earth, some with trees and brush still attached, then depositing them downstream. You now have to negotiate your way past this graphic evidence of stream erosion. Eventually, you reach the last area deep enough to prevent bottom scraping and maneuver your boat for the return paddle.

Upon entering the lake, make a right turn and head south along the shoreline. The tree-lined sandy beach that borders the south side of the creek and continues down the southwest shore is private property. Where the shoreline makes a bend, you begin to encounter the many homes that overlook the lake. If you paddle along the docks that front each home, keep a wary eye out for any fishing line which— almost invisible—may cause you to become entangled. This unfortunate event can escalate when the person fishing may either rain down curses or, even more humiliating, begin laughing hysterically.

If the problem of line entanglement is not enough to worry about, the speeding exit of a power boat will be. The quiet presence of a canoe or kayak gliding by is not always noticed by boaters exiting from their private docks. Some of these boats fly out from the small coves whose extended docks hide the view up and down lake.

Both of the problems are most likely to occur when paddling the lake during peak summer weekends. During my last paddle on a balmy fall weekday, I was the only kayaker present and one of only a small handful of boats on the entire lake.

When you get tired of viewing the different styles of cabins and their moored boats, turn your boat around and paddle back, using an outward tack, to view the stunning Sierra scenery. If the lake is calm and no adverse weather conditions are present, paddle out toward the middle of the lake, point your bow west, and drift a little. The panoramic view of the glaciated scenery is truly breathtaking.

At the end of the row of cabins, the boundary of Donner State Park begins. A small beach canopied by an arbor of trees provides a nice break area before paddling the shoreline around China Cove.

Donner Memorial State Park

From the sheltered beach, you will notice the buoy line stretching across the entrance into China Cove. During peak summer months, this area is off-limits to boats because of the numbers of swimmers in the cove. By September, especially after Labor Day, the entire shoreline of the park is usually deserted. The absence of people around the swimming areas allows you to paddle into places like China Cove and beach your boat with greater freedom.

At China Cove, there are toilet facilities and running water. Picnic tables are scattered around the area and a parking lot is located up above the beach. If you have additional vehicles, you may organize a shuttle between the launching facility at upper lake and the State Park.

The Donner Lake Interpretive Trail runs through here and ends at the parking lot. You can follow its course along the shoreline by large interpretive markers spaced at intervals along the trail.

A partially-overgrown road south of the parking lot is a bike path that connects with former South Shore Drive.

When you continue with your paddle, be wary of paddling close to the point rounding the northern tip of China Cove. The lake here is shallow with many partially submerged rocks. Upon rounding the point, however, a long narrow beach is revealed, stretching down the length of the shoreline. Trees and boulders hide small intimate coves where you can beach your boat to take a break, have a swim, or just enjoy the view.

Small groups of America's diving duck, the common merganser, may be spotted hunting for fish near the shore. As these birds cruise along, they lower their head into the water apparently looking for small fish, crayfish, or aquatic insects. Upon spotting their prey, the birds immediately dive and initiate a chase. I have watched these fast swimmers pursue their quarry in ever-tightening circles until the small fish are forced out onto the surface where they are quickly snapped up by the merganser.

At the far end of the shoreline, you come upon an open hummock of sand. If you take-out and walk up the sandy knoll, you will spot the entrance to the long, narrow lagoon that leads to Donner Creek and the Donner Lake Dam. Here you have a choice whether to conduct a short portage over the sand and into the lagoon or continue paddling around the large former island and enter the lagoon at its proper inlet.

If you elect to paddle around the island, the entrance is only a few hundred yards farther from the sandy knoll. When you reach the inlet,

Lovely picinic areas can be found at China Cove.

you have a nice view of a tree-covered sand bar and, depending on the water level, several smaller sand bars may be present. At first the scene is confusing, particularly when deciding which channel is the correct one to enter. Follow the far left shoreline, recognizable by its sandy tip. When you round this corner of beach, you have entered the former bed of Donner Creek. If you turn and look south down the long narrow channel, you can spot the sand bar that is part of the knoll on which you stood a few moments before.

As you continue paddling, the channel becomes even more narrow as the creek bed becomes more pronounced. Looking down into the water, you will spot large mats of waterweed. This common aquatic plant is a food source for muskrats, beaver and probably certain waterfowl. Smaller creatures use the foliage for shelter. Further down the channel, you will come to the site of the dam with its buoy line cordoning off any further entrance. If you were to walk to the other side of the dam, a natural creek bed with rushing stream, mossy cobbles and gravel banks will be in evidence.

If you are in no hurry, beach your boat and take the trail across the dam to the Donner Museum. The museum and Donner Memorial Statue are located a short distance down the road. Otherwise, enjoy a nice swim in the sun-warmed waters of the lagoon. Paddling back through the inlet, if you are going to continue to follow the shoreline, you will come to a small resort with a nice but small beach, lounging deck, and a boat ramp with canoe and kayak rentals. Inside is a bar and restaurant. At the end of a full day on the water, this is a nice way to reminisce about the paddle and watch the rosy tint of the setting sunbathe Donner Peak (8,019 feet) and Mount Judah (8,243 feet).

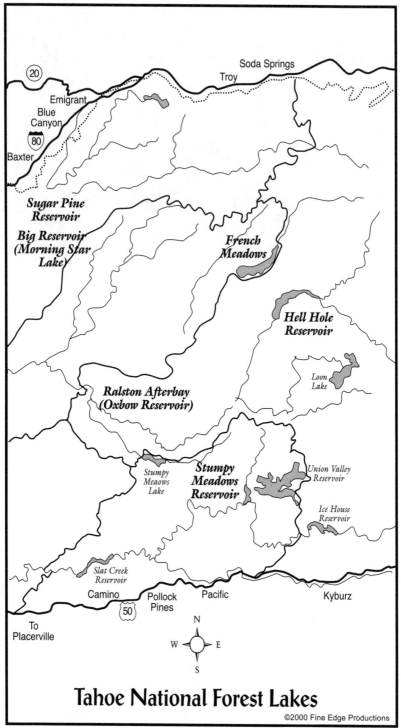

Tahoe National Forest Lakes

©2000 Fine Edge Productions

Tahoe National Forest Lakes
(Tahoe and Eldorado National Forests)

The old Lakota was wise. He knew that man's heart away from nature becomes hard; he knew that lack of respect for growing, living things soon led to lack of respect for humans too.
—Bill Mason, *Song of the Paddle*

Nestled among the pine-scented forests of the "High Country," man-made reservoirs have matured through the years to become a part of the natural landscape. Former meadows, deep gorges, and narrow river canyons have been replaced with sparkling lakes whose shimmering waters have started a new history of place.

Where grizzly bears once dominated the food chain, ospreys and eagles vie for nest sites and fishing territories. Mountain lions, while not a common sight, are prevalent enough to warrant posters warning the public of their presence. Deer still are plentiful, except during deer hunting season, but trout fishing has become the more accepted gateway into the out-of-doors.

Although the waters of these man-made lakes have erased the physical evidence of history, some flavor still remains in the names of the reservoirs: French Meadows, Hell Hole, Stumpy Meadows—a reminder of what once was. By paddling your boat on the waters of these lakes, you may still hear the echoes of the past.

French Meadows Reservoir

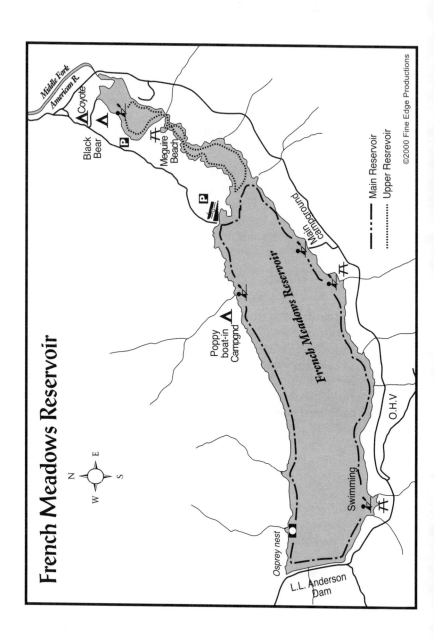

©2000 Fine Edge Productions

 **PADDLING AREA 1**

French Meadows Reservoir
(L. L. Anderson Reservoir)

Size: 1,408 acres or 134,993 acre-feet
Elevation: 5,300 feet
County: Placer

Trip Length: If you put in early, around 8:00 AM, You may paddle the entire length of the lake in one day. If you choose only one area to explore, the multitude of islands at the lake's upper end make a nice half-day destination.

Paddle Distances (one way):
From put-in at upper lake to Poppy boat-in campground: 2.5 mi.
From south shore parking area and boat ramp to Poppy Campground: 1 mi. *Note:* The USGS maps do not reflect the current water levels of the reservoir. I have added an approximate high-water level based on 1999 field research. Therefore all distances are approximate.

Difficulty: Although the lake is subject to strong afternoon winds, the upper lake is well protected and makes a great place to take the family or practice boating skills. This section of lake is suitable for paddlers of all levels.

The lower lake, because of its expanse and openness, receives a strong prevailing wind from the northwest. Conditions may rapidly deteriorate and turn the lake's surface into a mess of white-capped chop.

If paddling this section of the lake, a knowledge of paddle strokes and boat skills would be prudent.

Season: Weather and the lake's depth dictate the best paddling. Late spring, usually around late May, until late July or early August are the best times to enjoy French Meadows.

Maps:
USGS 7.5 minute series: *Bunker Hill; Royal Gorge*
USFS: *Tahoe National Forest; El Dorado National Forest*
Area/Road Maps:
Chamber of Commerce/Visitor Centers of Placer County, *Placer County ,California*. (800) 427-6463
Compass Maps Inc.: *Lake Tahoe Recreation Map*

Access: Take Interstate Highway 80 east. Exit onto the Auburn-Foresthill Road and drive to the town of Foresthill, approximately 20 miles northeast. Turn right onto Mosquito Ridge Road (Forest Road 96). (The turnoff is not well marked, so look on your left for the strip mall containing the Foresthill Post Office. The turnoff is on your right.)

The grassy put-in at upper French Meadows.

Twist and turn your way for the next 36 miles until you reach the French Meadows Dam. Cross over the dam, turn left (east) and drive along the lake on French Meadow Road (Forest Road 96) to either the boat ramp, the main campground or the campgrounds on the north shore.

To reach the put-in/take-out for the Islands Paddle described below, continue past the main campground for an additional 2 miles before the exit. Drive over the bridge, crossing the Middle Fork of the American River, and look for a sign just before the paved road ends and the gravel road begins. Turn left at the sign for Lewis Campground, McGuire Beach, the group campgrounds; and the boat ramp.

Look for a small dirt turnout on your left, 0.1 mile (or 0.3 mile from the turnoff) past the Black Bear Group Campground, but before the entrance to Lewis Campground. The put-in can be seen from the roadside approximately 80 feet down the trail leading to the lake.

Highlights:
- The upper end of the reservoir, near the mouth of the Middle Fork, contains many "islands" of high ground that provide protected lagoons, ready-made for canoes and kayaks.
- The lower end of the lake, particularly the south shore, has several sheltered coves located near the dam that make for excellent destination points.
- Best paddled in late spring through early summer, before the drawdown of the reservoir's waters.

- Last place for shopping and gas is the market in Foresthill.
- Bears may be a problem so pack smartly.
- **Camping:** There are two lakeside campgrounds, two group campgrounds, and one boat-in campground. Additional campgrounds are located along the Middle Fork of the American River off Forest Road 96 above the reservoir.

  Campsites surrounding the reservoir include gravel or paved parking spurs, piped water, picnic tables, and fire grill or fire ring. Both flush and vault toilets are in the campground. The main campground has a public phone.

  The fee for camping sites is: $10.00. For reservations, call (877) 444-6777 or online at www.ReserveUSA.com. A reservation fee is charged.
- **Fire Permit:** Required for any dispersed camping (this includes the use of the boat-in campground as well). Fire permits may be obtained at the Foresthill Ranger District Office in Foresthill, (530) 367-2224.
- The ranger office is open 9-5, seven days a week, closed 12-1 for lunch during the summer season. Inside you may purchase USFS maps and pick up some great free literature on the area. In particular, check out *Driving Tour Guide to Foresthill Road and The Placer Big Trees Grove.*

Description: Nestled in a valley surrounded by tall conifers, French Meadows Reservoir looks like a huge gem dropped from a broken necklace. After driving for over an hour on the narrow and twisting two-lane forest service road, the waters of the reservoir appear as if from nowhere, jump-starting your heart and clearing the glazed look from your eyes. This scene, however, occurs only—like the mythical city of Brigadoon—for a short span of time during the latter part of spring and the early months of summer. As the summer progresses, the waters of the reservoir decrease, leaving only a mud puddle to mark the location of the former reservoir. But, at its fullest, the beauty of this lake makes it hard to resist placing a boat on the water and paddling away.

Due to the unique physical formation of stacked granite boulders at the upper end of the reservoir, the lake has two distinct personalities. The first centers around the scenic spires and shapes composed of granitic rocks that form strings of islands in the waters of the upper lake. The lower end or main body of the lake presents a more typical lakeshore with coves of varied size surrounded by a mantle of red fir and ponderosa.

The Islands Paddle, Upper Reservoir

The best spot to put-in for exploring this part of the lake is the small beach down the trail that leads off the left side of the road immediately past the Black Bear Group Campground, before the entrance to the Lewis campground. Park your vehicle in the small gravel turnoff and portage your boat to the water's edge. A small intermittent stream is on your right as you hike to the lake.

At the lake's shore, you have a grand view of the many down-lake islands of varying sizes and shapes that give this end of the lake its unique personality. Directly across the lake and to your left is the mouth of the Middle Fork of the American River, which you drove across just before making the turnoff onto the road leading to this end of the lake.

Begin your day by paddling to the mouth of the river and viewing the wildflowers that grow along the river bank. Clusters of aspen dot the northeast shore of the mouth and their shimmering leaves seem to sparkle in the morning sun. With luck you may hear the delightfully melodic sound of the canyon wren as it flits about the granite boulders. In the clear pools beneath your paddle, the shape of trout can be seen as they dart away from your craft.

If you leave your boat and hike a short distance above the rapids, find a granite slab that offers a view of the river. Be still and quiet and you may observe the slate-gray, wren-like American dipper or "water ouzel" go about its unique hunt for food. This small bird ducks beneath the surface of the water and "runs" along the bottom with its wings half-open seeking small aquatic insects.

When the reservoir is at its fullest, your paddle will take you through brush and scores of small trees standing below the high-water table of the lake. One cove that contains many tops of drowned trees and brush is located north of the river mouth. Before entering, look for mergansers and other ducks that feed among the brush in the lake. Occasionally you may spot a band of Canada geese resting before they continue their northern migration.

Following the shoreline, as you backtrack to your put-in, you will pass a granite outcrop. In the late spring, carpets of red and blue penstemon decorate the alcoves bordering these granitic slabs. Hidden in the shaded rocky soil are the single white blossoms of the Sego lily (also known as Lechtlin's Mariposa lily). Lying along the ground in small dense clusters are pussy paws; sunning themselves or scurrying for cover at your approach are dark-colored Western fence lizards.

Be sure to take time to get out of your boat and get "up close and personal" with this beautiful display of spring. Some of the blooming penstemons show a mixture of color, attesting to hybridization.

Back in your boat, paddle past the dark green sedges of the swale near your put-in and head toward the nearest set of islands shimmering

These islands are dwarfed by the peaks of Granite Chief Wilderness.

in the morning sun. As you make your approach, be watchful for barely submerged granite outcrops that may scrape your boat's hull.

Hiding in the nooks and crannies of these outcrops, mergansers, Canada geese, mallards and other waterfowl will take flight at your approach or peer nervously until you glide by.

Sometimes you come across a family of parent birds and their young. If you do, *please back off and observe from a distance.* A good rule of thumb for judging the proper distance is to observe the parents. If they are swimming about nervously, making verbal sounds of distress, or attempting to shield their young from your boat you are too close. Back off until their actions appear normal, and you observe feeding, preening or resting behaviors.

The clarity of the water is such that you may spot the silhouettes of different-sized trout gliding by. Occasionally you can hear the "bark" and "plop" of a bullfrog startled out of its doze and hitting the water. Because of the shapes of the pools created by the granite outcrop, along with warmer water due to the relative shallowness of the area, searching for that perfect swimming spot adds to the fun of paddling among the islands.

As you wind your way into the maze of granite, notice the view that is taking shape to the northeast. The green conifers give way to the rise of barren, snowcapped peaks bordering the Granite Chief Wilderness. The lower lake comes into view as you continue to follow the line of boulders across the upper lake's end. The location of the main campground is defined by the wisps of smoke from smoldering campfires.

A broad conifer-covered ridge stretches for miles around the lake and flanks the road on which you drove; this is Chipmunk Ridge.

An unimproved ("rough") access road to the top of the ridge is located just off Forest Road 96 between the dam and the turnoff for the main campground. Look for the small sign indicating the turnoff. From the top you have an uninterrupted view of the reservoir below as well as the peaks of the Granite Chief Wilderness. The road also connects to Chipmunk Ridge Road (Forest Road 24) and the turnoff for Hellhole Reservoir [see Paddling Area 2].

The ridgeline that borders the lake from north to west and flanks the Poppy boat-in campground is called Red Star Ridge. It was named for the Red Star Mine located near Duncan Peak some miles west of the reservoir. Today, a remnant of the ditch that carried water to the mine can be seen on the right (north) bank of the Middle Fork below the dam.

The Tevis Cup Trail, a portion of the Western States Trail, follows the crest of the ridge. (The Tevis Cup is a one-day event that challenges horse and rider for 100 miles over the former Pony Express Trail, while the Western States Trail is the site of a one day, 100-mile endurance run.) [For more information, see *the American River: A Recreational Guide Book*, PARC (Protect American River Canyons), Auburn, CA.]

Eventually you will paddle across the chain of islands that border the upper reservoir. The water is shallower here then on the other side, so be alert for hidden outcrops of granite that may scrape or hang your boat. The shallow waters also attract water fowl, particularly the Canada geese that feed on the grasses on or near the shore.

When the wind begins to blow over the waters of the lower lake, here you can enjoy the sheltered bays nestled within the protected string of granite islands.

Main Reservoir (Lower Lake)

There are several put-in spots along the lower reservoir. To explore the north shore, launch from the boat ramp near the McGuire Day Use Area. From there you have ready access to the northern shoreline.

To explore the southern part of the lake, put-in either from the beach at the main campground or from the boat ramp at French Meadows Picnic Site.

Paddling along the north shore places you along the forest of firs and pine that grow right down to the rocky shoreline. This means that getting out of your boat does not happen often. Not only are the trees dense and difficult to hike through, but the shoreline is steep and loosely packed.

One area with a nice level area and a lovely stream bed to hike up is adjacent to the Poppy Boat-in Campground. The campground is located a mile west of the boat ramp at McGuire Beach. Look for a small inlet with a large boulder on the right side of the entrance. With careful scrutiny, you will spot the picnic tables and concrete fire circles indicating the campground. The stream borders the right end of the campground. Here you can pick up the hiking trail that follows the entire length of the north shore.

Paddling farther down, you pass many old-growth trees, some of impressive heights and notable girth. Allow your boat to drift silently and listen to the wind as it passes through the trees. During the lulls, you may hear the echoes from the rhythmic drilling produced by the woodpeckers. Occasionally the screech of a Steller's jay announces an intruder or register a complaint when a squirrel or another jay robs his food cache. On the lake, a small ripple or stream of air bubbles announces a fish lurking near the surface in wait for a low-flying insect.

Kayaks among the pines.

A shy merganser may suddenly pop out beneath a brushy spot near the shore, squawk and beat wings across the water.

As you near the dam, look for a tall bleached deadfall leaning slightly toward the lake. Located high on the tip is an osprey's nest. If it is late spring through early summer, you may see the parent birds arriving with a fresh "catch of the day" for the ever-hungry nestlings. With a set of good binoculars or a zoom lens, you can capture the feeding or at least obtain a glimpse of the youngsters.

Caution: To avoid stressing the parents, you must maintain a proper distance from the nest. Please do not attempt to land nearby.

Just before you reach the debris boom at the spillgate of the dam, look for a spot to beach your boat and hike to the dam site. The spillway leading from the reservoir down to the river below was drilled out of sheer granite bedrock. Those long thin grooves running down the surface of the granite wall are drill lines marking where the drill bit bore into the rock. The earthen dam, called the L. L. Anderson Dam, was completed in 1964 and is 236 feet high. Across the road, you will see the restrained Middle Fork of the American River reasserting itself after being captured within the confines of the reservoir.

South Shore

Paddling from either the campground or the boat ramp, head down-lake toward the dam. Although there are several nice beaches where you can put-in, it's worth the effort to stay on course until you arrive at a nicely-formed cove complete with a small stream cascading into the lake. Paddling distance is approximately 1.5 miles starting from the main campground. Inside the cove you are protected from the westerly wind that picks up in the late morning and blows until late afternoon. The cove has some nice swimming areas and, by mid-day, you will find shade at the southern arm.

When it is time to return to your take-out, you have the wind and waves off the stern instead of "in your face." As an added bonus, it's fun to catch and surf the waves generated by the wind.

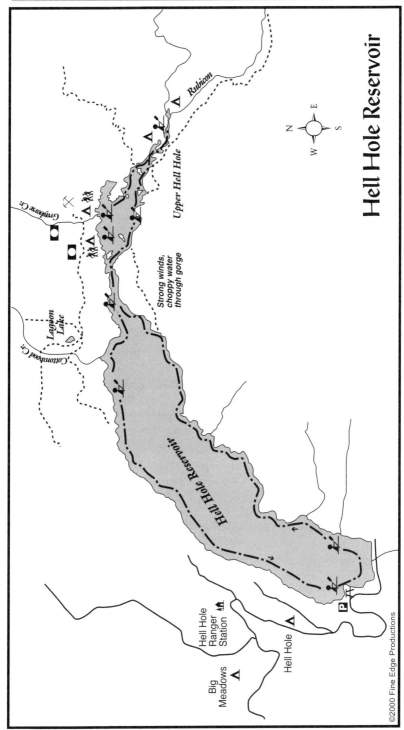

Hell Hole Reservoir

Rubicon

Greyhouse Cr.

Upper Hell Hole

Strong winds,
choppy water
through gorge

Cottonwood Cr.

Lagoon Lake

Hell Hole Reservoir

Hell Hole
Ranger
Station

Big
Meadows

Hell Hole

©2000 Fine Edge Productions

PADDLING AREA 2

Hellhole Reservoir

Note: Although located in Eldorado National Forest, this reservoir is described placed in this chapter because of its proximity to the other lakes in this region and its accessibility through the Tahoe National Forest roads.

Size: 1,300 ares
Elevation: 4,700 feet
County: Placer

Trip Length: Hellhole is best suited for a weekend paddle because of the disance to reach Upper Hellhole. If you attempt it as a day paddle, be sure to start early; it will be a full day's paddle.
Paddling Distances (one way):
Main boat ramp to entrance of narrow gorge into Upper Hellhole: 2.5 mi.
Main boat ramp to Grayhorse Creek outlet: 3.2 mi.
Entrance of narrow gorge to Grayhorse Creek outlet: 0.5 mi.
Grayhorse Creek outlet to Rubicon River outlet (Upper Hellhole): 1 mi.
Difficulty: Due to the reservoir's remoteness, size, and prevailing windy conditions, a knowledge of paddle strokes and basic boat-handling skills will prove to be prudent. Once the protected basin of the upper reservoir is reached, partially submerged rocks and the afternoon wind are the major concerns.

Do not underestimate the paddling time and conditions to reach the upper reservoir. Once you begin your paddle, there are few beaches available to put-in at for emergencies. The entire paddle to the upper reservoir is on open water with no shelter.

There is too much wind on the lower reservoir for paddle craft.
Season: Late spring when the road opens, usually around May, through the fall until the first snowfall. However, as summer progresses, the water level of the reservoir is drawn down, leaving the upper reservoir "high & dry." Day paddling on the main reservoir is not recommended because of the strong prevailing afternoon winds, and the lack of beaches for take-out.
Maps:
USGS 7.5 minute series: *Bunker Hill; Wentworth Springs*
USFS: *Eldorado National Forest; Tahoe National Forest*
Area/Road Maps:
Compass Maps Inc.: *Lake Tahoe Recreation Map*
Chamber of Commerce/Visitor Centers of Placer County:
Placer County, California. (800) 427-6463

The approach to Hell Hole boat ramp. Park and off-load in the day-use parking to the right of the restrooms.

Access: You can reach Hellhole Reservoir from two different routes; both are long and winding but the route from Foresthill is more direct and easier to follow.

1) <u>From Interstate 80 East:</u> take the Auburn-Foresthill Road exit past the town of Auburn. Continue on Auburn-Foresthill Rd. for approximately 20 miles into the town of Foresthill. Turn right onto Mosquito Ridge Road (Forest Road 96); this turnoff is not well marked. Look for a strip mall with the Foresthill Post Office on your left. The turnoff is on your right.

Continue for another 36 miles, down a gorge, then up a gorge. Eventually, you cross over the dam at French Meadows Reservoir and face a T-intersection. Make a right turn onto Forest Road 22 called French Meadows Road on the Placer County map. Continue for approximately 7 miles, then turn left onto Forest Road 2 (Hellhole Road on the Placer County Map). Go 6 miles to the boat ramp and parking area.

2) <u>Highway 50 via Georgetown:</u> from State Highway 50 East, exit onto State Highway 193 North at Placerville. Continue until you reach the town of Georgetown. At Georgetown, exit right onto Wentworth Springs Road (listed as Forest Road 1 on the Eldorado NFS map). Continue on this road for 22 miles. Make a left turn onto Forest Road 2 (Eleven Pines Road on the Placer Co. Map). Continue on Forest Road 2 for an additional 23 miles until the road intersects with Forest Road 22 (French Meadows Road). Continue right on Forest Road 2; the Hellhole boat ramp is 6 miles up the road.

Highlights:

- Be sure to inquire about the water level of the reservoir, particularly the availability to paddle into Upper Hellhole. If the level of the reservoir is drawn down, as is usual by late summer, then the paddling experience is greatly diminished.
- Parking and launching are confined to one small, steep site. For canoes and kayaks, use the small beach located at the bottom of the slope between the toilet facility and the picnic table.
- Last-minute items may be purchased either in Foresthill or Georgetown.
- If camping, park your rig at the overnight parking lot located above the day-use area. (You passed the turnoff for it on your way down to the boat ramp.)
- There are no adequate toilet facilities in this backcountry camping area, so plan to carry out your soiled TP (in a double-lined plastic bag). If paddling as a group larger then two, pack in a portable waste system, use a common latrine or properly bury your waste (but still pack out the TP).[1]
- **Caution:** Due to the remote location, be sure to have a proper first aid kit on hand.
- **Water:** No drinking water is available, so pack in enough water for your needs or invest in a water filtration system or a proper chemical treatment.[2]
- **Fire permit:** Required for any dispersed camping (this includes the use of the boat-in campground as well). Fire permits may be obtained free of charge at any ranger station in the Tahoe or Eldorado National Forests.

  The Foresthill Ranger District Office in Foresthill, (530) 367-2224 is open 9-5, seven days a week, closed 12-1 for lunch during the summer season. If you are arriving by way of Georgetown, you may pick up your permit at the Georgetown Ranger District Office, (530) 333-4312).

Description: Hellhole Reservoir is a long, open lake set in a deep gorge that tapers into the distance like a keyhole. (When paddling the length of the reservoir, I feel like I'm a key being inserted slowly into a lock.)

Hellhole Reservoir's name does not do justice to the setting. The reservoir is encased in a magnificent bowl of granite carved by ice and running water. Tall spires of conifers stand sentinel over the lake, providing a contrast to the black rock stained by weather and lichen. Close to the water's edge, the dark green of the conifers gives way to a lighter shade of green marking the presence of manzanita, California black oak and other deciduous plants. An occasional burst of bright color marks the location of wildflowers. To the northeast, caprock—an eroded remnant from a former lava flow—marks the location of

Steamboat Mountain (7,347 feet) and Little Steamboat Mountain (6,840 feet).

On a quiet morning, as you prepare for your paddle, stop and listen to the constant lapping of water against the granite shore. The location of the reservoir creates a wind tunnel, and this wind agitates the water so that the lake is in constant motion. Even in early morning, the wind is strong enough to initiate the rhythmic sound of wavelets washing onto the shore.

As you leave the rocky beach of your put-in, head toward the southern shoreline. Because the wind blows the entire length of the reservoir, there is no leeward or wind-free area that protects your time on the water. The southern shore has the best beach access if you need to make a landing.

Note: If you arrive late in the afternoon and wish to camp on the lake, there is a nice level area approximately 0.5 mile up the lake from the put-in. Use the pipeline located on the opposite shore as your reference point. The beach is located just before the pipeline, but on the southern shore. The camping site is a small cove on the inside leg of a short rocky point. Additional pockets of sloped granite gentle enough to beach your boat become scarce past this cove.

Even though it may be windy, the blow is on your back and the scenery unfolding in front of you makes the paddle worthwhile. Unlike some other mountain lakes, the depth of this reservoir makes the water seem opaque and the only time you can glimpse the bottom is at the immediate edge of the lake. This lack of clarity creates interesting

Bow-on to a glacial erratic; Hell Hole Dam is in the background.

Climb the granite outcrop for a great view of the reservoir.

surprises as you paddle along. Just when the rhythm of your paddling begins to lull you into complacency, the surface of the water erupts with a splash, a portion of a fin momentarily appears and, just as quickly, disappears beneath the dark surface of the lake. Less commonly, the eruption of water is followed by the graceful leap of a fish snagging an insect before re-entering the choppy lake.

When you begin to get used to the intermittent splashing of feeding fish, you may be surprised again by the sound of sea gulls voicing their distinct calls as they swoop overhead. The occasional errant gull may be seen either fishing the surface of the lake or resting on a granite outcrop.

Eventually you near the end of the main lake and the entrance to the narrow channel that leads into the upper half of Hellhole.

Upper Hellhole Reservoir

As you enter the narrow channel that separates the lower, main half of the reservoir from the smaller, upper half, look for a level beach above the waterline on the left side of channel. This is a nice two-person camp site with a view of both ends of the reservoir. Continue on and you enter the rocky bowl of the upper half of the reservoir.

The beauty in this hidden end of Hellhole takes your breath away. Rising above the dark blue water are majestic slabs of granite whose surface is spotted with "rugs" of conifers. Stretching to the southern end of the lake are islands bleached white of various sizes and shapes. Some hold lone pines or junipers while, on others, huge rounded boulders sit stranded on the island's surface. A thin white "ring" surrounding the bowl-shaped reservoir demarcates the water from the rocky shoreline.

As the visual stimuli begin to recede, you hear the sound of water rushing over rocks. Tucked against the forest-covered flank of a ridge, Crazyhorse Creek tumbles down, spilling into the reservoir just to the left of the narrow channel entrance. Paddle to the right of the creek mouth, beach your boat, and walk up to the tree line where you will find a ready-made campsite complete with tables, cutting board, high-stacked rock fire ring and a million-dollar view.

Take time to follow the creek upward, and you will be enchanted with the tumbling waters, multi-colored boulders, and flower-decked copses of oak and pine. *Note:* If you wade in the deep pools near the rushing waters, be extremely careful of the slick granite at the edge of the stream.

The cobble-strewn dirt road and marks of large tires at the sandy mouth of Grayhorse Creek are indicators of off-road vehicles that use the jeep trail located above the ridge. It is worth the time and exertion to hike the dirt and rock-strewn jeep road until the point where it breaks away from the pines. After a short uphill hike, the switchbacks end and the trail opens onto a small meadow. Look for a bare surface area of granite with a prominent lip that masks the view of the reservoir. At the edge of this lip of dark granite, you have a clear view of the reservoir with its light-colored islets as well as the glaciated peaks bordering the Rubicon River Gorge.

This clean granite slope makes a perfect spot for sunbathing.

With binoculars, you can view the details of the caprock that makes up Steamboat and Little Steamboat Mountains towering overhead to the northeast. This dark rock is probably basalt, a remnant of former volcanic activity in the area. Because of its composition, the rock has a high resistance to erosion and thus became a prominent landmark to the early visitors in the region. By late afternoon, you may make out the sharply-defined vertical lines running the length of the rock. These vertical columns are a mark of basalt flows. As the lava cooled, it shrunk, forming the geometrically-shaped, spaced columns along fractures created during the cooling process.

Back on the water, paddling among the small islets, notice that many of them contain large boulders that seem out of place. These "erratics" are the rubble that was left behind by retreating glaciers. Many of these "lost rocks" were plucked by the glacier and carried miles from their place of origin. Some of the islets are used by Canada geese, mergansers, dippers (or Ouzels), and sandpipers as nesting and rest areas. *Do not disturb nests or nesting birds.* Don't be surprised as you paddle past a barren outcrop of granite when the long neck of a wary goose suddenly pops up, followed by a series of "honks," and the entire flock lifts up, wings beating, high into the sky.

Paddling through the narrow channels that separate some of the islets, observe the oval spots of darker rock imbedded in the matrix of the parent granite. The geological name for these pieces of country rock is *xenoliths*.[3] When the rising magma came in contact with the parent rock, pieces fell into the molten magma (rising *batholith*) cooled

Drifting logs form a carpet near the entrance of Steam Boat Canyon Creek.

into granitic rock. Some of these xenoliths are as small as marbles and others may reach the size of a cow.

One of these islets, located near shore on the west side, contains a fairly level area that provides a nice campsite. If you use it, put your camp fire in one of the pre-existing fire rings so the scant soil won't become "dirty" with the mixture of charcoal and ash.

Eventually, you reach the far end of the reservoir and pass by the water-carved bedrock of the Rubicon River. Flowing through the sculpted rock, the river pours over a ledge and swirls into the waters of the reservoir. Small grottos hide groups of mergansers diving for fish. Cutting a zigzag wake, young snakes—most likely aquatic garter snakes—swim from one wet ledge to another in search of prey.

Just past the Rubicon's channel is an exposed shelf of granite with a small level area large enough for one canoe or two kayaks. Above the bench is a campsite nestled among pines and straddling the river's gorge.

To the left, and past the sandy islet, is the entrance to the drowned channel of Steamboat Creek. As you enter it, you will gain an appreciation of the power of the surging waters that flow down this creek during the spring runoff. Piles of smashed and gouged wood that litter the banks to a height of six feet or more are spread out over the entire channel. To the left of the now-placid creek is a large sandy beach.

Blocking the way to the upper part of the creek is a thick raft of logs. If you enter the log jam, let your boat drift silently as you peer down into the clear depths below. Schools of fish, varying in size dart in and out of the wood. If you remain still and do not move abruptly, they will think your boat is just another log and you will soon be surrounded by pan-sized trout. Along the banks, small flocks of evening grosbeaks dart among the piles of debris.

Along the east side of the reservoir are small coves containing suitable campsites. Some have been used for so long that they have been "improved" by each visitor. Others are the "official" kind containing the required picnic table, fire grate and ever-popular vault toilet—if you are lucky. When it is time to start your return journey, be sure to time it so you have a minimum head wind and use the south shore to block against the stronger gusts.

[1, 2] Hart, John, *Walking Softly in the Wilderness: The Sierra Club Guide to Backpacking* (this outstanding guidebook is invaluable as a learning tool for developing proper ethics and habits for all outdoor activities).

[3] McPhee, John, *Annals of the Former World*.

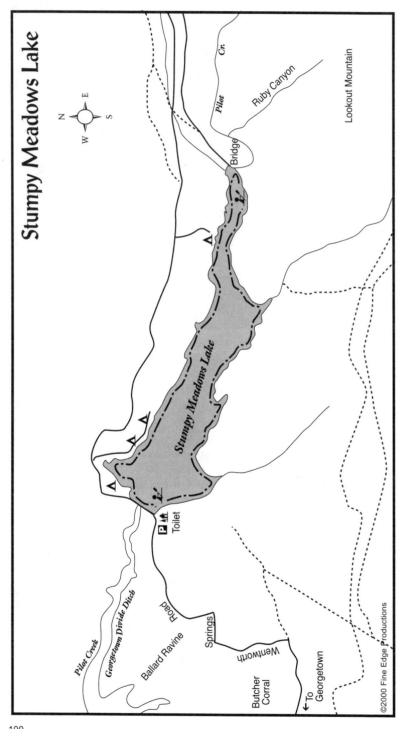

PADDLING AREA 3

Stumpy Meadows Reservoir

Size: 325 surface acres or 20,000 acre-feet
Elevation: 4,262 feet
County: El Dorado

Trip Length: Considering the time it takes to drive out here, give yourself at least a day to soak in the beauty of the forest and the clear, clean air. If you are having a good time, spend the night. On a moonless night, the stars are incredible.

Difficulty: Stumpy Meadows is an exposed reservoir with few places that provide shelter from afternoon winds. At low water, be on the lookout for partially-submerged stumps and rocky outcrops.

Season: From spring, when the snow melts, to fall or until the snows block the road (no county snow removal this far from Georgetown). However, the **best** time to paddle this lake is mid-fall when the leaves turn and you have the lake to yourself.

Maps:
USGS topo, 7.5 minute series: *Devil Peak, Calif. Quadrangle*
USFS: *Eldorado National Forest, California; Mt. Diablo Meridian*
Area/Road Maps:
De Lorme: *Northern California Atlas & Gazetteer* (section 88)
Compass Maps Inc.: *Western El Dorado County*
Chamber of Commerce/Visitor Centers of Placer County:
Placer County, California. (800) 427-6463 (Free; covers the majority of lakes and reservoirs described in this book. Available at the Folsom Lake State Park HQ off Folsom-Auburn Dam Road.)

Access: From Sacramento, take Interstate 80 East to Auburn; exit at the Highway 49/193 junction (south, also marked Placerville.) Drop down into the American River Canyon, make a right at the bridge crossing the North Fork of the American River, and continue up the canyon to Cool. At the first intersection (the only intersection), make a left onto Georgetown Road (Highway 193) and follow the road to Georgetown. At Georgetown, turn left onto Main Street and follow it through the town. Main Street turns into Wentworth Springs Road outside town. Continue on Wentworth Springs Road for 20 miles; you see the reservoir as you top the crest just before the drop into the basin holding the reservoir. Turn off into the Day-Use Parking Area and Boat Ramp located on your right just before the dam. (For camping in the established campgrounds, cross over the dam and follow the road to the signs indicating the turnoffs for each campground.)

From State Highway 50 East, exit onto Highway 193 North in Placerville and follow the road for 12 miles into Georgetown. [From Georgetown to the lake, follow the directions.]

Highlights:
- Fall paddling at its best.
- 5-mile-per-hour speed limit on the lake.
- Free access.
- Directly off of the main road.
- Last minute shopping at Camp Virner, Chiquita Lake.
- Concrete parking area and boat ramp with vault toilet.
- Free 3-day limit to overnight parking if boat camping.
- Campgrounds with 40 sites containing piped water, vault toilets, tables and fire places are adjacent to the reservoir.
- Campground use in summer months requires a reservation.
- **Fire Permit:** A campfire permit is necessary for any dispersed camping.

Description: To appreciate the subtle beauty of fall, try a paddle on Stumpy Meadows Lake. The crisp, cool, pine-scented air will take away the road weariness of your drive out here, and the fresh, clear air will dazzle you with views of the tree-covered forests surrounding the lake. If you are the only one at the lake, the stillness will cause you to speak in whispers.

Packed and ready to go, dockside at Stumpy Meadows.

The best route for this lake calls for a paddle toward the mustard-and ketchup-colored banks visible to the south (on your right) and down-lake. By staying in the shade as you begin, you avoid having the sun in your eyes on the return leg of the paddle.

Even before you launch the boat and paddle to the first landmark, you will probably notice all the small ripples, faint splashes and constant streams of bubbles throughout the surface of the lake. These are a sure sign of fish rising to the surface and feeding on the many insects that alight or are blown onto the water. Listen for the loud, croaking squawk of the common raven as it flies overhead; its impudent call is as grating as that of the Steller's jay that keenly observes all your moves from a nearby pine.

As you approach the multi-colored, eroded banks, look for a majestic Ponderosa pine standing precariously on the edge of the bank. The root system growing out of the exposed soil base keeps this mature giant from toppling into the lake, but it won't last forever. Sooner than later a strong wind or combination of heavy runoff and dense snow on the branches will cause the tree to succumb to the law of gravity. Until that sad day, enjoy its splendor and salute the pine's daily battle for survival.

The small cove to the right of the lone Ponderosa has a small intermittent stream at its end. At times, especially in the early morning, I have seen deer satisfying their thirst at the edge of the stream where it runs into the lake.

If curiosity gets the best of you, paddle to the edge of the exposed banks and examine the make-up of the stones eroding from the sides of the bluff. The majority of the rock appears to be *quartzite,* a "sugary-textured," crystalline metamorphic rock derived from sandstone. The coloration in the bluff (mainly the reddish hues) is staining caused by the leaching out of certain minerals as water percolates through the soil and deposits the minerals on the surface of the rock. The other colors are inherent to the individual rock types, particularly the gray tones of some *igneous* (volcanic) rock. Paddling away from the bluffs, look down-lake and admire the way the lake's horizon gradually recedes to a point, is blocked off by a dark wall of forest, and then reappears as twin peaks of stone that form a Sierra backdrop.

In the fall, the American bald eagle makes its appearance on many of the Sierra's lakes and reservoirs. Look for these large, shy birds perched on limbs of conifers overlooking the water. These birds, primarily carnivores, feed on fish, some waterbirds, and carrion. They like to blend into the foliage, so look for their outline or silhouette. Like the osprey, another visitor to Stumpy Meadows, the bald eagle cruises low over the surface of the water. With a "bit-o-luck" you will see one snag a fish from the lake's surface and fly to a nearby tree-branch to eat it, or you may come across eagles fighting ravens over a

This bridge crosses lower Pilot Creek.

piece of offal left behind by a careless fisherman.

Keep a lookout for a small, compact, dust-colored bird with yellowish feet that will fly ahead of your boat, alight on a rock or limb at the water's edge, and proceed to bob up and down to a beat of its own. This bird is a dipper (or water ouzel) ". . . the only aquatic perching songbird in North America. It is the size of a thrush and shaped like a wren, having a stubby tail. It dives like a Grebe, and feeds along the stream edges like a Sandpiper . . . The name comes from its habit of bobbing its entire body."[1]

With patience and slow movements, you can draw your boat close to the bird or birds and observe their hunting habits. (A pair will work as a team.) After a few bobs, the bird will either dive beneath the water for a choice morsel or swim to a spot and again dive or pluck its prey from the surface. Intermittently, one or both of the birds will stop and look you over; if no threat appears imminent, they will go back to their quest. Occasionally, another dipper will attempt to hunt on the birds' territory. Immediately both birds will chase the intruder away, tweet between each other, and go back to work. I have followed a pair of dippers from the down-lake edge of the bluffs all the way to the shallow cove near the mouth of Pilot Creek.

Paddling down the shady side of the lake becomes chilly after awhile. When you round the point of the second small cove before Pilot Creek, there is just enough of a clearing to allow some sunshine onto the beach. The water's edge is a gentle, shallow bank composed of gravel rather then mud. This is a good spot to warm up and take a break from the cold.

Back on the water again, you enter the cove where Pilot Creek empties into the lake. Since the 1960s, when the creek was dammed to create the reservoir, piles of silt have accumulated on the bottom of this part of the lake. Be alert for shallow areas as you make your approach; don't ground your boat on a shallow pile of muddy silt—as the author did when he was paying more attention to a cud-chewing cow than his paddling.

(Yes, I do mean cow! The area around Stumpy Meadows is leased to ranchers who graze cattle here from late spring through summer. On your drive up to the lake, you passed several loading/unloading chutes used to move the cattle into the forest from the trucks or vice versa. One such chute is located on the left side of the road across the dam as you reach the campgrounds.)

The best landing area is across the cove on the sunny side near the rocky outcrop at the edge of the grassy swale. From here you can hike to the forlorn-looking concrete bridge that crosses Pilot Creek. Somebody took pride in its construction, or maybe it was built as a reference point for a survey marker. Anyway, the evidence for both are set in the concrete that makes up the rail of the bridge.

This sunny, open area makes a great lunch spot. Afterward, you can take a short hike, following the stream bed or the overgrown former road that leads into the forest. The section of road heading east leads to a locked gate and a string of *No Trespassing* signs. The surrounding forest land is privately owned by a commercial lumber company and you will come across their posted signs bordering the lake.

As you explore the area, notice the small stunted tree growing on the edge nearest the lake at the end of the bridge abutment. This is a black cottonwood, a tree that normally reaches heights of 80 to 125 feet. Indeed, it is "... considered the largest Poplar in North America, perhaps in the world.[2] Unless luck is on its side, the chances of this specimen reaching such grandeur appear slim. However, we can enjoy its fall color and, in summer, take delight in the shimmering intensity of its leaves.

When you are ready to head back, follow the sunny side of the lake, along the wooded shoreline back to the boat launch and your take-out.

[1] Pickett, Edwin R., *Birds of Central California*.
[2] Peattie, Donald Culross, *A Natural History of Western Trees*.

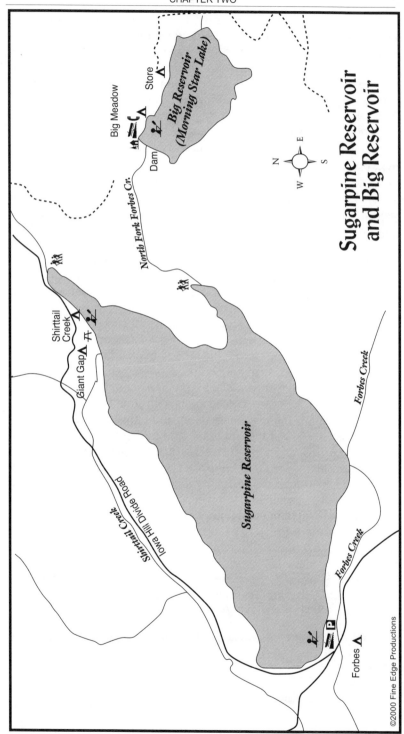

Sugarpine Reservoir
and Big Reservoir

Big Reservoir
(Morning Star Lake)

Store

Big Meadow

Dam

North Fork Forbes Cr.

N
W — E
S

Shirttail
Creek

Giant Gap

Sugarpine Reservoir

Shirttail Creek

Iowa Hill Divide Road

Forbes Creek

Forbes Creek

Forbes

PADDLING AREA 4

Sugar Pine Reservoir

Size: 160 surface acres,
Elevation: 3,618 feet
County: El Dorado

Trip Length: Can be paddled in a day.
Difficulty: Sugar Pine is somewhat exposed and receives gusty afternoon winds.
Season: From late spring through fall (summer brings out the crowds and motorized water craft).
Maps:
  USGS, 7.5 minute series: *Dutch Flat* quadrangle; *Westville* quadrangle
    USFS: *Tahoe National Forest, California; Mt. Diablo Meridian*
  Area/Road Maps:
    De Lorme: *Northern California Atlas & Gazetteer*
    Compass Maps Inc.: *Placer County/Western Placer County*
    Chamber of Commerce/Visitor Centers of Placer County: *Placer County, California.* (800) 427-6463
Access: From Sacramento, take Interstate 80 east to the Foresthill-Auburn Road exit, located past the turnoff for downtown Auburn and Highway 49. Continue on Foresthill-Auburn Road, crossing the bridge overlooking the American River Gorge. (You will pass the exits for

The end of the line until next season.

Lake Clementine, a finger-reservoir described in Volume 1 of *Up the Lake with a Paddle.*)

Continue for 20 miles to the town of Foresthill. Drive through, staying on Foresthill Road. Drive an additional 8 miles and make a left turn onto Sugar Pine Road (Forest Route 10). Follow the road for about 4 miles to Parker Flat OHV Staging Area. The road forks at the large clearing on your left. The road straight ahead of you (recently-paved Forest Road 24) leads to Big Reservoir and Morning Star Resort 2 miles away.

Take the left fork (paved) which is still Forest Road 10 (Sugar Pine Road) to the reservoir approximately 2 miles ahead. You will pass Forbes Creek Campground, one of three campgrounds surrounding the lake; 0.5 mile past Forbes Creek Campground is the right exit for the Sugar Pine Reservoir Boat Ramp and Day Use Area.

To reach Giant Gap and Shirttail Creek campgrounds, stay on Sugar Pine Road for an additional 3 miles, cross over Sugar Pine Reservoir Dam, and turn right onto Sucker Peak Road. Dropping down toward the lake, Manzanita Day-Use Area and beach, with parking area, are ahead. Shirttail Campground is to your left and Giant Gap Campground, and the campground host, is on your right.

Highlights:
- Sugar Pine is nestled in a small basin surrounded by a full, diverse forest.
- The reservoir is a comfortable driving distance from Sacramento.
- Sugar Pine Reservoir is scenic to paddle *but* is open to all boaters. There is a 10 mile an hour speed limit law which discourages most power boaters.
- Big Reservoir is only 2 miles by road from Sugar Pine Reservoir.
- There are full camping facilities.
- For information, call the Foresthill Ranger Station at (530) 367-2224.

Description:

On a warm Indian Summer day, you can almost hear the leaves fall as you paddle on the clear water of this picturesque reservoir. With the arrival of fall, the bright hues of the changing leaves give this area a look of Vermont.

Mid-fall or the month of October is the best time to paddle the lake. You may find the lake—except for a few bank-fishermen—empty of people. This has happened to me on several occasions and has made for some memorable views of local wildlife.

The best place to launch is the boat ramp; or if you wish to stake a spot by the shore, park in one of the spaces closest to the lake in the upper parking area. From there, it is a short walk with your boat to one of the many shady areas located below the parking lot.

The main beach, Manzanita Day-Use Area.

To make your return paddle a little easier, circumnavigate the lake in a clockwise direction; if you do, on your return leg you will be protected from most of the wind that comes up in the afternoon. In addition, paddling on a cool fall day, the warmth of the sun falling along the north shore feels mighty fine on your shoulders.

As the breeze picks up, close your eyes and you will hear the rustle of the falling leaves. Steller's jays appear suddenly, broadcasting their presence with loud boisterous cries. The softer tones of a small flock of sparrows complements the throaty hoarseness of the jays. Paddling past the dense screen of trees that border the shore, you may notice a reminder of last summer—the frayed length of a rope swing gently swaying in the breeze.

As you admire the different trees growing near the lake's edge, you can pick out the reddish shredded bark of incense cedar and, if it is warm enough, the faint piney aroma of all the conifers. The large-lobed leaves turning yellow in autumn identify the California black oak, a name given to it by the esteemed pioneer botanist, Dr. Albert Kellogg, because of its dark gray bark. According to many of the California Native Americans, the acorn of the black oak tasted best. As Sabina Norris, a Norfolk Mono, recalled:

"Acorns are everywhere, but we like the ones in the mountains, the black oak acorns . . . They taste the best, they cook the best—get nice and thick. That's what we ate—*ekibay* (a thick, congealed acorn pudding)—we had it every day."[1]

Orange-colored leaves set against the wine-red peeling bark are sure indicators of the Pacific madrone. This tree is considered by many one of the most beautiful flowering broadleaf evergreens. The name originates from the Spanish *Madrono* meaning "the strawberry-tree," a similar species that grows in Spain and the Mediterranean Region. The tree was named by Father Juan Crespi, a member of the Portola expedition of 1769.[2]

Paddling past the lush growth along the lake's banks, suddenly you come across an extensive clearing where only short grasses and manzanita grow. Examining the area closer, you notice the milky-green sheen of the exposed rocky outcrop. If you pick up and examine one of the rocks, it has a soft soapy feel to it. This greenish rock is *serpentine*, the California State Rock. An outcrop of serpentine indicates a special type of nutrient-poor soil base that harbors a unique plant community given the term *edaphic*:, " . . . where soil is the principal factor to which the community must adapt."[3]

Paddling still farther, you spot a large clearing that shimmers in the autumn sunlight. This is the Day-Use Area and the campgrounds are on either side of the beach and picnic tables. If the area has not been closed for the season, you will find a clean restroom tucked behind the manzanita just above the beach area. The path seen winding its way through the area leads to the Giant Gap Campground located among the pines to the south.

As you round the extensive serpentine outcrop, you enter a small finger channel. This is the mouth of Shirttail Creek. If you get out and hike up to the upper bank, you will cross the Sugar Pine Shore Trail, a hiking trail that circles the entire reservoir. Beyond the trail, following Shirttail Creek, is a small scenic log bridge. Just over the bridge is Shirttail Campground. Located a few yards up the creek and past the trees are open meadows with outcrops of serpentine.

After getting back into your boat, follow the trees lining the left shoreline to the point barely visible in the shade of the conifers. Upon reaching the point, be careful of the rocky headland. As the water level drops, the rocks just beneath the surface may scrape against your boat.

Working your way past the point brings you into view of a cobble bar that stretches from the far shore to the edge of the trees that border the upper parking lot of the day-use area. On your left, approximately 100 yards from the rocky point around which you paddled is a small sandy beach, the only beach on this side of the lake with a decent level area on which to beach your boat and take a break.

When you are on your way again, paddle into the second stream channel that enters the lake. This drowned stream channel belongs to the North Fork of Forbes Creek. The water flowing into Sugar Pine

Forbes Creek is a good spot to beach your canoe and explore.

Reservoir from this stream is released from the dam on Big Reservoir. The channel narrows as you approach and the pines seem to enclose the light in dark patches of deep shade. Notice the hue of the soil here. It is a deep red, almost rust in color. This soil base, often called *lateritic*, is derived from the type of soils—*laterites*—which are often found in the tropics. The deep red color is a result of many years of weathering of the parent rock—andesites, basalts and other igneous rock. Over time, many of the minerals were leached out and heavy concentrations of iron oxide were left behind creating a process not unlike the rusting away of a metal object left to the elements.

When you reach the end of the channel, beach your boat and follow the same Shore Trail you first saw at the junction of Shirttail Creek and the reservoir. If you follow this trail as it winds its way upstream, you will reach the heavy-duty bridge that spans the creek and allows you to continue on the trail to the day-use parking lot near the boat ramp.

If you hike the trail back toward the lake, you will reach the high ground where Shirttail Creek Channel becomes part of the lake. From here you have an unobstructed view of the upper reservoir and dam.

Back in your boat, paddle out of the channel and, using the cobble bar as a wind break, follow the shoreline to the boat ramp or your put-in.

[1] Pavlik, Muick, Johnson, and Popper, *Oaks of California.*
[2] Peattie, Donald C., *A Natural History of Western Trees.*
[3] Schoenherr, Allan A., *A Natural History of California.*

PADDLING AREA 5

Big Reservoir
(Morning Star Lake)

Size: 70 surface acres
Elevation: 4,050 feet
County: El Dorado

Trip Length: May be paddled in one day.
Difficulty: Aa family paddle at its best. Some afternoon wind may present a problem, as well as submerged tree stumps at the southern end of the lake that may become a hazard to unwary paddlers.
Season: From late spring through early fall.
Maps: [See *Sugar Pine Reservoir* above.]

Access: From Sacramento, take Interstate 80 east to the Foresthill-Auburn Road exit, located past the turnoff for downtown Auburn and Highway 49. Continue on Foresthill-Auburn Road, crossing the bridge overlooking the American River Gorge. (You will pass the exits for Lake Clementine, a finger-reservoir described in *Up the Lake with a Paddle, Vol. 1*.)

Continue for 20 miles to the town of Foresthill. Drive through the town, staying on Foresthill Road. Drive an additional 8 miles and make a left turn onto Sugar Pine Road (Forest Road 10). Follow the road for about 4 miles to Parker Flat OHV Staging Area.

At the junction of Forest Road 10 and Forest Road 24, continue straight on Forest Road 24 toward Parker Flat. Follow the newly-paved road for 1.6 miles, then turn right at the sign for Morning Star Lake, which is about 0.5 miles from this turnoff.

Stop at the entrance and pay your fee, then follow the road down to either the Day-Use Area or the campgrounds at the end of the lake.

Highlights:
- Big Reservoir is small, but it has a nice family atmosphere.
- Sailboats, canoes, kayaks, row boats and windsails **only**; no outboards allowed.
- Big Reservoir is privately owned and has a better campground (a camp store and hot showers) than Sugar Pine.
- Owned and operated by De Anza Placer Gold Mining Company who renamed the reservoir and campground Morning Star Lake. For reservations, call (530) 367-2129 during normal office hours, April through October. (Office closed November through March.)

•California Fishing License is <u>not required</u> if you stay here, but you must purchase a private fishing permit from the operators).

Description: If a camping trip with the family is on your agenda and just happens to include a canoe or kayak, then a visit to Big Reservoir may be a smart choice. This small, rather unimposing lake has a charm that fits the image of a "family camping spot." Because it is privately owned and maintained, families can expect a set of rules and regulations to insure the safety, comfort, and pleasure of all the guests at the campground.

The small oval lake is ideal for teaching children the basics of canoeing and kayaking; the water is warm enough in summer for swimming; its size permits a paddle away from the hustle and bustle of the campground while still in view of family members.

A short distance from the entrance is the day-use area shaded by trees. Farther down the lake on the shoreline you will pass the general store and campground showers. The campgrounds are at the end of the lake. If you plan on staying for the weekend or longer, sites 1-3 seem the best bet; sites 42-51 border the forest (site 42 is closest to the lake) and have ample morning shade. Each site has wooden shade bowers, but also bring a tarp or other means of providing shade.

The northwest shore, across the lake from the main entrance, is forest-covered and contains some deep holes where the trout lurk. At the far southern end of the lake, the forest has been cut back, creating an open sunlit area. Here, among tree stumps and deciduous trees bordering the lake, blackbirds nest, deer come to drink, and the coyote howls.

Need an extra boat? Rentals are available at Morning Star.

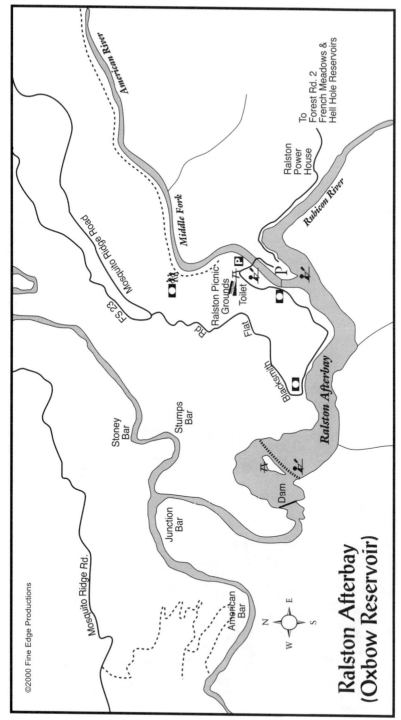

Ralston Afterbay (Oxbow Reservoir)

©2000 Fine Edge Productions

PADDLING AREA 6

Ralston Afterbay
(Oxbow Reservoir)

Size: 2,519 acre-feet covering 83 acres
Elevation: 1,200 feet
Counties: Placer and El Dorado

Ralston Afterbay Reservoir is named after Ralston Ridge, part of an extensive region called Ralston Divide. This locality also includes Long Canyon and the Nevada Point Ridge areas. Ralston Ridge is the predominant geologic feature in the vicinity of the reservoir. In the , the entire region was a well-known placer-gold district. The ridge was reportedly named after William Chapman Ralston (1828-1875), one of the principle founders of the Bank of California.

The name, Oxbow Reservoir, comes from the Oxbow Powerhouse and Dam that holds back the waters of the afterbay.

Trip Length: Great for a day paddle.
Paddling Distances (one way):
Put-in at Ralston launch ramp to boom-line: 1.0 mi.
Put-in at Ralston launch ramp to Ralston power plant: 0.5 mi.
Difficulty: As the water level drops, current from the exposed river channel increases, causing some difficulty in paddling to the upper areas of the reservoir.
Except for this section, the remaining part of the reservoir may be paddled by boaters of all skill levels.
Season: From winter through late spring water levels are high enough to paddle. By mid-June, too much fluctuation from draw-downs makes Oxbow Reservoir unpredictable.
Maps:
USGS 7.5 minute series: *Michigan Bluff* quadrangle; *Tunnel Hill* quadrangle; *Forest Hill* quadrangle.
USGS County Map Series: *Placer County, CA.* 1:100 000 series
USFS: *Tahoe National Forest; Mt.. Diablo Meridian*
Area/Road Maps:
Sowarwe-Werher: *Auburn State Recreation Area Topographic Trail Map* (1998) [a new map based on information from USGS topographical maps, USFS maps, Bureau of Land Management (BLM) maps and California Parks & Recreation maps. Data shown includes: hiking, equestrian, and mountain biking trails, as well as whitewater boating].

Ox Bow lies deep in the confluence of the American River Middle Fork and the Rubicon.

Compass Maps Inc.: *Western Placer County; Western El Dorado County*

Chamber of Commerce/Visitor Centers of Placer County:
Placer County, California. (800) 427-6463 (a free map that covers the majority of lakes and reservoirs described in my books. Pick one up at the Folsom Lake State Park headquarters off Folsom-Auburn Dam Road.)

Access: From Sacramento, take Interstate 80 East to Auburn. Exit onto Foresthill Road, and continue for 20 miles to the town of Foresthill. Look for a small strip mall with the Foresthill Post Office on the left. The exit onto Mosquito Ridge Road will be on your right immediately past the Smugglers Inn restaurant. Follow this ribbon of a road through many twists and turns as it descends into the Canyon of the Middle Fork of the American River. Just past the 9 mile marker, you will cross a graceful and picturesque steel span bridge across the North Fork of the Middle Fork, a tributary of the Middle Fork of the American River. Immediately across the bridge—if you are interested in hiking this historic canyon (there are many mining tunnels in the adjacent side canyons)—park your vehicle in one of the few turnouts located on either side of the road. The trail starts on the east side approximately 40 feet past the southeast bridge abutment.

To reach the turnoff for Oxbow Reservoir, continue for an additional 1.5 miles. The turnoff is on your right immediately past the

11 mile marker. After you exit, you'll be looking down at the tail end of the reservoir with Ralston Powerhouse abutting the canyon on the left. Continue on Blacksmith Flat Road (National Forest Road 23) until you come to a Y intersection. Follow the road on the left. At approximately 0.2 mile is the turnout for Ralston Picnic Ground and boat ramp.

The road continues across the bridge, follows the channel of the Rubicon River past the Ralston Power House, and climbs upward onto Ralston Ridge; eventually, the road intersects Forest Road 2 that leads to French Meadows and Hellhole reservoirs, and Georgetown.

Highlights:
- Day-use only.
- Free access.
- Ralston Picnic Area contains picnic tables, grills and a vault toilet.
- Easy put-in from two boat launch ramps.
- In the late spring and early summer, the shallow reservoir contains some great swimming areas.
- Water levels fluctuate and by late summer, the reservoir may be drained.
- Weekdays and during the winter months, it is not uncommon to have the reservoir to yourself.
- If paddling in winter, the sun seldom reaches the depths of the gorge; therefore, dress *warmly* and bring a thermos with a favorite hot beverage.
- Good trout fishing and hiking along adjacent Middle Fork of American River Canyon accessed from Ralston Picnic Area.

Mosquito Ridge is reflected in the still afternoon waters.

Description: It is the middle of winter, you have paddled all the local lakes and reservoirs that still have water in them to the point of boredom. So where can a paddler get his or her "fix" paddling something new, without a lo-o-ng driving time? Check out Ralston Afterbay, better known as Oxbow Reservoir.

Located only a couple hours driving time from Sacramento, this small finger reservoir will delight you with its wintry mood and tranquil waters. The reservoir is nestled at the bottom of a deep gorge carved by the mixed waters of the Middle Fork of the American and Rubicon rivers. If you arrive after a recent snowfall, the sight of a white-cloaked canyon gorge, with dazzling sunlight reflected by ice crystals hanging from bare branches, will take your breath away.

Upon stepping out of your vehicle, your breath will cause steamy vapors to billow around you. With each intake, the sharp scents of winter, the smell of new snow and the tartness of wet rock mixed with damp vegetation, will excite the senses.

If the reservoir is full, use the boat ramp located in the Ralston Day-Use area. Sometimes a rime of ice covers the surface of the stream below the bridge. I have paddled through it without difficulty. If you feel uncomfortable about working through the ice, there is an ice-free boat ramp a short distance across the bridge and on your right.

As you begin your paddle, look down at the water, its clarity is amazing. I have always been astounded by the clarity of the streams and rivers flowing out of the Sierra backcountry. I realize a water's clarity sometimes masks the toxins and harmful chemicals that abound in our lakes and rivers; nevertheless, this clear, running water is a joy to behold.

A high, mass of exposed rock face juts out on your right just before you enter the main body of the reservoir. Paddle close and slowly examine its weathered, incised face. This block of rock is a piece of the bedrock that makes up the geology of the area. It is composed of sandstone and slate that underwent intense heat and pressure to become *metamorphic* or "re-crystallized and changed" rock. This deformed assemblage of rocks became part of the geologic feature called the *Shoo Fly Complex*: a sequence of sedimentary deposits originally laid down on the continental shelf, approximately 400 million years ago. The assemblage underwent a change caused by heat and pressure, then subsequently was squeezed upright by mountain-building episodes, and became the basement rock for the ancestral Sierra-Nevada Mountain Range.[1]

If you examine pieces of similar slate found along the road you will see small square holes set into the rock face. This occurred when *iron pyrite*, also known as fool's gold, weathered out, leaving an empty space where it had been. If you place the rock in sunlight or shine a flashlight on it, bright crystals shimmer and sparkle in the light. On some pieces of the slate, you will find the yellowish cubes of pyrite still embedded in the matrix. Their shine fooled many a "tenderfoot" or novice miner into thinking they had "struck it rich," only to realize that they had been "fooled" by Mother Nature."

The grooves, or joints, running the width of the rock were caused by weathering, an erosion process that aids in the breakdown of rock. Ferns took advantage of the small soil base that was established and their root systems eventually enlarged the cracks.

Paddling past the rock outcrop, you enter the main body of the reservoir. Directly across the water to the southwest is the shadow world of the gorge. Dark green canopies of oak, pine, and dogwood stand sentinel on the rocky escarpments of upthrust slate. Interspersed between the larger trees, a light green mantle of moss hides the surface of any exposed rock. As you paddle farther across the reservoir, the shade grows darker and colder. When you reach the other side and look back, your pupils—having adjusted to the dim light of the gorge—focus painfully on the sun-drenched hills of the upper canyon.

The current of the river slowly pushes your boat down into the gorge of the reservoir, so you take up your paddle and, pointing the bow back upstream, begin your day.

Foliated black slate is part of the "Shoo Fly Complex," a metamorphic assemblage found on the road to Ox Bow entrance.

Stay close to the shoreline as you make your way up the reservoir. The many-layered texture of the exposed rock resembles a marbled cake, with moss as the icing. Air bubbles, breaking the surface, are followed by the rising head of a small diving duck. One glance in your direction and it disappears back into the clear but sunless water.

Just before you round the bend, look across the reservoir and up to the saddle silhouetted against the skyline. The sharply-delineated layers of metamorphosed rock angle skyward from the depths of the water, run upward to the top of the gorge, only to disappear abruptly at the outlined edge of the canyon.

Looking up past the bend, you spot the small structure of Ralston Power House standing on the sunlit southeast side of the canyon. The pull of the current is stronger here, but you welcome the workout because it warms your body against the cold. As you get closer, you can see the cascade of water as it exits the concrete structure. In silhouette in the foreground is a turbine wheel that is on display and acts as a backup to the primary turbine. The road running past the power house is Blacksmith Flat Road (Forest Road 23).

On your return from exploring the tail of the reservoir, use the current flowing against the rip-rap of the east shore to push you back into the shadow of the main body of water. The feeble sunlight will provide adequate warmth to numb fingers and stiff limbs. Just before you pass the bend from where you viewed the sunlit saddle, look for a lone pine whose root system has attached itself to the bare rock. creating a precarious anchor for the main trunk.

The sunlight disappears and you are back in the shadowed atmosphere dominated by steep canyon walls covered with trees, shrubs, moss and rock. The utter stillness of the water reflects the sunlit distant hills that appear telescoped at the far end of the lower reservoir. Only the sounds of passing airliners are heard echoing off the high walls of the gorge. Slowly, you dip your paddle and break the tension as the boat moves deeper into the shadows. From somewhere, the cackle of a lone raven, followed by the of a feeding fish, provides the background music for your day on the water.

Soon you pass the mouth of the Middle Fork of the American River and round the first bend in the main body of the lake. Looking north, you spot a nice sandy beach—the only beach—on which to enjoy a short break. Above you is the narrow two-lane road that brought you to the reservoir. Hopefully, you remembered to bring that thermos with something hot and satisfying.

After your body has thawed out and you are ready to paddle, you seat yourself as comfortably as possible and continue the outing. Staying to the east bank, you paddle around the oak-covered point and the upper body of the reservoir opens up onto a broad landscape

This steel bridge spans the north fork of the Middle Fork, American River.

of bright sun highlighting the upper foothills, contrasted by a sharp line marking the deep shadows of the lower canyons.

A small island covered with a sparse growth of pine, oak and various shrubbery sits in the center of the lake. Paddling to the island, you run into a logboom stretched across from the shore nearest the dam to the western tip of the island, and from the island to the eastern shoreline. Unfortunately, this boom prevents boaters from paddling to the dam site. Sudden discharges from the outflow pipe create a vortex in the lake nearest the intake pipe which is located against the cliff to the right of the dam.

I sometimes beach my boat on the shallow east tip of the island. From there, it is easy to find a nice picnic or rest area with a fine view up and down the canyon. If you visit this same area in summer, the "island" becomes a hill surrounded by sand in a half-circle of water.

To explore the dam site, follow the boom to the western shore, secure your boat, and follow the road cut to the platform with an overview of the dam's concrete face. The dam was completed in 1966 as part of the Middle Fork of the American River Development Project. It stands 79 feet high and is 570 feet in length.

On your return paddle, check out the mouth of a small stream located on the west shore just up from the log boom. You can hear the rustle of the water as it cascades over the rocks before entering the reservoir. The large trees growing on the right bank are California laurel, sometimes called mountain laurel. In Oregon, the same tree is known as the Oregon myrtle. If you crush one of its leaves, a spicy, pungent aroma tickles your nostrils. The scent is not unpleasant and, hopefully, will become a reminder of pleasant times past.

[1] Protect American River Canyons (PARC), *The American River North, Middle & South Forks A Recreational Guide Book.*

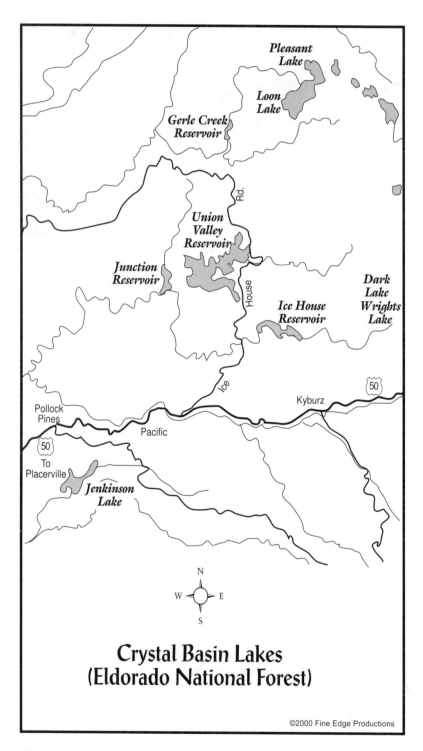

Crystal Basin Lakes
(Eldorado National Forest)

©2000 Fine Edge Productions

CHAPTER 3

Crystal Basin Lakes
(Eldorado National Forest)

The Old Man: "Ain't nothing like a boat to teach a man the worth of quiet contemplation."
The Boy: "Like the Old Man said, there is nothing like being alone on the water in a boat of your own to learn the value of peace, quiet, and responsibility.

—Robert Ruark, *The Old Man and the Boy*

Bits of doubt may creep into your thoughts as you begin the ascent up Ice House Road into Crystal Basin; the sight of vast acres of burned forest with standing ghost trees is hardly appealing. However, when you first reach Ice House Lake your hopes are restored. The effects of the Cleveland fire that devastated so much of the forest are not present here. Instead, a lush canopy of tall conifers surrounds the sparkling lake. This friendly scene is repeated at all the lakes within the basin.

If one lake does not appeal to you, there are six other lakes within a short driving distance of each other. If weather or road conditions make the drive to these lakes impractical, you still have the option of paddling to Jenkinson Lake, five miles south off Highway 50.

Although all these lakes are a short distance from crowded cities and foothill towns, you can find solitude along with many plants, birds and animals to observe. As your canoe or kayak carries you beyond the campground or boat ramp, vistas of green-canopied forest, shimmering snow-capped mountains, and glaciated valleys work their magic upon your senses. The piercing cry of a hawk, an osprey's talon upon a fish, or the soaring flights of turkey vultures—and even an eagle—will become a vivid memory. In the heat of the sun, the rich scent of pine and cedar mixed with the subtle perfume of blossoming wildflowers tickles your nose. As the day wanes, the granite peaks that border Desolation Wilderness give credence to their name, The Crystal Range, as they come alive with sparkling intensity.

If you are camping on one of the many beaches along a lake's shore*, the sight of the Milky Way and the occasional falling star provide a fitting finale to a day's paddle.

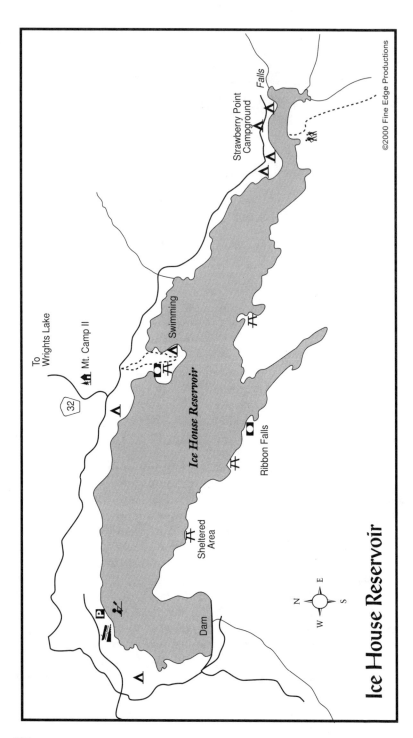

Ice House Reservoir

Ice House Reservoir

To Wrights Lake

32

Mt. Camp II

Swimming

Strawberry Point Campground

Falls

Ribbon Falls

Sheltered Area

Dam

N
W E
S

©2000 Fine Edge Productions

PADDLING AREA 1

Ice House Reservoir
(Crystal Basin Recreation Area)

Size: 678 surface acres
Elevation: 5,500 feet
County: El Dorado

Trip Length:
Give yourself a full day if planning on an overnight stay, consider hiking/biking the old logging road that follows the south side of the lake.
Paddling Distances (one way):
Boat ramp to Day Use Site 1: 2.5 mi.
Boat ramp to Day Use Site 2: 2.5 mi.
Boat ramp to Strawberry Point Campground: 3.0 mi.
Boat ramp to Day Use Site 3: 3.5 mi.
Season: Spring through early summer (by late summer the water is too low to enjoy the beauty of the reservoir).
Difficulty: Suitable for paddlers of all skill levels. Afternoon winds may present a problem, as can overzealous boaters—the lake is too small for fast boats.
Maps:
USGS 7.5 minute series: *Kyburz* quadrangle; adjacent sections are: *Riverton* quadrangle; *Robbs Peak* quadrangle; *Loon lake* quadrangle; *Pyramid Peak* quadrangle.
USFS: *Eldorado National Forest, California; Mt. Diablo Meridian*
Area/Road Maps:
Sacramento Municipal Utility District (SMUD): *Crystal Basin Recreation Area* (1995 ed.)
De Lorme: *Northern California Atlas & Gazetteer* (sections 88 and 89)
Family Fun Publications: S/E 35: *Crystal Basin* and S/E 35A: *Desolation Wilderness*
Compass Maps Inc.: *Western El Dorado County*

Access: From Sacramento, drive 65 miles on Highway 50 East to the turnoff approximately 1 mile past the Bridal Veil Waterfall turnout. Take the first left turn upon crossing the South Fork of the American River onto Ice House Road (Forest Road 3) at Riverton historical town site. Drive an additional 10 miles and make a right turn onto the Ice House Access Road (Forest Road 32), approximately one mile past Ice House Resort. The parking area and boat launch is located 2 miles from the turnoff. *Note:* Ice

House Road is a narrow winding road with many blind turns. The road carries heavy traffic consisting of logging trucks and heavy duty repair vehicles belonging to SMUD.

Highlights:

- Summer draw-downs are common.
- Paved parking area and boat launch equipped with vault toilets and piped water.
- Overnight parking in self-contained vehicles is allowed in the parking area for a $10/night fee (1998).
- Camping is permitted only at designated campgrounds.
- 83 camping units.
- Ice House Resort, a full-service resort, is 4 miles from the lake. You pass it on Route 3 just before turning off onto Forest Road 32. Phone (530) 293-3321.
- **Fire Permit:** Any overnight camping in non-designated campsites requires a fire permit, even if using only a self-contained stove.

Description: From the moment you arrive at the boat launch, you know this is going to be a fun paddle. The smallness of the lake gives it a feeling of intimacy, unlike the overpowering breadth of some of the larger lowland reservoirs.

Note: Do not paddle this gem if the water table has been drawn below the boat launching area; the bathtub effect mars the beauty and

A monument to the crew of Air Tanker 61 who died fighting the fire is at the Corral Visitors Center.

The aftermath of the 1992 Cleveland Fire.

won't be able to explore the many finger coves of the lake. Be sure to launch early to avoid the wind blowing out of the northeast.; the strong head wind, while providing you with a healthy workout, will prevent you from soaking in the scenic splendor of the lakes setting. This is the type of paddle where you should take your time and paddle slowly.

If you are launching on a clear, early morning, remain along the near and shady shore. The south shore, while sunny, will be uncomfortable as you paddle into the rising sun. Photography becomes difficult as you constantly turn your boat to prevent your highlights from becoming light-drenched.

As you paddle your way down the lake, the campsites visible on the north shore are part of the Northwind Campground. You can drive there by taking the Wrights Lake Road (Forest Road 32) which cuts to the left near the main entrance of Ice House camping area.

One cove over from the camp area is a beach with a variety of small paddling craft spread. This is a private beach belonging to Mountain Camp II, located off Forest Road 32.

A few coves over from the private beach is a small finger of land extending out into the lake. Paddle around the point and you will find a pleasant, sheltered gravel beach. This is the first of two day-sites that I consider the best on the lake. If you are planning an overnighter, this site is definitely one to aim for. Beach your boat and walk up to the old fire circle. (Before increased use of the lake forced the Forest Service to close the shoreline to camping, this and the other sites I mention were considered the ideal camp sites on the lake.)

From here you have an overview of the lake and a nice breeze to keep the "skeeters" and other annoying insects from feasting on your body parts. The small grove of pines and oaks provides you with shade and privacy. Sunbathing on the rounded granite boulders as you enjoy the view adds to the contentment of the moment.

Looking east toward the Sierra.

A trail leads up past the boulders of granite and into the vegetation zone. These large boulders, some as big as a Volkswagen, are called *erratics*; a term given to debris carried by the movement of glaciers, then dumped as the glacier melted. The trail cuts through a grove of manzanita; if the berries are ripe, try one; they have a pleasantly tart taste that quenches your thirst. Wind your way to the top of a small ridge with an exceptional view of the whole lake. Look across the lake to the southwest, where you will see a gently sloping clearing in the small grove of pines along the shore; at the point, just before the small finger cove there is another exceptional day-use spot. If you continue on the trail, you come to a road and the camping sites that are part of Strawberry Point camping area.

Back at your boat you can take a dip; because of the shallow depths the water warms to a comfortable temperature. The local Canada geese favor this cove, and it is not uncommon to share your swim with a gaggle of geese as they paddle in line, following the leader; you will probably run across this same gaggle on different parts of the lake during your paddle. The geese like to stay near shore following the shoreline as they hunt for suitable feeding areas. They appear to make a complete circumnavigation of the lake during their daily hunt for edible grasses.

Continuing on, you will notice campsites all along the shore. The road to Strawberry camping area follows this side of the lake. Many of the camp sites are nestled in the pines and manzanita that provide privacy and act as a wind break. The clarity of the water, especially near the shore, allows you to spot varieties of fish at different depths. By letting the boat glide and casting your eyes onto the forest lining the shore, you can see individual trees moving to the rhythm of the approaching breeze. Look closer, you may notice the scars or blisters on the main trunks of some of the taller trees. The older scars are grayish and the fresh ones have sap still oozing from the lower edge. If the scar is fresh, see if you can spot a deadfall near by. These scars are formed when neighboring trees lose their stability—either from the strong winds or a heavy snowpack—and fall, glancing off the trunks of nearby trees.

Eventually you hear the sound of rushing water as you approach the mouth of the South Fork of Silver Creek where it empties into Ice House Reservoir. This is a favorite gathering spot for campers, hikers, bank fishermen and passing tourists. It is also the terminus for the Strawberry Campground Road.

If you want a bit more privacy, paddle toward the smaller cove on the southwest end of this section of the lake. Round a small, bare point and enter another drowned creek drainage. If a longer visit is on your agenda, beach your boat and hike up the cleared path into the pines growing along the rim where you will come upon a former fire circle and a nice sheltered spot with your own creek and view of the upper lake. This third site that was formerly used for shoreline camping on the lake.

Back in your boat, follow the west shore and take time to explore the long finger cove located mid-way on the lake. Just as you enter the cove, on the right (west) shore, look for a small, thin waterfall that has created a delightful set of "ribbons" falls in the exposed boulders of the steep shoreline. Paddle close to the falls where you can observe colorful wildflowers such as the red columbine. In the late spring, watch for a common merganser flying overhead and follow it to a lone standing tree trunk where the bird has built a nest and is raising its young.

When you reach the upper (northwest) entrance to the finger cove, you will spot a large granite boulder with a noticeable channel carved into the rock. Imagine this rock as molten matter slowly rising like a small plume from a larger parent of magma deep beneath the surface. As the distance from the heat source increased, this mass began to cool and solidify. Crystals formed and the molten pile began to take shape and form. In time, a moister climate eroded the layers of soil covering this granitic mass. Eventually, the climate cooled and glaciers began to form. As the glaciers scraped their way downslope, they scooped the remaining overburden covering the now-solid mound of rock. For the first time, this small representation of plutonic rock, that we call granite, made its appearance on the surface.

An unobstructed view from the water allows you, the paddler, to appreciate the beauty of this small version of granite majesty that was formed in the same way as the Sierra Nevada Mountain Range. [For an up-to-date description on how this portion of the Sierra Nevada

The waters of Ice House and the peaks of the Desolation Wilderness.

was formed, see Jeffrey Schaffer's *Desolation Wilderness and the South Lake Tahoe Basin.*]

This side of the lake is much steeper, therefore there are fewer landings. The only places where a boat can be beached are adjacent to exposed granite boulders. These boulders, which have been eroded to a fairly level surface, create a suitable spot for exiting gracefully from your boat. However, these same steep banks give you a clear view of the tall pines and cedars growing down to the water's edge.

As you round the point toward the view of the dam and its spillway, take one last look up the lake and at the majesty of the trees; breathe deeply the piney scent permeating the breeze, and aim your boat toward dock and home.

IN THE EDDY

Naming the Land I

Ice House Reservoir is one of several multi-use reservoirs created in 1957 under the Upper American River Project, a joint effort of Sacramento Municipal Utility District (SMUD) and the U. S. Forest Service. Consequently, Ice House Dam was dedicated to the memory of Albert Elkus, first president of SMUD, director of the American River Project, and former mayor of Sacramento. This project succeeded in meeting the needs of business and recreation without destroying the beauty of the area.

The name Crystal Basin comes from the fact that the rock has a crystalline sparkle when the sun's rays glisten off the glaciated granite which was carved during the last Great Ice Age approximately two million years ago.

El Dorado was a Spanish phrase used to describe California that comes from a story about a mythical kingdom called El Dorado, famous for its beauty and wealth. This term was applied to the present county area by Charles Preuss, the cartographer on Fremont's expeditions who placed the legend "El Dorado or Gold Region" on his 1848 map.

El Dorado was the name given to one of the original 27 counties created by the State legislature in 1850. When the national forest was created in 1910, the spelling was run together as Eldorado. The county uses the correct Spanish spelling.

The name Ice House comes from the use of the basin just below the present location of Ice House Resort for collecting ice for residents of the communities along the present-day Highway 50 corridor. Silver Creek—the major stream in the basin—has cut a deep channel that receives little sun; consequently, the area registers some of the coldest temperatures in the region.

Granite is an intrusive (formed and crystallized beneath the surface), igneous(created by intense heat) rock composed primarily of feldspar and quartz, giving it a salt-and-pepper look.

As the origin of this rock was better understood, the term *granite*—when applied to the rock of the Sierra Nevada—became controversial. In modern "geology-speak," *granitic rock* or *grandodiorite* are more common terms.

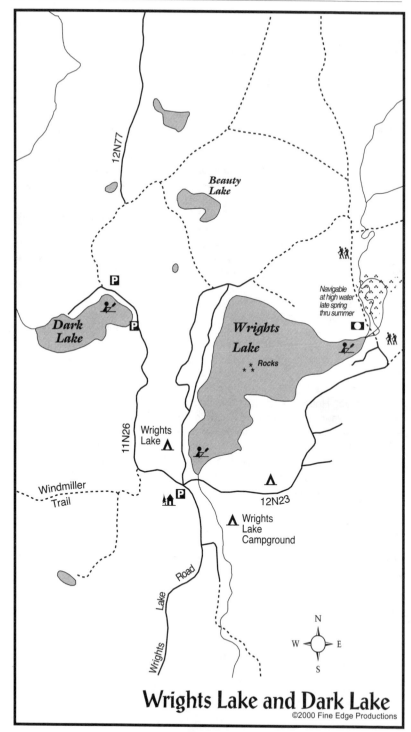

12N77

Beauty Lake

P

Dark Lake

P

Navigable at high water late spring thru summer

Wrights Lake

★ ★ ★ Rocks

11N26

Wrights Lake △

Windmiller Trail

△ 12N23

P

△ Wrights Lake Campground

Wrights Lake Road

N
W ✦ E
S

Wrights Lake and Dark Lake
©2000 Fine Edge Productions

PADDLING AREAS 2 & 3

Wrights Lake & Dark Lake
(Crystal Basin Recreation Area)

Size: 65 acres
Elevation: 6,941 feet (Wrights Lake)
Elevation: 6,900 feet (Dark Lake)
County: El Dorado

Trip Length: Wrights Lake consists of lower and upper lakes. The lower lake is the main lake, the one that the paddler first glimpses upon arrival. The upper lake is reached by paddling to the upper northeast end of the lower lake and entering the upper lake via a small stream channel that connects the two lakes. The upper lake contains many narrow channels leading into small marshy ponds on its borders.

Almost the entire lake is visible as you drive down to it. Although the lake may be paddled in its entirety in a couple of hours, its beauty and charm should be savored and appreciated by spending a morning or late afternoon quietly paddling and drifting on its surface.

Dark Lake can be paddled in its entirety in one hour, but take your time.

Paddling Distances (one way):
Boat launch at Day-Use Area (Wrights Lake) to Upper Lake entrance: 0.5 mi.

From the put-in (Dark Lake) off the access road to the west end: 1,500 ft.

Season: From spring (when the road is plowed), through fall or until the first snow threatens closure of the road.

Maps:
USGS, 7.5 minute series: *Kyburz, Calif.* quadrangle; *Pyramid Peak, Calif.* quadrangle.
USFS: *Eldorado National Forest, California; Mt. Diablo Meridian*
Area/Road Maps:
Compass Maps Inc.: *Western El Dorado County*
De Lorme: *Northern California Atlas & Gazetteer* (sections 88 and 89) Family Fun Publications: S/E 35: *Crystal Basin* and S/E 35A: *Desolation Wilderness*
Sacramento Municipal Utility District (SMUD): *Crystal Basin Recreation Area* (1995 ed.)

Access: Drive 65 miles from Sacramento on US Highway 50 east to the turnoff located approximately 1 mile past the Bridal Veil Fall turnout. Take the first left turn upon crossing the South Fork of the

You get a good view of Table Rock from the Wrights Lake Road.

American River onto Ice House Road (Forest Road 3) at the Riverton historical town site. Drive an additional 10 miles and make a right turn onto Ice House Road (Forest Road 32) located approximately one mile past Ice House Resort. Turn left just before entering the Ice House Campground onto Wrights Lake Road (you are still on Forest Road 32) and drive for approximately 9 miles to the junction of Forest Roads 32 and 4. Turn left onto Forest Road 4 and continue for approximately 2 miles to the Wrights Lake Information Center.

Highlights:
- Close access to the Desolation Wilderness hiking area.
- A wilderness permit is required even for day hikes into Desolation Wilderness.

- Don't leave without paddling Dark Lake (preferably in the later afternoon)

  The best put-in for Dark Lake is the parking spot adjacent to the no parking access point immediately past the first parking area.
- **Camping:** Highly popular for family camping—reservations are a must.

  Campgrounds at Wrights Lake contain vault toilets and faucets. Each campsite has a picnic table, grill and fire ring. Campsites 8 and 5 are nearest the lake
- The visitors' center provides free literature and maps of the area and their is a knowledgeable staff on hand to answer questions.

Difficulty: Except for gusty afternoon winds bringing the chance of rain and threat of lightning, the mosquitoes are more of a problem than anything for a paddle on Wrights Lake.

Dark Lake is a small, oval moraine lake that can be paddled easily by anyone in a canoe, inflatable or kayak. The best time to appreciate the mirror-like smoothness of the lake's surface is in the early morning or late afternoon. By 10:00 AM, the wind is up and ruffles the lake's surface. A windblock exists on the far end of the lake, probably created by the tall pines and high rock wall.

Description: Paddling Wrights Lake or Dark Lake without knowing their historical context is akin to watching a movie without the sound; you may see the activity but not understand the dynamics. To better

Area information is available from the Wrights Lake Visitors Center.

IN THE EDDY
Wilson Meadow

As you approach the intersection of Forest Roads 4 and 32, the large clearing on your right is Wilson Meadow. Before you turn onto Road 4 and head for Wrights Lake, take some time to explore this outstanding clearing situated in the middle of the forest.

An early settler, probably Egbert Livingston "Bud" Wilson, cleared the area for grazing land to run dairy cows thereby creating the meadow. The Wilson Ranch still stands at the junction of Silver and Lyons creeks at the south end of the meadow. To explore the meadow (the ranch is private property), park your vehicle alongside Road 4 near the concrete ford-crossing, approximately 0.25 mile south of the junction.

On a hot summer day, you can take a swim in one of the many deep pools downstream from the ford. If fishing is your passion, sneak up the creek and try your luck on the trout visible in the clear cold water. Watch for frogs and snakes that hunt along the bank. If you have not already felt them, the mosquitoes make the meadow their home and your presence is welcome!

Hike past the creek and into the meadow proper. Carpets of wildflowers grow so profusely that you feel guilty stepping on them as you make your way. This is a photographer's delight! The blue lupine mixes with the red paintbrush against a ground cover of yellow buttercups. Close to the stream, you will find clusters of blue camas flowers, an important food source early Native Americans. Small earthen cores, running in all directions are the handiwork of pocket gophers. [See pg. 338, *Sierra Nevada Natural History* for an account of the digging habits of the pocket gopher).

Outcrops of granitic rock show like islands glistening in the sun. Growing in the crevices and niches of the rock are clusters of mountain pride, a penstemon and member of the figwort family.

Interspersed through the meadow are lone stumps of trees that were cut to enlarge the clearing. Many of them still bear evidence of saw cuts on their trunks. Now they serve as perches for the many birds that come to the meadow to gather food. They also make handy benches for sitting and admiring the view.

Before hiking back to your vehicle, make your way to the southwest end of the meadow and catch a view of Blue Mountain and Pyramid Peak glistening in the sun. Their bright, sparkling surfaces provide you with the best example of why this part of the Sierra Nevada is called the Crystal Range.

appreciate the these lakes and their origin, stop off at the Eldorado National Forest Information Center just off Highway 50 and pick up a copy of *The Wrights Lake Story*. The book provides a fascinating background on the people and events that helped shape the cultural and physical makeup of Wrights and Dark lakes.

Wrights Lake is a small *moraine lake* that formed when the natural flow of nearby streams, Silver Creek being one of them, was blocked by the piles of rocky debris (*moraines*) left behind by a glacier. The lake is nestled near a *cirque* or former glacier valley head.

The drive to the lakes, through a forest of tall pines and cedars, with ever-nearer glimpses of the broad, granite Crystal Range, will heighten your expectations for the paddle. The steep ridges of granite boulders and gravel that line first one side of the road and then the other are *lateral moraines* (the soil and rock scraped, then pushed aside by an advancing glacier). It is these former alpine glaciers that created many of the depressions that eventually filled with water and became lakes.

These moving walls of ice also helped form the lay of the land. The large boulders and piles of soil heaped at random throughout the area contribute to the majestic splendor of the forest. Sometimes glimpsed through a break in the trees or seen standing alone in a clearing, these lichen-covered monoliths (given the term *erratics* by

Looking across the lake from the boat launch.

geologists) look like remnants of a city built by a now-forgotten civilization. The trees hide their bulk and bracken ferns provide a carpet of cover that accentuates the rock's form.

Wrights Lake Campground

Caution: The last section of Forest Road 4, although a two-lane road, is very narrow and contains many blind curves. Be extremely cautious driving this section of road and be ready to pull out for vehicles larger than yours. When you reach the information center, look for the campground directory located on your right. To your left is a charming pine cabin with an open deck that serves as the ranger station. The campground directory provides you with instructions on how to locate, secure and pay for your campsite. The information center has maps of the area and other materials for sale or free.

If the rangers are not available, the center is also staffed with local volunteers. Many of these volunteer staffers are also long time residents of the area, either cabin owners or individuals who have been coming to Wrights Lake for many years. Their knowledge of the area is unsurpassed and many a fine tale of the lake and its history may be heard if you take the time to "hang around."

Wrights Lake Paddle

The best boat access to Wrights Lake is from the boat launch located below the day-use parking area. From here you also have your first clear view of the Crystal Range which is a backdrop for your paddle. I recommend you plan to start as early as possible. Watching the sun rise above Pyramid Peak, silhouetting the entire Crystal Range, is a powerful way to start your day at Wrights Lake.

Note: The depth of the lake decreases as the summer progresses. Although you can paddle the lake through the fall, shallow spots with granite exposures become prevalent and demand careful attention.

From the boat launch, head toward the point with the tall pines on the right (east) end of the shoreline. When you round the point, notice that the lake is larger than it appears from the visitors center and campground. The cabins that you see surrounding the lake are part of an agreement going back to 1916 between early campers at the lake, the U. S. Forest Service (which owned only the north and west sides of the lake) and the principal landowner, Western States Gas and Electric Company.

To access the ponds that are at the upper end of the lake, paddle across the eastern arm of the lake, aiming for the upper left (northeast) corner. As you paddle, look down at the water's depths; you will be astounded at the lake's clarity. Fish of all sizes may be spotted as they cruise past your bow. The silty bottom is an indicator of age; the more shallow the lake, the closer it is to becoming a bog and eventually a meadow.

Paddling at Wrights Lake is fun for the kids too.

In the early part of summer, the passage from the lake under the footbridge and into the upper marshland is rather straightforward and without incident. Not so in late summer, when the shallow areas of the lake become covered with mats of green sedge. To reach the marshes, you must pick a path by following the channels of deep water that lead to the footbridge and beyond. A deep water channel that provides the easiest passage is located on the far left adjacent to the shoreline.

One of the benefits of paddling through these sedges is the sight of so many waterfowl feeding, nesting and cavorting among the grassy bunches. As you make your approach, the long neck and dark head of a Canada goose will suddenly appear above the stalks of grass. Farther down the channel, a flotilla of fuzzy ducklings may be seen paddling behind their mother. On the shore, what at first appears to be a bunch of brown feathers is a resting brood of juvenile mallards. Blackbirds flit among the grasses and the strident cry of the Steller's jay can be heard from the pine forest.

Paddling under the footbridge and making a hard left turn will grant you access to the upper marshes above the lake. You may notice several canoes banked on the shore. Many of the locals or campers familiar with the area will paddle their craft to this area before hiking into the Desolation Wilderness area. (Many smaller alpine lakes are located in the high country and are accessible by trails leading from Wrights Lake.)

As you follow the channel into the marshland—the water level will dictate what area can be paddled—you will be rewarded with a stunning view of the Sierra peaks. If you follow the channels, you will pass through the pines and firs growing around the marshland.

Woodpeckers, deer and other animals may be spotted through the trees. If the mosquitoes are not biting, find some dry ground and have a picnic or just enjoy the view.

Before heading back to the take-out, keep a sharp eye out for ospreys circling overhead as they hunt for fish near the lake's surface. Near the shoreline, an occasional nighthawk may be seen performing an aerial ballet as it hunts for flying insects.

If you're tired of paddling, find a good rock and cast out your line.

Dark Lake Paddle

Dark Lake is a small, oval moraine lake paddled easily by canoe, inflatable or kayak, but it is best suited to the canoe. I enjoy my kayak, but the canoe shines on these small Sierra lakes. The size and temperament of Dark Lake make for a slow, lazy stroke that can be achieved only in a canoe. But hey! kayaks also do just fine. The best boat put-in is the parking spot adjacent to the *No Parking* access point, immediately past the first parking area upon sighting the lake.

The best time ("bar none") for paddling Dark Lake is late afternoon when the sun starts its descent, shadows lengthen and the light changes to a golden hue. If a breeze is blowing, don't worry; at the far end of the lake the trees provide a windbreak and the lake's surface is pure glass.

After launching your boat continue paddling until you have passed the last cabin. Then, sweep-stroke your craft until you are facing your put-in and enjoy the view. The high broken wall of rock on your right provides a dramatic backdrop to the forest surrounding the rest of the lake.

Many small clearings on the northwest side of the lake allow you to explore the lake. Although the bottom may look sandy and firm, often the beaches are composed of silt and you will sink to your ankles in the muck. Watch for submerged granite boulders and the ends of tree limbs near the shore as well as for fishermen casting from the banks.

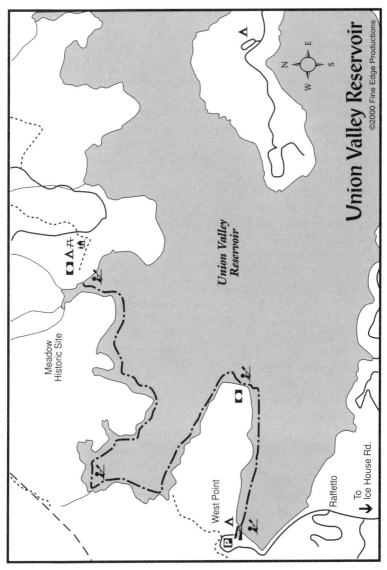

PADDLING AREA 4

Union Valley Reservoir
(Crystal Basin Recreation Area)

Size: 3,000 surface acres
Elevation: 4,900 feet
County: El Dorado

Trip Length: Day paddle minimum, or overnight and spend longer.
Paddling Distances (one way):
West Point boat ramp to former ranch site: 1.5 mi. (3.75 mi. if following route on map.)
West Point boat ramp to Robbs Peak Powerhouse (Tells Creek Arm): 4 mi.
Difficulty: This paddle is suitable for paddlers of all skill levels. Except for afternoon winds that blow over the lake, no additional hazards are encountered. With that said, Sierra weather is known for its fickle nature, changing from a mild sunny morning to snow flurries by mid-day.
Season: Year round; spring and fall are prime times to ensure a quality time on the water without pressures of weather and crowding. In the spring, you have the wildflowers and nesting birds, while the changing colors of the deciduous trees along with flocks of migrating birds make a fall paddle memorable.
Maps:
    USGS, 7.5 minute series: *Robbs Peak; Riverton, Calif.; Loon Lake.* [*Note:* The Robbs Peak and Riverton quadrangles help locate the destination points for the paddle.]
    USFS: *Eldorado National Forest, Mt. Diablo Meridian.*
    Area/Road Maps:
        Sacramento Municipal Utility District (SMUD): *Crystal Basin Recreation Area*
        De Lorme: *Northern California Atlas & Gazetteer*
        Compass Maps Inc.: *Western El Dorado County*

Access: Take Highway 50 East past Pollock Pines. Exit left immediately after crossing the bridge over the South Fork of the American River at the Riverton Historical Town Site. You are now on primary Forest Road 3 (Ice House Road). Continue on this road for approximately 8 miles and exit left onto primary Forest Road 31 (Peavine Ridge Road). After 2.5 miles, you come to a fork; take the right fork onto Forest Road 31 (Bryant Springs Road). Follow this road to the dam and the West Point Boat Ramp and campground.

Highlights:
- Located centrally to six other lakes within the same region.
- Breathtaking view of Desolation Wilderness Sierra peaks.
- May be setup as either a day or an overnight paddle.
- Access to boat-in camping spots bordering the lake.
- A Fire Permit is necessary for any overnight camping in non-established camping areas. This rule applies even if using only a camp stove.
- Fall and late spring are best for paddling this lake.
- In spring, many of the coves contain families of Canada geese, along with their goslings, feeding on the sprouting vegetation along the shoreline.
- Ice House Resort open year-round is located off Ice House Road has a small store for groceries, (530) 293-3321.

Description: There are numerous spots where canoes or kayaks can be launched to enjoy the scenery surrounding Union Valley Reservoir. However, one location stands out from the rest because of the variety of features and scenery all centered within a day's paddle. By putting-in at the West Point boat ramp located near the dam, you have access to one of the most "postcard-perfect" areas of the reservoir.

As you cross the dam, you'll be struck by the view of the Sierras––be careful! Upon arrival at the dam road, be sure the driver is not distracted by the awesome view of the Sierras as the vehicle slowly crosses over the dam.

Storm clouds over the Sierra darken the waters of Union Reservoir.

Note: Looking down the gorge to the left below the dam you can see the put-in for the Junction Reservoir paddle [see Paddling Area 7] as well as the tail of the reservoir.

Follow the road to the right, drive past the quarry located above the rocks on your left, and proceed down to the boat ramp. The site in the pines opposite the ramp and closest to the dam is the best campsite. To spend the night at a boat-in site, park in the designated parking area near the restrooms after off-loading your boat and gear.

Depending on the water levels, the area to the left of the cement boat ramp allows you to equip your boat without causing someone else to wait for the ramp.

If you are launching in the afternoon and the wind is up, don't worry; upon rounding the point to your left you are in the lee of the wind and, when you cross the open cove, the prevailing wind should be a westerly and on your back.

When you reach this first point that resembles a thumb on the map, take time to study the rock-strewn beach and incredible view of the Sierras. You can beach here and make adjustments to your boat or repack any gear to improve the boat's trim. I enjoy this spot because of its geological feature: the remnants of what looks like a *volcanic mud flow*. The tectonic pulses that created the present day Sierra initiated episodes of volcanism far greater than what we have experienced in modern times. As Mary Hill, in her book, *Geology of the Sierra Nevada*, describes:

> *The first part of these last 20 million years would have been awesome, had we been alive to see them. Those were the andesitic days, a time of hot volcanic mud flows, pouring from vents in the highlands and cascading down the streams and mountainsides. The mud flows were many, from different centers in the Sierra, piling on top of one another and merging to form a sea of steaming mud . . .*
>
> *. . . The mud flows poured down the mountain slopes as jumbled masses of large rocks and small, of boulders of granite and metamorphic rocks, of torn and shattered trees, mixing and churning coming to rest when they had stiffened too much to move farther or had reached the bottom of the slope.*
>
> *Eventually the old landscape was inundated, only ridges of resistant greenstone in the foothills, a few peaks in the middle zone [of the Sierra] and some high country along the crest remaining as islands.*

A small portion of this chaotic jumble of mixed rocks and boulders cemented into a matrix of former ash, defined by geologists as a *lahar*, is now slowly eroding; subsequently, rocks large and small, igneous and metamorphic in origin, litter the beach of the exposed point.

Looking up at the eroding cut of the former flow, you can detect the direction of movement that the mud flow took. The sharp angles

Head around this point after you leave the West Point boat ramp.

of the individual rocks show evidence of being crushed into various-sized chunks by the churning movements of the mudflow. These cemented fragments of rock, called *breccia* (Italian for broken) are the only large exposure of vulcanism located along the reservoir's shoreline.

From this point, continue along the shore and round the point into the large cove that stretches to the north. As you paddle around the point, look for families of Canada geese browsing high on the edge of the scrape zone where the grasses grow. Chances are that the appointed goose "lookout" will already have spotted you and with loud "honking and carrying on," be shepherding her down-covered goslings to the safety of the water. Allow your boat to drift quietly so you can watch them paddle by.

At the end of the cove, the patches of dark green that extend up from the water's edge mark the small streams that feed into the reservoir. What appear to be carpets of thick grass are actually sedges that form near the water-saturated soil. Examine the stems of these plants; they are triangular in shape, a defining characteristic of the sedge family.

If you beach your boat at the southwest end of the cove, note the change in soil color and its overall composition. While the shore of the point contains many of the eroded rock from the former ash flow, it is duller in color than the light-colored, gravel-based soil of the northern shoreline. Look for an outcrop of rock near the water's edge. From this side of the point and on the remaining shoreline, the majority of exposed rock is primarily granitic.

Spring on the reservoir, but winter in the Sierra.

Following the edge of the cove along shore, you pass two smaller pocket-coves and enter a narrow cove whose large expanse of meadow is a delight . Feeding on the shore will be large numbers of geese, ducks and other birds, notably the Brewer's blackbird. Look for an outcrop of granite near the northeast end of the cove. To the right (easterly) of this outcrop is a lovely mixed gravel and sand beach that appears to be made expressly for the beaching of boats.

Walk to the top of the outcrop and gaze across the meadow. In the spring time, you may enjoy its beauty without the annoyance of mosquitoes that normally frequent this wet land. Resist the urge to walk into the meadow where the earth is saturated with water—you would leave imprints that would remain for a long time and your walking will put undue stress on the fragile mosses and green plants that grow in the area. Instead, look for the drier high-ground where the earth is more compact and follow to the southeast over the small ridge where the fence line is located.

At the top of the incline, you will see an old wooden structure that may have been a ranch house or a line shack for housing men and gear when the cattle were brought up to spring pasture. It now serves as a favorite spot for camping and enjoying the view of the bay below. Take time to explore; look for the corral with its lichen-covered cattle chute. More than likely this was the place were the young heifers were gathered to be castrated, inoculated, notched and branded in the yearly roundup.

Looking over the area, you can understand why it was chosen: the streams provided a wet area that created a rich meadow for the cattle; forested ridges protected the area from direct wind, yet there was enough breeze to keep the area clear of mosquitoes.

If you want to hike the meadow, follow the old logging road above the ranch house (northerly). At the fork in the clearing, take the lower road. You soon come upon another small clearing with a path leading to the edge of the meadow. Using the high ground, follow the deer trails that skirt the wet areas. You'll see wildflowers, birds and other animals in the meadow. Eventually, you come out at the pathway that leads to the granite outcrop and the beach where you beached your boat. Linger here or explore the shore and coves that eventually end at the Robbs Peak Power House approximately 3.5 miles up the lake.

The anvil-shaped cloud is a good indicator of a coming change in the weather.

The word *granite* comes from the Italian *granulo,* meaning grain or particle. The different salt-and-pepper patterns of granite are readily apparent identifying characteristics.
    –Philip L. Fradkin,
    The Seven States of California

147

IN THE EDDY

A View of Spider Lake

Stepping out of the boat on a cool, overcast autumn morning, my intention was to hike the granite ridge bordering the northeast shore of Pleasant Lake. From there, I was going to route-find my way to the top of a saddle which promised a view of Spider Lake. On my hike, I would occasionally run across cream-colored veins of rock running in long straight lines, hugging the surface of the barren granitic floor. These dikes were formed when molten matter was "squirted" under pressure into weak cracks or fissures in the parent rock.

Making my way past the first ridgeline, I reached an expanse of woodland. These dense groves of trees and brush form wherever soil had a chance to build. I was fortunate to cut across the narrow trail that leads off from the larger Loon Lake Trail which terminates at Pleasant Campground on the northeast shore of PleasantLake. My chance encounter with this section of the trail eliminated the need to bushwhack through the thick brush growing in the adjacent depression.

Following the trail upward, I noticed that it paralleled a wide stream bed overgrown with pines, manzanita, bracken ferns and assorted wildflowers. Eventually, the trail intersected the larger Loon Lake Trail. Making a right turn (southeast) onto this main trail, I followed it through a recent blow-down. (These occur when strong gusts of wind flow through an area, usually a narrow canyon, and uproot whole trees that are in the path of the wind gust). Just past the downed trees, the trail opened onto a barren expanse of glaciated granite. Looking west, I saw the wide expanse of Loon Lake.

A breeze blowing off the water felt cool and carried a mixed scent of pine and wetness. Peering up toward the saddle (easterly), I scouted the terrain looking for an easy route to lead me to the crest of the saddle. Spotting a stream-cut ravine that appeared less rugged and steep than the surrounding talus, I slowly made my way along the flank of the stream bed. The yellowing leaves of several deciduous trees marked the beginning of Fall in the Sierras. As the climb became steeper, The brush began to clear and the pines gave way to junipers. Higher still, the junipers took on a dwarfish, stunted appearance termed krummholtz ("crooked wood.")

One more pitch over a blocky granite ridge and I would reach my destination. I completed this last leg of the climb and peered over the ridge line to the valley below. Spreading like fingers of a hand, the waters of Spider Lake sparkled in the misty sun. Small islands of granite with mantles of pine dotted the surface of the lake. As I ate my lunch the wind rapidly cooled the sweat on my shirt. I shivered, finished eating and, with a last look at Spider Lake, began the long, steep descent back to my canoe.

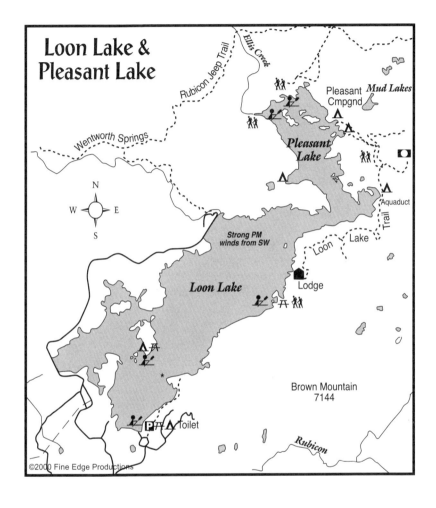

Loon Lake & Pleasant Lake

Rubicon Jeep Trail

Ellis Creek

Pleasant Cmpgnd

Mud Lakes

Wentworth Springs

Pleasant Lake

N
W E
S

Strong PM winds from SW

Aquaduct

Loon Lake

Loon Lake

Lodge

Brown Mountain 7144

Toilet

©2000 Fine Edge Productions

Rubicon

PADDLING AREA 5

Loon Lake and Pleasant Lake
(Crystal Basin Recreation Area)

Size: 600 surface acres
Elevation: 6,378 feet
County: El Dorado

[handwritten notes: 5/27-30/04 notes: $61/night for overnight parking next to ramp. Pay ranger in trailer. winds start ~ recommend: Start @ 0830. Strong by 11…]

Trip Length: You can paddle the length of the lake in one full day; however, it is better as an extended overnight stay.

Paddling Distances (one way):
South boat ramp to large island: 0.5 mi.
South boat ramp to rocky point and hazardous area: 0.5 mi.
South boat ramp to sheltered cove and chalet: 1.5 mi. (chalet is 0.2 mi. beyond the cove).
South boat ramp to Pleasant Lake entrance: 2.0 mi.
South boat ramp to aqueduct tunnel and campsite: 3.5 mi.
South boat ramp to campsite on granite bench: 3.3 mi.
South boat ramp to Pleasant Boat-In Campground: 3.7 mi.
South boat ramp to the mouth of Ellis Creek: 4.5 mi.

Season: Spring, after the road is plowed, and the lake thaws through late fall before the first snow.

Maps:

USGS 7.5 minute series: *Loon Lake* quadrangle; *Wentworth Springs* quadrangle.

USFS: *Eldorado National Forest, California; Mt. Diablo Meridian*

Area/Road Maps:

Sacramento Municipal Utility District (SMUD): *Crystal Basin Recreation Area.* (1995 ed.)

De Lorme: *Northern California Atlas & Gazetteer* (sections 81 and 89)

Family Fun Publications: S/E 35: *Crystal Basin* and S/E 35A: *Desolation Wilderness.*

Compass Maps Inc.: *Western El Dorado County.*

Access: From Sacramento, take Highway 50 east to the Ice House Road (Primary Forest Road 3) exit (on your left immediately past crossing the highway bridge over the American River). Follow the Forest Road for 30 miles. Make a right turn at the small sign indicating Loon Lake South Campground. The boat launch is to the left of the campground host site.

The boat ramp at Loon Lake.

To find the North Campground, stay on the Forest Road, cross over the dam and take the first right. The North Camp also has a boat ramp.

Highlights:
- Concrete boat ramps accommodate low-water launches.
- No fee (as yet) for vehicle parking (if you boat camp).
- Primitive boat-in camping with exceptional views.
- Fee for self-contained (RV or other) parking in boat ramp parking area; there are 15 units.
- Loon Lake Campground, adjacent to the lake, contains 53 units and one first-come, first-served double unit, No. 43. Reservations are *highly recommended,* especially in summer.
- To reserve the Loon Lake Chalet, contact the El Dorado National Forest Information Center at (530) 644-6048 (the chalet off the entrance road, not visible from the water). *875/night 180 day advance res.*
- Campground has piped water, picnic tables, fire pit and vault toilets;
- Camp Host located at South Campground.
- Safeway Store at Pollock Pines (Sly Park Exit) for last full service groceries; Ice House Resort ((530) 293-3321 and Robb's Valley Resort—both off Forest Road 3 have limited supplies.
- **Fire permit:** Permit is required even for camp stoves for backcountry or wilderness camping. No permit required for camping at a designated campground.

- You are in bear country, so think and pack smart. [See "Bear Safe Camping," June 1998, *River Magazine*]
- An added activity includes hiking the Loon Lake Trail, a 14-mile scenic trail bordering the lake [see "Before you go loony," *Sacramento Bee*, August 25, 1999].

Difficulty:

0900

Crossing the lake requires intermediate boating skills necessary for handling a boat on rough, choppy waters. Loon Lake is known for its strong wind gusts that begin in late morning and continue throughout the afternoon, and eventually die down in the early evening. The wind blows predominately from the northeast and creates a strong head wind as you begin your paddle, but it gives you a nice "push" on your return leg.   *5/27-30/04 wind up lake (toward Mensual)*

On a spring paddle, be prepared for snow and extreme drops in temperature. During the summer, afternoon thunderstorms bring strong winds, thunder and lightning. If paddling to the upper lake area, plan your crossing either in the morning or early evening.

0830

Description: A star-filled night—an occasional meteor streaks soundlessly across the sky—the stillness broken only by the lapping of water on the shore; the smell of wood smoke and the taste of coffee as good-hearted conversation flies around the camp. Sound good? Thought so! Loon Lake in spring and summer is that kind of place. The paddle to the end of the lake is long enough to give personal

Loaded canoe, complete with rain cover, ready for a weekend on Loon Lake.

Looking west toward your put-in; around the point on the right is Upper Loon Lake (formerly Pleasant Lake).

satisfaction, yet close enough for boaters to test their paddle skills or for kids on their first serious wilderness paddle.

For those of you who have time restraints, or if you just want a day paddle, I suggest a trip around the group of islands visible from the campground and boat launch; the two largest islands can be seen clearly from shore. Both have several easy landing beaches and clusters of trees for shade. From there, you can paddle to the smaller islands scattered around the northern section of the lake. The cove and islands that make up this end of Loon Lake provide a good wind break for late morning or afternoon paddling. Do not stray past the northeast point of the largest island unless you are comfortable paddling in windy, choppy waters.

However, if you plan to visit Pleasant Campground or do some wilderness camping at the extreme northeast end of the lake, launch either in the early morning or late afternoon for a calm-water crossing. From the cement ramp, aim your bow for the small finger of land jutting out from the southern shoreline. Depending on the depth of the lake, clusters of rounded granite boulders jut out from the point.

As you begin the paddle, look right where you can see campsites beyond the tree line that make up a small portion of the 53 units of the Loon Lake Campground. As you approach the rocky point, watch for granite boulders hidden below the surface. It is easy to ground your bow or glance off a rough section of rock that could scratch or fracture your hull.

Resting on the rocks through which you steered, or paddling nearby, are families of common mergansers. The males have a black back, white chest and underparts, with a black head; the females are gray with a rust-colored head and neck; both sexes have a long, thin reddish bill. These are diving ducks, capable of catching even fast-swimming trout. Speaking of trout, by now you will have spotted fish jumping as they prey on low-flying insects on the glassy surface of the lake. When the air is still and the lake calm, keep an eye out for an osprey cruising overhead in search of fish.

Note: If you cross in the early morning, you will paddle into the rising sun. Be sure to wear a pair of sunglasses. On your return leg, unless you leave late in the afternoon, the rays of the setting sun shine directly into your eyes. The harsh reflection off the water may disorient you or create discomfort that takes away from the joy of your paddle.

Rounding the point, you pass the entrance to a small cove with a sheltered beach—a nice spot to take a break and have a swim. At low water, a long sandy beach provides a nice landing spot with shelter from any wind, and a view down-lake. Eventually, you pass the small building or chalet on your right.

From here the lake narrows and you enter the former body of Pleasant Lake. Prior to 1967, when the dam blocking Gerle Creek was completed, a ridge line at this narrow bend of the lake separated Loon Lake from Pleasant Lake. In the late afternoon, I have spotted mule

The four-mile tunnel leads through the granite to Buck Island Lake.

deer making their way down from the forest bordering the steep and rocky southwest shore.

Just before you round the elbow and enter Lake Pleasant, look for the mouth of a tunnel at the base of the high granite ridge in the cove to your right. The mouth of the tunnel is part of a four-mile underground aqueduct carrying water from Buck Island Lake to Loon Lake, part of the massive Upper American River Project. The project was started in 1957 to provide water and hydroelectric power to Sacramento. The completion of Loon Lake Reservoir in the early 1960s was the final phase of this project. Located above the tunnel is a small segment of the Loon Lake Trail, a hiking trail originating at the Loon Lake Horse Camp and providing entry into the Desolation Wilderness. To the left of the tunnel is a small beach. As the summer progresses and the lake level decreases, a nice beach is exposed, creating a small camping site suitable for three or four boaters. To explore the area beyond the rocky shelf of the shore, beach your boat at this small cove and hike inland. Although you can't see it from the lake, a lovely

Campsite on granite sand beach; Devils Peak in the background.

rectangular pond covered with a carpet of yellow pond lilies lies nestled against the base of the ridge that holds the Loon Lake Trail.

The first notable cove located on the southwest side 0.25 mile from the point marking the elbow of Pleasant Lake contains a great campsite. As you pull into the cove from the down-lake (south) end, look up (if paddling at low water) and to your left where you can see the campsite on a granite bench shaded by several pines. In front of you is a gravel beach with a strand of green grass that hides a medium-sized pond. In summer, your presence would alert the ever-vigilant Canada goose. Here, the grassy swale provides them with ample food and the quiet waters of the pond are good security against any predators. *Note:* By October, and certainly November, the waters of the pond may be evaporated. Only in exceptionally wet years, such as 1998, do these small ponds remain filled into fall.

Hike up the small ridge bordering the lake, where you can see the path that the last active glacier took. The polished surface contains tiny striations that mark the angle of the glacier's movement. Deeper grooves were created as small boulders and debris-laden ice slid over slabs of rock. The oval-shaped circles adjacent to the patches of polished granite bedrock that resemble burst blisters are called *chatter marks*. These semi-ovoid wedges of rock were formed by the *juddering* (stop and go) movement[1] of the glacier. The erratics of various shape and composition that you see scattered about the granitic bedrock should now be a familiar sight to you. Walking toward the lake, you come across a large pile of driftwood, some for the fire and some for beach sculptures. Back at the campsite, see if you can spot the weathered stump standing near the granite ledge; the oval-shaped holes of various size are the work of woodpeckers.

Continuing with your paddle, the next area of interest is the drowned inlet of Ellis Creek. From the cove with its picturesque pond, paddle northward following the western shore. For the next quarter-mile, a steep bank extends from the tree line to the waterline. As you round a small shoulder of the boulder-covered shore, the view up-lake reveals a level beach and a small inlet. Paddle into the inlet and beach your boat. The small stream cascading over small boulders and merging into the waters of the lake is Ellis Creek. If you have time, the hike the creekbed onto the granite domes for some outstanding views of the lake and the forest that extends out toward the Rubicon River Valley.

As you paddle away from Ellis Creek heading north toward the end of the lake, look for a tall pine with a bare crown growing on a high granite ledge that juts out from the lake on your left (northwest). Not only does this tree provide you with a reference point for the next cove to be explored, but it also serves as a perch for osprey. I have frequently spotted the birds resting on the upper dead limbs of the pine. Despite the lack of cover, the birds are difficult to spot as they blend with the whitish dead wood of the tree limbs. I have not been able to spot a nest in the area, but if you turn your boat so that you have the same view as the birds do, you can understand why they favor this location—the entire portion of the lake here is protected from wind, providing a good vantage spot for sighting fish.

The next finger cove from the inlet to Ellis Creek gives you the chance to hike past a large meadow and up to the Rubicon Jeep Trail. If you follow the trail into the granite, notice the telltale tracks of tires on the surface of cobble-strewn trails and on huge slabs of granite, evidence of drivers having pushed their vehicles to incredible limits. Paddling this end of the lake, particularly the entire northern section,

Deep vertical fissures create the appearance of a granite cityscape.

brings you into contact with the jeep trail. Just beyond the boulders of the lake shore, you can get occasional glimpses of the "road."

Turning south, you pass numerous exposed islands of granite. These outcrops continue to "grow" larger as the level of the lake recedes in the upcoming months. As you paddle past these barren rock piles, the shoreline on your left becomes more rocky and open. The tree line is farther back now due to the lack of soil. Small fingers of narrow, water-filled channels tempt you into further exploration. If have you timed your paddle in the correct season, the water level will be high enough so that each of these mysterious small coves ends on a bench of fairly level granite. Each of the finger channels contains deep, clear water at just the right temperature for a swim and the large level slabs of granite give you a warm spot where you can lie down and dry off.

Eventually, you reach a large conical island flanked with pines. Enter the inlet, where you can beach your boat on a nice level outcrop. For a campsite, follow the path up to a small clearing under a pine canopy. From here, you have a terrific view of the lake and the forest-covered lands beyond. Coincidentally, the Pleasant Boat-In Campground is located in the adjacent cove north of your camp. From here, you can hike up to the area described in *In the Eddy,* or explore the surrounding ridges with their own small alcoves of trees and plants. Just remember to make your return paddle before the wind picks up by mid-morning.

[1] Hambrey and Alean, *Glaciers.*

IN THE EDDY
Gerle Creek

As you make your way around the bend, the tail end of the reservoir abruptly gives way to Gerle Creek. The sound of the rapids and the sight of huge boulders lets you know that your paddle has come to an end. But don't quit just yet! If you beach your boat and explore past the boulders, a delightful surprise is in store.

The first 100 yards is the hardest, but the deep water pool at the end makes this struggle worthwhile. Refresh yourself with a swim in the pool, then locate and follow the upstream trail on either side of the creek. After a short hike through the trees, you come out at the base of a large granite outcrop extending into the creek. The dynamic shapes of the boulders with their grottos and rounded forms gives the spot an air of magic. Boulder-hopping from one granite sculpture to another provides you with a new and different view of this fairy-tale landscape.

Resting on a water-sculpted boulder, close your eyes and listen to the creek speaking a symphonic language as it rushes and cascades over dissimilar rocky gradients. Somewhere from a nearby conifer, the scolding chatter of a squirrel is met by the indignant cry of a Steller's jay; the ongoing, ultimate shell game is very much in play.

As you look around the water-worked rock, a question comes to mind. Why here? How did these boulders form? By studying the area, you arrive at a hypothesis. The exposed granite is an outcrop that was revealed due to the work of Gerle Creek and the action of a small tributary stream flowing just below the outcrop on the north side of the creek. The exposed granite contains many cracks or *joints* that divide the rock into different-sized blocks. Water, as ice, and other agents of *weathering,* worked on the joints until each block separated. Then, the creek, acting as an agent of *erosion*, removed the weathered debris and carved a channel through this stack of fractured boulders.

Hiking farther upstream, you can see that this hypothesis may have merit because the sizes of the boulders decrease the farther away you are from the exposed outcrop. Only in the next layer of granite to be exposed by the action of the creek, do similar-sized, weathered boulders appear.

As the shadows of the forest grow longer and the mosquitoes become more profuse, it is time to hike downstream, back to your boat and the short paddle to the take-out.

[1] Gilluly, Waters, and Woodford, *Principles of Geology.*

PADDLING AREA 6

Gerle Creek Reservoir
(Crystal Basin Recreation Area)

Size: 57 surface acres
Elevation: 6,500 feet
County: El Dorado

Trip Length: An hour.
Paddling Distances (one way):
Put-in at Day Use Area to the dam: 0.5 mi.
Season: From spring through summer. By early fall, the water level is drawn down, revealing rocky outcrops and a muddy shoreline.
Difficulty: A good family paddle, Gerle Creek Reservoir (pronounced *grr-lee*) is situated in the former small Gerle Valley and enjoys some

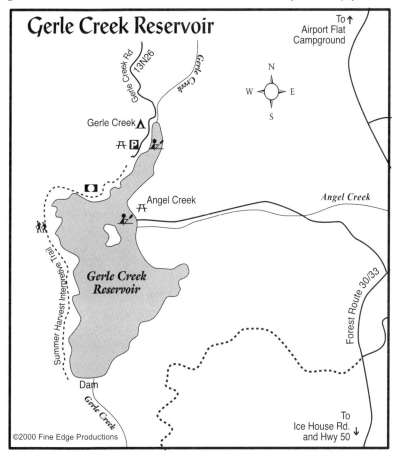

protection against strong winds that make the larger reservoirs more hazardous during a "blow." The only hazards come with the decrease in water levels as summer progresses. If you paddle on Gerle in late summer, keep an eye out for barely-submerged stumps and granite outcrops.

Maps:

USGS 7.5 minute series: *Robbs Peak* quadrangle. (*Note:* The name, Gerle Creek Reservoir, is not shown on the map, only the shaded outline of the reservoir.)

USFS: *Eldorado National Forest, California; Mt. Diablo Meridian.*

Area/Road Maps:

Sacramento Municipal Utility District (SMUD): *Crystal Basin Recreation Area* (1995 ed.).

Family Fun Publications: S/E 35: *Crystal Basin* and S/E 35A: *Desolation Wilderness.*

De Lorme: *Northern California Atlas & Gazetteer* (section 89).

Compass Maps Inc.: *Western El Dorado County.*

Access: From Sacramento, take State Highway 50 east to the Ice House Road (Forest Road 3) exit (on your left immediately after crossing the highway bridge over the South Fork, American River). Follow the forest road for approximately 33 miles. Where the road forks to Loon Lake, take the left fork (Forest Road 33) for an additional 3 miles. The exit (marked as Forest Road 13N 26B) for Gerle Creek Reservoir/ Campground is on the left just past the Airport Flat Campground.

Second-growth forest of Jeffrey pine and other conifers.

Note: If you are driving up for just the day, or want a less-crowded put-in, take the left exit for Angel Creek Picnic Area. The exit is 1.1 miles past the Loon Lake turnoff. Additional information on Angel Creek is included in the text.

Highlights:

- No power boats allowed, human powered craft only!
- No fee for day use
- Nature trail (Summer Harvest Interpretive Trail) with views of the lake, old-growth stands and bedrock mortars.
- Angel Creek Picnic Area has numerous day-use sites, each with a grill, picnic table and vault toilet, but no running water.
- **Camping:** Gerle Creek Campground contains 50 units and is operated by L & L, Inc. For reservations call the National Forest Reservation Center at (800) 280-2267.

  If you arrive without prior reservations and a site is available, you can pay in cash **or** check. Fee $13/night (1998). The best sites are numbers 31-33 (facing Gerle Creek with view of the reservoir); 34-40 are also in close proximity to the creek and have excellent views. Each site has a grill, fire pit and picnic table. Vault toilets and faucets with running water are provided.
- Bring firewood.
- A camp host is on the premises.
- Non-designated camping along the shoreline is not permitted.
- **Bears abound, so camp smartly!**
- **Fire permit:** Permit is required outside official campgrounds.
- Robbs Valley Resort is located off Forest Road 3, approximately 23 miles from Highway 50/Ice House Road exit and 10 miles before the Gerle Creek turnoff, for last minute shopping.

Description: Upon your arrival at the parking area for Gerle Creek Reservoir, the first thought that comes to mind is, "So, where's the water?" A glance through the screen of vegetation bordering the parking area provides you a tiny glimpse of shimmering water. This may be discouraging until you walk to the edge of the shore just past the screen of trees and shrubbery.

WOW! A granite ledge rising from the water across the narrow channel sets the scene as you follow it to the wider opening of the small, but picturesque, reservoir. Growing along the floor of this dome of granite are mature incense cedars, tall Jeffrey pines and other old-growth evergreens. As you acquaint yourself with the lake's scenery, you will notice a small island with several small pines growing out of the sculpted granite. Stretching out beyond the island is the main body of the reservoir, small yet inviting, with just enough surface area for your to explore comfortably without becoming overwhelmed. The unobtrusive dam at the extreme southern end does not detract from

Boulder-strewn Gerle Creek.

the setting. If you follow the narrow channel upstream, you will find that it disappears around the bend—a promise of future discovery and scenic splendor.

Before you hurry and paddle out, be sure to read the informative interpretive display at the water's edge nearest the parking area. The first sign describes the *Summer Harvest Nature Trail* which I highly recommend. The second sign explains the *Gerle Creek Fishery Project;* the third sign does a nice job of describing the *Brown Trout Life Cycle* that occurs in the reservoir.

Since the prevailing wind is from the south (from the dam), in the early morning, I recommend that you paddle to the dam first and allow the wind to give you a "push" homeward. When you reach the center of the lake, make a 360-degree turn with your boat, and you will see that the lake is set in a small valley covered by forest. Behind you, the topmost peaks of granite make up the extreme northern edge of Desolation Wilderness. Lone dead skeletons of conifers provide perches for ospreys or other birds of prey. Drilled holes girdling these standing dead trees provide graphic evidence of work by woodpeckers. Steller's jays flit from one deadfall to the other hunting for food.

If you are fortunate enough to be here in late spring, look for the osprey nest on top of the tall deadfall above the building at the base of the granite cliff to the left of the dam. With a set of binoculars, you may spot one of the adults on or near the nest. *Note:* Please do not stress the birds by hiking to the base of the tree.

On your return leg, paddle into the small cove located on your left (northwest). In the late summer, be wary of stumps lying just beneath the surface. This is the area where herons can be spotted hunting for small fish and frogs that live in the shallow waters. A small grove of box elders provides a nice area for a rest stop.

From the small cove, paddle directly to the island. On a warm summer day, the deep water around the granite boulders offers good swimming; as a bonus, use the smooth, rounded surfaces of the granite for sunbathing. As the sun dries you and the warm granite lulls you into a doze, listen to the sounds of the forest. If the area is not crowded with campers, you should hear the sound of the wind as it moves through the tops of the trees. The occasional splash on the surface of the lake signals the leap of a trout. In late summer and early fall, as a new crop of dragonflies takes wing, lie still and listen for the crisp sound of wings beating as darners flit over the lake. Far off, the sharp cry of a Steller's jay warns the forest of an approaching intruder. A slow rumble that grows in intensity brings you back from the sounds of the forest as an airliner slowly flies overhead, then recedes beyond the tree line. Time to move on.

Angel Creek
Directly across from the island is a small cove with a stream emptying into it. This is Angel Creek, and the picnic tables you see tucked into the base of the granite are part of the Angel Creek Picnic Area. If you arrived by car, claim one of the picnic spots to the left of the restroom close to the water. If you are beaching your boat, use the small sandy area adjacent to the granite outcrop situated to your right. (In spring, the waters of the creek flow into the reservoir, covering the sandy flat and making it difficult to beach a boat.)

Once you have beached your boat and found your picnic site, hike up the weathered dome that blocks the view down the lake. As you start your climb, notice the condition of the granite. Instead of the smooth polished surface found at Loon Lake, the rock here is crumbly and composed of coarse, rounded fragments—partially weathered particles of granitic soil called *grus.*

The absence of obvious glacial action—the polished "mirror surface" of the granite found in Desolation Wilderness—does not mean that Gerle Valley was free from the work of ice. It just may be harder to spot from casual observation.

Up from the two picnic sites on the south side of the creek mouth is an alcove of granite overlooking the lake. The alcove, with thin sheets forming layers underneath, are a form of weathering, a process is called *exfoliation* the ". . . 'leafing away' of layers of granite much as layers of onion peel away from the center."[1] On a larger scale, this form of weathering, as well as the work of moving ice, is responsible for much of the scenery found in the Sierras. From this particular vantage point you have a clear view of the lake with its island below and the

A natural granite sculpture.

surrounding forest stretching out like a giant green mat.

Cross over Angel Creek and hike through the trees to the edge of the lake-filled granite gorge that marks the channel of Gerle Creek. On a warm day you can catch the faint whiff of vanilla or pineapple in the air, a scent characteristic of Jeffrey pine, one of the principal trees within the Yellow Pine Forest. From the edge of the overlook, you can spot the former channel of Gerle Creek as it makes a left bend around the point where Gerle Creek Campground is located. From Angel Creek, finish your excursion by paddling up this channel to explore Gerle Creek.

[1]Alt, David D., and Donald W. Hyndman, *Roadside Geology of Northern California*.

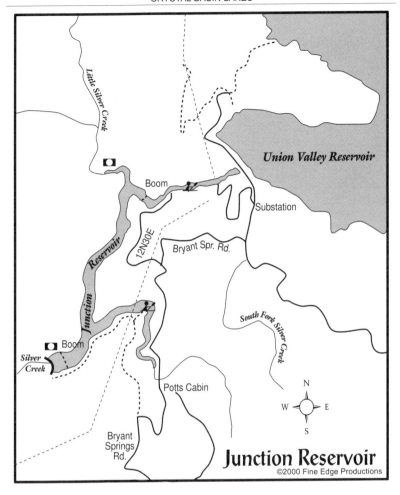

Junction Reservoir
©2000 Fine Edge Productions

PADDLING AREA 7

Junction Reservoir
(Crystal Basin Recreation Area)

Size: 64 surface acares
Elevation: 4,400 feet
County: El Dorado

Trip Length: The entire reservoir could be paddled within one hour.
Paddling Distances (one way):
Put-in near power plant to Little Silver Creek: 0.5 mi.
Put-in off Junction Reservoir Dam Road to Little Silver Creek: 1.0 mi.
Put-in near power plant to dam: 1.5 mi.

Junction Reservoir from the dam road.

Difficulty:
Paddlers should have a knowledge of basic skills and carry a proper first-aid kit before venturing out. Remote access and wind blowing through the narrow canyon are concerns. *Caution:* Do not use the put-in at the power house gate during times of water release at Union Valley Dam. A sudden surge through the narrow channel could become life-threatening.

Season: Early summer through fall.

Maps:
USGS 7.5 Minute series: *Riverton* quadrangle; adjacent section: *Robbs Peak* quadrangle

USFS: *Eldorado National Forest, California; Mt. Diablo Meridian*

Area/Road Maps:

Compass Maps Inc.: *Western El Dorado County*

Access: From Sacramento, take Highway 50 east past Pollock Pines and exit to your left immediately after crossing the highway bridge over the South Fork of the American River at Riverton Historical Town Site. You are now on Primary Forest Road 3 (Ice House Road). Continue on this road for approximately 8 miles and exit left onto Primary Forest Road 31 (Peavine Ridge Road). After 2.5 miles you come to a fork; go right onto Bryant Springs Road (Forest Road 31). Continue on Bryant Springs Road for 4.1 miles and exit onto an unmarked gravel road located near a road sign that shows mileage to Union Valley Dam and the West Point Boat Ramp. [This unmarked gravel road is not shown on the Eldorado Forest map. On the Riverton Quadrant, the road is shown but not marked.] *Caution:* The gravel road to the put-in is steep; be sure weather conditions are dry and your vehicle is able to make the grade.

You are now on the road that ends at the Junction Reservoir Dam. Drive for an additional 0.2 mile. Look for an abrupt right turn that drops off below the level of the road you are on. This last section of road leads to the edge of the reservoir and your primary put-in.

If you want to launch from the pump house built directly below Union Valley Dam, stay on Bryant Springs Road and exit left onto Forest Road 12N/30E. [Forest Road 12N/30E is not marked on the Eldorado Forest map, but it is shown on the Riverton Quadrant.] Drive 0.5 mile to the gate of the pump house, park offroad and launch from the gradient cut into the road embankment at the foot of the gate.

Highlights:
- Limited and remote access.
- Rugged beauty.
- Not suited for motorized boats.
- Primarily day use/no fee.
- No camping facilities available.
- **Fire permit** required for overnight camping.
- To understand how costly the Cleveland Fire was, visit the Information Board and memorial to the crew of a USFS aerial tanker at the Cleveland Corral Information Center as you start your climb on Ice-House Road.

Description: Sometimes pretty things *do* come in small packages! Hidden in a gorge surrounded by tall pines and cedars and overshadowed by the immense size of Union Valley Reservoir it's no wonder that little Junction Reservoir has been ignored by boaters. It is this remote quality, coupled with its intimate size, that makes this reservoir a paddler's delight.

Powerhouse Put-In
If you put-in at the power house, before you launch, look across the channel and up to the top of the lighter rock wall. The stains on the rock are caused by mineralization created when water cascades down the face of the rocky wall after heavy rains or snow melt. Imagine how spectacular the waterfalls are in early spring.

Due to the fast current, in a short time you pass the narrow gorge and enter the slower pool that is part of the upper end of the reservoir. This part of Junction Reservoir bears a striking resemblance to the scenery at Slab Creek Reservoir. [See Volume 1, *Up the Lake with a Paddle*, page 71, for a description.] The dense forest grows down to the water's edge, while tall conifers create a skyline that casts deep shadows on the shore. Rounding the first bend, you may be startled to see an orange

The mouth of Little Silver Creek.

boom straddling the width of the lake. If you paddle to the far right of the boom, you'll see a small exit with just enough negotiating space for a single boat. Once you clear the boom line, notice that the reservoir opens up into a Y. The right channel leads to the mouth of Little Silver Creek where, at low water, you can beach your boat and walk to a delightful set of falls. The upper terrace of the creek is also one of the few places to find a campsite. The last time I was here, I found bear tracks on the wet sand and scat in the grassy cover of the terrace. If you spend the night, store your food carefully.

The left channel opens to the main body of the reservoir. Peering down the narrow finger of the lake, reminds me of similar sights on the lakes of Oregon and Washington. The dense belt of trees is pierced by thin shafts of sunlight.

Working your way up the lake, notice that the right (northwest) shore contains a thin screen of pines behind which are whole sections of silver skeletons of conifers destroyed in the Cleveland Fire—the same fire that ravaged the forest on both sides of Highway 50 past Ice House Road, and the hills bordering Union Valley Reservoir. (The fire began as a result of man's carelessness, on Tuesday, September 29th, 1992.) Fortunately, the belt of forest around Junction Reservoir was spared, insuring stability of the slopes and preventing heavy erosion from runoff and weathering.

Occasionally, you pass outcrops of grayish, lichen-encrusted rock jutting out from the steep banks; the dark coloration creates a somber mood. This rock, a metamorphosed series of sedimentary layers, is one of the ". . . oldest sequence[s] of sedimentary rocks exposed on the western slopes of the Sierra Nevada. These rocks were first deposited in the ocean between 200 and 300 million years ago . . . they form a broad belt along the higher foothills of the Sierra Nevada . . ."[1]

For a good look at this rock, drive to the dam at the toe of the reservoir and look across the gorge below the dam. Individual specimens of these rocks found at the mouth of Little Silver Creek form a broad bar at the foot of the falls, just past the high-water line of the reservoir.

Eventually you pass the second down-lake arm that marks the inlet of the South Fork of Silver Creek. (Forest Road 31 Bryant Springs Road) parallels the fire-scarred gorge of this rough-and-tumble stream and eventually crosses it as the road continues to Union Valley Reservoir Dam.)

Ahead of you are the concrete wings of Junction Reservoir Dam. Paddle to the center of the boom crossing the lake to have a good view of the dam and the main body of the reservoir behind you. One happy note is that the wind blows up the lake from the dam, ensuring a welcome assist on the return leg of the paddle.

Primary Put-In

On your return, paddle into the channel of the South Fork where you will find the broad terrace that marks the primary put-in. Above the terrace is the gravel road that connects with the road that exits Bryant Springs Road and ends at the Junction Reservoir Dam. If you explore the channel further, the toe of the lake is around the left bend. If the water level is low enough, a sandy bar is exposed where you can beach your boat. By hiking up the stream bed, you can reach the small bridge where Forest Road 31 crosses Silver Creek.

Once out of the channel, the breeze off the dam should help carry you back to your take-out and vehicle.

[1]Alt, David D., and Donald W. Hyndman, *Roadside Geology of Northern California.*

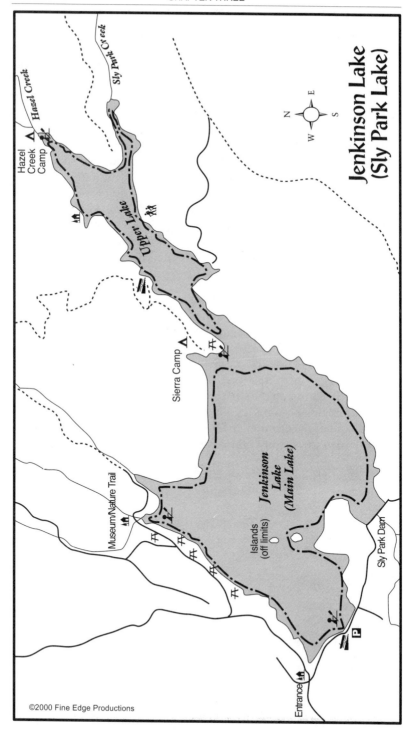

Jenkinson Lake
(Sly Park Lake)

Hazel Creek

Sly Park Creek

Hazel Creek Camp

Upper Lake

Sierra Camp

Museum/Nature Trail

Jenkinson Lake
(Main Lake)

Islands
(off limits)

Sly Park Dam

Entrance

©2000 Fine Edge Productions

PADDLING AREA 8

Jenkinson Lake
(Sly Park Lake)

Size: 640 acres, 8 miles of shoreline
Elevation: 3,500 feet
County: El Dorado

Trip Length: A day-paddle or as part of a weekend outing.
Difficulty: All levels of experience. The wind blowing down the lake may cause a problem, particularly when you cross the channel and it blows on the side of your boat. In the late spring or summer, keep a lookout for motorized boats, especially if they are towing water-skiers.
Season: The lake is open year round. To miss the crowds paddle in early spring, April through May. The fall, when the leaves turn, is a fine time to enjoy this lake. A sunny day in late winter, especially around March, is also a good time to enjoy a quiet paddle.
Maps:
 USGS 7.5 minute series: *Sly Park* quadrangle; *El Dorado County*
 Area/Road Maps:
 Compass Maps Inc.: *Western El Dorado County*

Access: Take State Highway 50 East to of Placerville. Continue for an additional 11 miles to Pollock Pines. Exit onto Sly Park Road (look for a sign for Sly Park Recreation Area) and follow the road for 5 miles down to the lake. The kiosk is located on your left. To reach the upper end of the lake, follow Lake Drive to Sierra Camp located 2 miles around the lake. The area described below is the upper end of the lake.

 (If you want to paddle the main part of the lake, upon payment of fees, take the first right and drive down to the mooring facility and boat ramp. You may park next to the breakwater and launch near your vehicle.)

Highlights:
 • Well-run private lake ideal for family paddle trip.
 • There is an access fee.
 • Boating rules are strictly enforced; as of 1999, no jet skis or 2-stroke gas motors are allowed on lake.
 • The upper lake is better suited for canoes or kayaks (there is a 5-mph speed limit); however, you still have access to the main (lower) lake.

Here you can put in for the main lake (West Shore).

- Bicycles are allowed on the hiking trails and roads. Riding the trail around the lake on a mountain bike offers some beautiful scenery.
- Due to past vandalism, and to ensure a secure nesting area for birds, the islands are off-limits to people.
- If planning a camping trip to the lake in spring, reserve one of the campsites—69, 70, 71, 72, 73, 74, 78, 79—in the Sierra Campground. They are nearest the water and you may launch from them. In the Hazel Creek Campground, sites 141, 142 & 143 are the best bets.
- For information on the Eldorado National Forest and other nearby lakes, visit the Eldorado NF Visitors Center a few miles past Placerville off Highway 50 at the Camino Exit (phone: (530)644-6048). The center stocks USGS 7.5' maps, US FS maps, and assorted guidebooks to the area.

Description: Jenkinson Lake has a split personality, not only from confusion about its name, but also from differences in temperament. The lower or main body of the lake is where all the action takes place--the rumble of powerful engines and the screams of towed skiers become the sounds of the day. There are coves and small niches where you can get out of the way of these "fast boats and loose skiers," but the noise and wakes are ever-present. In addition, by late morning the wind on the open body of the main lake makes paddling more a chore than a pleasure.

The upper lake, which begins at the spot known as the Narrows and stretches down to the Hazel Creek area, has a 5-mph speed limit which creates an entirely different feel. Here you can may glide silently up to a dozing turtle or view the antics of a fuzz-covered gosling hatched only hours earlier. "Yup, it's the same lake, but at a whole lot slower pace."

Now what about the name? Well, for the folks living in Sacramento and vicinity, going to the lake is voiced as, "We're going to Sly Park." Since Sly Park Recreation Area encompasses Lake Jenkinson, it has become the term for the lake as well. [For more on names, see *In the Eddy* below.]

In the spring, before the lake fills with people, the best launching spot is the Sierra Camp Day-Use Area or one of the campsites at Sierra Campground. (I park my vehicle at the trailhead sign for Chimney Trail.) There is a picnic table near the water and a nice level spot for a boat. From this location, it's a comfortable paddling distance either into the upper lake or the main lake.

Upper Lake

Paddle this narrow portion of the lake in the early morning or late afternoon and you can escape the noise and confusion of the day-to-day grind. Just you, the boat, other fishermen, and the tall pines bordering the lake. If the lake level is high, glide through the naked boughs of drowned trees that stand forlorn near the shore. Occasionally, a small diving duck or the honk of a passing Canada goose break the stillness of the setting. The water has a clear, greenish hue with good visibility near shore. As you approach the small cove on the west shore just past the buoy line, raucous Steller Jays announce your arrival. If you are early enough, you may startle a deer on the shoreline taking a drink before it disappears again into the forest. Look for a wooden bench near the lone pine that grows near the water's edge. If you have time, step out of your boat for a quiet moment in this peaceful cove.

This finger marks the entrance to the Narrows and the Upper Lake Paddle.

Paddling farther up the lake, don't be surprised if you see someone on horseback or bicycle negotiating the narrow, twisting trail. When passing the inlets whose streamlets are covered with brush, look for the shy common mergansers that hide among the branches. The male is easily recognizable by his breeding plumage—a black-and-white body and wings, shiny green-black head and a long thin red bill.

Eventually you reach the channel of Sly Park Creek, the first of two major creeks that flow into the lake. Upon negotiating the many trees standing in the channel, you reach the end of the lake where you hear the rushing sound of the creek. A small footbridge adds a delightful touch to the forest where it crosses the creek. The water here is clear, and if you allow your boat to glide slowly without casting many ripples, you may spot trout in the deeper depths of the pool. Near the edge, where the rock outcrop slopes into the water, look for the California newt or "water dog." In April and May, the male amphibian enters the water to prepare for mating. He develops a fin on his tail with which to propel himself through the water, where the mating ritual takes place.

Rounding the point past Sly Park Creek channel, you pass a mound of earth along the shore. In the limbs and deadfall resting on the surface of the lake, look for mud turtles silently sunning themselves. Be silent and observant and you may pick out their forms outlined on the branch. Once startled, a quick but silent plop, and they're gone.

Past the brush-covered shore, you will sight several picnic tables and a clearing at the edge of the lake, the location of Hazel Camp and Hazel Creek. Beyond Hazel Camp are the Youth Group Campgrounds.

Past Hazel Creek and the camping spots, the next area of interest is the lone chimney that rises out of the water in the small cove flanked by a lovely grassy beach. At one time, before the dam was built, this valley meadow or "park" was the site of several structures, including a ranch, hotel, school, post office, and even a saw mill. Which building this historic chimney belongs to, nobody is absolutely certain. Iin her book, *Pollock Pines Epic, Marilyn Parker* writes:

"The chimneys in the eastern portion of the lake are said to be remnants of a house started by a Mr. Bishop in 1911."

The chimney adds a charming touch to the tranquillity of the cove. Unfortunately, as the summer months progress, this portion of the lake dries, exposing a grassy meadow.

Look for a lone picnic table under a pine on a bed of green. If you beach your boat here, you will be able to observe families of Canada geese and their goslings feeding on the grasses nearby. A short walk past and above the table is a toilet. Flitting around the blooming wild flowers are several species of butterfly. I have spotted the small but colorful Northern blue and the larger stunning Western tiger swallowtail.

A picturesque footbridge crosses Sly Park Creek.

From here it is a short paddle past the Stonebreaker Campground boat ramp to your take-out.

Main Lake (West Shore)

There are many accessible spots where you can launch and paddle along the shore of the main (or lower) lake. However, almost the entire northern and eastern shore is dedicated to either camping or day-use. This means that there is no hope of a quiet paddle to observe the birds or animals of the region. If you do launch in the main lake, I suggest the area nearest the mooring facility at the southwest corner of the lake. From here you can paddle along the less-frequented southeast shore, away from the hustle and bustle of the north shore. Otherwise, using the same location, you have a variety of choices for a paddle route.

If the urge to paddle comes upon you at the Sierra Camp Day Site, launch and aim your bow toward the two islands visible to the west. Unless the wind is blowing exceptionally hard, your boat breaking through the smooth surface of the lake and the scent of pine will put a huge grin on your face. Around you, the water sparkles from the droplets cast away by your paddle as you rotate its shaft in the water. The distance between you and the islands decreases with each stroke and, before you know it, pine-covered shores lie before you.

Unfortunately, the islands are off-limits, but you can circle them and observe the birds, particularly the Canada geese that use the islands for nesting. Paddle between the two islands where the shallow depths prevent powerboats from blasting through.

This peaceful sport near the chimney is ideal for a lunch break.

From here, decide if you want to explore the south shore or paddle farther down to the lake where the mooring facility and boat ramp are located. If you paddle across the lake in a northerly direction, paralleling Sly Park Road, you reach the small cove where a creek empties into the lake; adjacent to the creek is a small mooring dock. From here a trail following the creek, leads to the James Calvin Sly Museum and the Miwok Nature Trail.

To return, follow the northeast shoreline where the different campgrounds border the lake.

IN THE EDDY
From Land to Lake

Jenkinson Lake sits in what was a large meadow or forest clearing whose openness was termed a "park" or "flat" by early settlers. The name did not reflect the use of the land; rather the open land reminded the pioneers of the cleared sects owned by rich European landowners. These large, cleared areas of land were set aside as hunting preserves by the gentry.

Before the lake was formed, the large meadow with its blanket of wildflowers and small, bisecting streams served as a summer home for the Nisenan-speaking Native Americans, part of the larger Maidu Tribe. This land was also used by the Miwok, a tribe living primarily in the lower elevations, and some overlapping of territory probably occurred. Like the majority of Native Americans residing in California before the arrival of the White man, "They were hunters, gatherers and fishers and preferred territories that crossed the differing life zones from lower to higher elevations to allow for a greater variety of food." [For more about these people, read Marilyn Parker's *The Pollock Pines Epic*.]

Reminders of their presence can be seen in numerous outcrops of rock that contain round mortars ground into the parent rock by generations of women grounding acorns into meal. In 1848, the Mormon Battalion, a group of Mormon-Americans who were stationed in California during the Mexican War, were returning to Salt Lake City. Scouting ahead for a pass to the east, on July 5, 1848, they came to a "lush green valley" which they named Sly's Park after James Calvin Sly, the scout who first found it.

Settlement of Sly Park began in the early 1850s and continued until 1927 when the land was purchased by the El Dorado Irrigation District to build a dam on Hazel Creek. Due to financial difficulties brought about by the Great Depression and, subsequently, World War II, construction of Sly Park Dam did not start until 1951. The lake behind the dam was named in honor of Walter E. Jenkinson, a former Secretary-Manager of the El Dorado Irrigation District who persevered in the dam's construction.

Today, Sly Park Recreation Area and campground is owned by the Bureau of Reclamation but operated by the El Dorado Irrigation District.

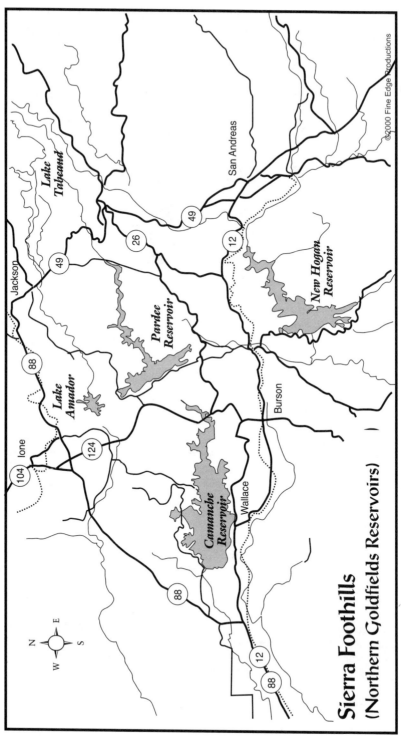

Sierra Foothills
(Northern Goldfields Reservoirs)

©2000 Fine Edge Productions

Reservoirs of the Foothills
(The Northern Goldfields)

You must not know too much, or be too precise or scientific about birds and trees and flowers and watercraft; a certain free margin, and even vagueness—perhaps ignorance, credulity—helps your enjoyment of these things.

—**Walt Whitman**

Paddling the reservoirs of the Sierra foothills gives you the chance to explore sites abandoned by either miners of the Gold Rush era or Native Americans. Where else can you beach your canoe or kayak to explore a grove of oaks, observe the comical antics of an acorn woodpecker, marvel at the subtle beauty of a blooming elegant brodiaea and trace the oval depths of a group of bedrock mortars—all within view of each other?

The lakes covered in this chapter were created by filling former river channels whose drowned canyons once echoed to the workings of Man. The sound might have been from the clang of a shovel followed by the swish of water in a pan, or a mano (pestle) used to grind acorns in stone mortars. Traces of these activities can still be found.

Many of the reservoirs have broad expanses to cross and numerous pockets and coves to cover. The rewards, are numerous and satisfying.

To observe the communal feeding tactics of the Western grebe, paddle first across the main bay of Camanche Reservoir to the quiet shelter of East Cove. It's a full day's paddle to the narrow gorge of the Mokelumne River at the upper end of Lake Pardee. Your reward? Towering walls of rock, splashed with bright patterns of color—yellow, orange, and multiple shades of green lichen cover the bare rock. Bracken ferns grow in many small rocky niches. On the plateaus, where a soil base exists, Digger pines thrust their trunks precariously over the water. In the spring, a profusion of scents from blooming wildflowers permeates the air. As a finale to this visual spectacle, the sound of cascading water from numerous falls provides a fitting accompaniment to the flute-like sound of a canyon wren's song.

Crossing Lake Amador on a wind-free spring morning, you observe the paddle blade as it quietly slips into the water; feel a subtle tug as the blade "bites" and moves cleanly through your stroke cycle. While the lake in front of your bow maintains a glassy, oil-like sheen; a growing V-like bow wave breaks the tension of the surface. Jumping fish increase as you progress farther across the lake. Occasionally you catch site of a Great blue Heron standing motionless awaiting its prey. Deer pause to observe your passing, before completing their morning drink. You smile, maybe laugh out loud, as your muscles work in rhythm to the smooth glide of your boat.

The numerous coves and drainages of New Hogan Reservoir await your exploration. Paddling on this lake brings you into contact with bedrock mortar sites, Miwok middens and abandoned miner's stone-cabins as well as many plants and animals living.

While water-skiers scream on the main body of the lake, posted speed zones in the coves are a canoeist's or kayaker's delight. It is within these long, narrow coves that history and nature intermingle and await your discovery.

A typical California oak knoll in spring.

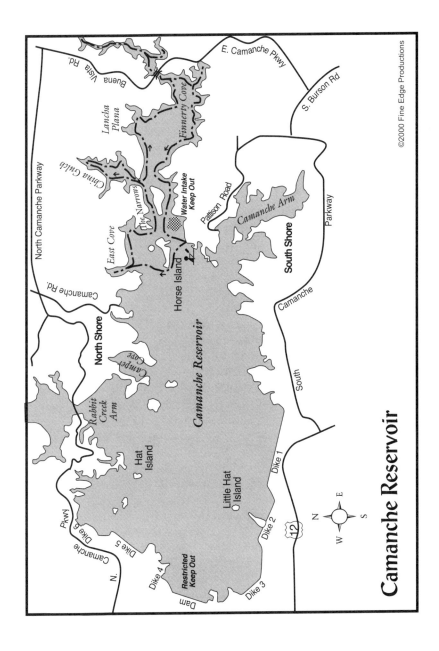

Camanche Reservoir

PADDLING AREA 1

Camanche Reservoir
(South Shore Recreation Area, Mokelumne River)

Size: 7,700 surface acres; over 50 miles of shoreline
Elevation: 325 feet
County: Amador, Calaveras and San Joaquin

The name *Camanche* (a reference to the Comanche Indian Tribe of the Southern Great Plains) came from a town that was built in 1849, grew to a population of 1500 , and was destroyed by fire in 1873. The remains of the town site are now beneath the waters of the reservoir.

Trip Length: A minimum of one full day to explore the upper lake between East Cove and the lower gorge of the Mokelumne River.
Paddling Distances (one way):
Rearview Campground to western tip of Horse Island: 0.5 mi.
Horse Island to southwest tip of East Cove: 0.5 mi.
Rearview Campground. to East Cove: 1.1 mi.
East Cove to China Gulch: 1.1 mi.
Rearview Campground to China Gulch: 0.5 mi.
China Gulch to Sue Island: 0.4 mi.
Rearview Campground to Sue Island: 1.0 mi.
Sue Island to northeast tip of Finnerty Cove: 1.0 mi.
Rearview Campground to Finnerty Cove: 2.0 mi.
Finnerty Cove to the Buena Vista Road Bridge: 0.6 mi.
Rearview Campground to Buena Vista Road Bridge: 3.0 mi.
Buena Vista Road Bridge to upper end of Penn Mine site: 0.1 mi.
Rearview Campground to Penn Mine site: 3.1 mi.
Penn Mine site to entrance of Mokelumne River Gorge: 0.3 mi.
Rearview Campground to Mokelumne Gorge entrance: 3.6 mi.
Difficulty:
Except for a strong afternoon wind blowing from the northwest, the major problem will be budgeting your time in order to complete the paddle before dark. There is so much history and so many places to explore, both in and out of your boat, that it is easy to lose track of time.

Camanche Reservoir is noted for extreme water fluctuations; if the water level drops below the 200-foot level, be cautious about exposed or partially submerged rocks near the shoreline. *Note:* To obtain the current reservoir depth, call (209) 763- 5121 (North Shore) or South Shore (209) 763-5178.

Season: Year-around; the ideal time is spring to early summer.

Maps:
USGS 7.5 minute series: *Wallace* Quadrangle; *Clements* Quadrangle
Area/Road Maps:
FHS Maps (Fishing Hot Spots, Inc.): *Lake Camanche* (A131)
Fish-n-Map Co.: *Camanche Reservoir/Folsom Lake*
De Lorme: *Northern California Atlas & Gazetteer*
Compass Maps Inc.: *Alpine, Amador and Sacramento Counties; Calaveras and Tuolumne Counties*

Access: From Sacramento, you have two choices; a "straight and narrow" route or the "scenic meander."
Direct Route:
Take State Highway 99 South to Lodi and exit onto Highway 88/12 heading northeast into the town of Clements. To explore the North Shore, head north on Highway 88 for approximately 2 miles and turn right on Camanche Parkway North. Follow the parkway signs to the entrance.

To reach the South Shore and the start of the paddle, continue on Highway 12 for approximately 6 miles and exit left (just past Goodmans Corner) onto Camanche Parkway South. Follow the parkway for an additional 8 miles to the entrance station.

Upon payment of fees, request the campgrounds map and follow the directions to Riverview Campground. Once there, pick a spot that provides easy access from which to launch.

At Camanche, your put-in comes complete with picnic table and view.

Highlights:
- Many coves and inlets to explore.
- Historic Gold Rush sites located around the reservoir.
- A variety of wildlife and wildflowers can be seen.
- Fee area (For latest rate, call (209) 763-5121 (North Shore) or South Shore (209) 763-5178.)
- Easy access from vehicle to the water.
- Full service resort with motel, campgrounds, full-sized bathrooms, showers, laundry facilities and well-stocked store.
- To save time and energy, use the facilities at either the Oaks Campground or Rearview Campground when paddling the upper lake.

Scenic Meander Route
For local scenery and history, from Sacramento take Highway 50 East for 30 miles; take the Latrobe/El Dorado Hills Boulevard exit toward Latrobe; it is 8.5 miles to Latrobe.

Pass through lower foothills covered with oaks, small creeks and various ponds. This Ranch Country—with its grazing cattle and horses and deer browsing among the groves of oaks is rapidly disappearing. The open hills and grasslands stretching to the horizon without a human structure are the last such sights in this county. Signs of future development are already evident—survey markers and billboards advertising future home sites or industrial parks.

Latrobe, the small community of houses and ruins, was once the terminus for the Placerville-Sacramento Railroad, with eight daily stages connecting to all parts of El Dorado County. Because of its transportation links, the town also controlled the entire trade of Amador County. [See *Historic Spots in California: Three Volumes In One* by Hoover, Brooke, Rensch and Rensch.]

From Latrobe, it is another 8.5 miles to your turnoff onto Highway 16 West (a right turn). Drive approximately 8 miles west and turn left (south) onto Ione Road. As you cross the Amador County Line, Ione Road becomes Michigan Bar Road. Continue on the same road until it stops at the entrance to State Highway 104. Take State Highway 104 South into the town of Ione.

During the Gold Rush, Ione was called "Bed Bug" and "Freeze Out." Its name was later changed to Ione after a heroine in Bulwer Lytton's novel, *The Last Days of Pompeii*. The prominent church on the hill, visible from the highway as you enter the town, is the Methodist Episcopal Church built in 1862. In its heyday, Ione served more as a busy supply center than a mining community although gold was mined in the nearby foothills.

Highway 104 becomes Preston Avenue. Cross over Dry Creek, pass the Mule Creek State Prison, named after Mule Creek which flows along the south boundary of the prison. Bank right as you pass the entrance to the California Division of Forestry Academy. Continue on Preston Avenue to Main Street. (At the corner, look for a rock slab containing a number of bedrock mortars on display.) Make a left turn onto Main Street, drive 2 blocks and turn right onto Church Street/ State Highway 124 South. [Refer to the insert, on the Compass Map of Alpine, Amador & Sacramento counties.]

Continue on Highway 124 for 11 miles; to reach Camanche's North Shore, make a right turn onto Liberty Road/Camanche Parkway North and follow the directions on the signposts.

To continue to the South Shore, drive 2 miles farther and make a left (east) turn onto Highway 12 East. The left (north) turn onto Camanche Parkway South is approximately 5 miles from the 124/12 junction. Follow the parkway road for another 8 miles until you reach the entrance station.

Description:
Camanche Reservoir, a full-service resort with a first-rate campground, is run by the Camanche Recreation Company (subdivided as Camanche Recreation Company North and Camanche Recreation Company South.) The entire company is under contract to East Bay Municipal District (EBMUD) which owns and operates the reservoir/ dam. Because Camanache is privately owned, there is a fee for its use but it's worth the fee; the campsites are neat and well maintained; there are showers and laundry facilities; the bathrooms are spacious, clean and well placed. Small mini-marts are located near the various campgrounds. If you want to pamper yourself or make an extended stay, cottages and motel rooms available. The full service-marinas contain well-stocked stores and decent restaurants.

Camanche Reservoir teems with Man's history. Unfortunately, most of the Gold Rush history lies underwater; however, you can still find evidence of that era tucked in the brush and oak groves that border the coves and drowned gulches of the reservoir.

Upon putting in, paddle across the lake toward Horse Island, skirt around the western tip of the island and catch a glimpse of the cattle shading themselves under a large oak tree overlooking the island's tip. If the wind is up, skip the island tour and instead use the leeward side as a buffer against the wind.

Note: When the water level is below 220 feet, Horse Island is connected to the mainland by a strand of hard-packed mud which requires a short portage of about 80 feet. The portage is faster and less exhausting than paddling against the wind. When you cross the lake, you will recognize the entrance to East Cove by the white beach on the left bank.

Cut stone with reinforcing bars at the ruins of Penn Mine.

East Cove

As you enter East Cove, stop paddling and wait quietly for the appearance of the feeding Western grebes. Try to second-guess where a bird will appear after it dives. If you are fortunate, you might spot a group of these birds working as a tag-team, herding the fish. According to William Sleuter, a Sacramento local and long-time student/ photographer of grebes, the birds group together and drive the fish into shallow water where they then take turns picking them off.

As you watch for the grebes, listen to the sounds of the many birds in the area. One bird you will hear throughout your paddle is the mourning dove; almost every cove and canyon carries the plaintive cry of this small, dust-colored bird.

You will also hear the acorn woodpecker, a resident of the tree-covered hills. You will recognize this small, colorful bird by its undulating flight and distinctive markings—black body, patterns of white on forehead, cheeks and throat, and head crowned with red. Overhead, clusters of black turkey vultures soar on the thermals and hawks cruise the hillsides looking for prey.

In the springtime, from April on, clusters of wildflowers begin to appear. Look for the tell-tale blue or cream of the ground lupine that bloom in open spaces above the shore. Mixed in with the lupine are smaller, ground-hugging flowers, some yellow, others white; clustered among exposed rocky outcrops are bunches of red paintbrush.

From East Cove, it's faster to follow the shore and double back through the shallow area between Horse Island and the mainland than to paddle around the island. After you enter the Narrows you will see signs posted *No skiing, jet skis or personal water craft, 20 MPH*. Here you won't have to worry about jet skis or bass boaters ripping past your small craft.

If you enter the Narrows in the morning, stay along the far left wall, where the sunshine highlights the plants and colors of the rock. This deep-water stretch of the drowned Mokelumne River Canyon has the feel of sections of the Grand Canyon. The high, multi-colored quartzite walls are stained by mineralization; assorted alcoves are eroded into the face of the rock. Clusters of bushy, orange-yellow monkey flowers grow out of clefts that pierce the rocky side walls. High on the rim, the skyline is broken by silhouettes of Digger pines and oak trees. Swallows flit about carrying mud to their nest sties or hunting for insects.

China Gulch and Little China Gulch

After passing through the Narrows, make a quick left turn into the entrance of China Gulch where you can see a cove rimmed by gradually-sloping white beaches. As you gaze up from the shore, the beaches give way to a carpet of green grasses mixed with bunches of small yellow flowers. Grassy slopes, in turn, blend into bands of dark oaks, manzanita, and Digger pines.

Two smaller pocket coves lie to your left as you paddle into the main cove; both make excellent camping spots. You can gauge their popularity by the remains of fire rings above the high-water line. My favorite camp spot or break area is Little China Gulch, the second pocket cove. Look for turtles sunning themselves on the dead brush piles on either bank of this small cove. Don't be alarmed if the water suddenly erupts and you spot a shadowy object speeding by your boat; these are golden carp that feed in the shallows; your approach has startled them.

On shore, the small cement and cobble structure is the remains of a barbecue pit; if you look around, you may spot several concrete fire rings hidden in the grass amongst the oak trees. To explore the area you can beach your boat and hike up the bed of the small creek that flows into the cove.

If you follow the creek, you intersect the hiking and equestrian trail that follows the north side of Camanche Lake. In spring, look for

Little China Gulch from the lakeside trail.

clusters of yellow Sierra iris that grow in the shady spots. Watch where you step in late spring or early summer; rattlesnakes like to warm themselves on the sunny, open trail and their coloration makes them difficult to spot.

When you have children with you, it's fun to guess the identities of the animals tracks. You're sure to come across deer, raccoon, coyote, skunk, turkey, the ever-present cow and horse, and maybe even a mountain lion.

With binoculars, find a shady spot under an oak with a view of other oaks; you can spot the busy acorn woodpecker in the trees. Look for their "granaries," dead standing trees or living trees, drilled with thousands of holes where they cache their acorns. These woodpeckers live in groups of up to 15 birds, sharing their territory, relying on cooperative behavior. (For a description of these birds, see Walter Koening's insert in *Oaks of California* and Verna R. Johnston's *California Forests and Woodlands; A Natural History*.)

Paddle to the opposite shore directly across from the entrance to China Gulch. (You can spot the entrance to a small cove by a reddish outcrop of eroded soil. Here the terrain is more exposed and you can find interesting rocks that provide a clue to the geologic history of the region. Hike up the old road to the top of the hillside where you have a great view.

Lancha Plana

From China Gulch, the next leg of the paddle covers the coves and shore of what was known during the Gold Rush as Lancha Plana ("flat boat" in Spanish) and Poverty Bar. According to *Historic Spots in California*, the site of Lancha Plana—a small mining town now underwater—was ". . . a mooring place for the flat-boat ferry which carried miners from the north side of the river across Poverty Bar and the mines of Calaveras County." You will paddle over this now-vanished town site as you follow cliff banks along the north shore.

Note: Do not follow the shore too closely, partially-submerged quartzite boulders present a hazard.

Watch for a cove entrance as you pass the quartzite bluffs on your left. Head for the beach at the base of the single steep peak that separates two drowned stream beds. On the east (right) side of the lone peak look for a trail along the small stream that empties into the reservoir and follow it inland into the oak woodland. You are hiking in the vicinity of an infamous hangout—Camp Opra—that in the 1850s saw the likes of Joaquin Murieta and other bandits. In the 1860s, when copper was discovered nearby, the short-lived mining towns of Copper Center and Townerville (Hotel de Twelve) were established in the vicinity of Camp Opra. Now, as you hike, the only clues to man's presence are overgrown piles of stone, odd pieces of metal, and occasional bits of shiny glass.

Continue along the stream to its source approximately 0.5 mile inland where you come to a meadow lake, covered with a blanket of aquatic plants—a pretty sight nestled in the middle of an oak and pine woodland. In late spring and early summer, you can hear the sounds of frogs along the lake and spot Great blue herons, egrets, and other waterbirds.

Sue Island/Poverty Bar

Continuing on, look for the small island in the center of this part of the lake. What was once a dredged river bed but is now exposed high ground is Sue Island, a great place to stop for a break. Between you and the island is a ghost forest whose tips seem to be growing out of

Canada geese raise their young on the shores of Sue Island.

the lake; take care paddling this area; the branches are brittle and break away very easily.

Just past the southern tip of the island is a small cove where you can beach your boat on a sandy bar and be protected from the wakes of motorized boats. In the spring, the island becomes a nesting site for families of Canada geese that use the tall, dense grasses to shelter their nests. By May, you may spot their fuzzy goslings feeding alongside the parents on the banks of the island or bobbing on the lake's surface. *Caution:* Do not approach too closely; small birds will panic and may become separated from parent birds; this also places unwarranted stress on the adult birds.

The paddle from the island to the south shore and former location of Poverty Bar is a short one. As you come closer to the shoreline, you will notice remnants of a pipeline and small tunnels running parallel to the shore. These are the remains of an aqueduct built to obtain water for local hydraulic mining operations. A small cove to your left as you face the shore hides a delightful swimming area and a shady grove of oaks.

Moving up the lake, follow the south shoreline. You will pass a small cove whose drowned entrance is covered by a bristling surface of dead trees. Kingfishers use the branch of the dead trees as perches from which to spot and dive for fish.

By now you will have paddled around the lake's bend, past Finnerty Cove, and caught your first view up-lake to the Buena Vista Road Bridge. Turn and scan the north shore, to see the bright red and cream-colored soils eroding from the steep cliffs. This erosion is, in part, the result of dredging operations that took place on the Mokelumne River prior to the construction of the reservoir. (See *Gold Districts of California*, Bulletin 193.) The area along the south shore was known as Winter's Bar.

In spring, as you pass under the bridge, you will see hundreds of swallows passing overhead; don't tarry or they will provide you with an unpleasant souvenir.

Oregon Bar/Penn Mine Site

Past the highway bridge, a small finger cove lies to the right. Investigate it for a delightful paddle under an umbrella of overhanging branches where you can watch kingfishers, egrets, and an occasional heron feeding in the muddy shallows.

In the morning or late afternoon, you can spot white sparkles on the north shoreline stretching from the bridge up the lake to just past the Penn Mine Site. Paddle closer to see that the sparkle comes from hundreds of quartz crystals imbedded in the white matrix of exposed *milky quartz.* The quartz chunks are eroding from larger beds of quartz veins that make up the area's geology.

Paddle along the south shore to the left of the entrance to the finger cove where you can see reminders of former mining operations. This vicinity was formerly Oregon Bar. Scan the exposed rock to see a slight green tinge in the soil layers, the copper once mined at the nearby Penn Copper Mine.

The large, flat area extending from the banks of talus was created by the dumping of *slag* (residue left over from the smelting of metallic ore) into the former river gorge.

Caution: Do not paddle too close to the piles of slag; the water is opaque and you may scrape your hull on a partially submerged slag heap.

In the late afternoon or early morning, take time to stop and watch the fish jumping; they fish appear more active here than at other parts of Camanche. When paddling close to the north shore, look just forward of your starboard (right) bow for groups of large carp swimming slowly just below the surface.

To explore the mine site, beach your boat at the upper end of the buoy line at the small beach next to a stream. This spot has the only sandy bottom. The entire area surrounding this site is frequently covered with a carpet of yellow-orange monkey flowers.

Mokelumne River Gorge
Paddling away from the Penn Mine site, look to the hillside on your right where you can see *talus piles* from abandoned mines of the mid-1800s. When you reach the debris pile—a "raft" of floating wood and other flotsam—look to the left to spot standing slabs of upthrust *schist* called "tombstones." A clear channel lies through this floating debris on the far right before the left bend of the river.

Almost hidden by the pines, these talus piles mark the site of old mines.

191

Just before the bend where you enter the gorge, look for the road cut that angles down to the edge of the reservoir's scrape zone. Remains of the foundations of the old wagon road that followed the gorge and the bridge that once stood here can be seen on either side of the gorge. The massive concrete abutment blends into the neighboring rocky slope.

As you enter the Mokelumne River gorge, shadows of the rock walls on the surface of the opaque water may disorient you momentarily. It is difficult to tell where the rock ends and the river begins. Let your eyes follow the angles cut into the rock by faulting and erosion; the harsh lines are softened by vegetation that grows precariously in eroded clefts; the skyline is broken by the shapes of Digger pines and oaks growing along the rim.

Here swallows hunt or carry bits of mud to their nests under high alcoves of rock. The green of the brush is broken by the sharp colors of red, yellow, orange and purple wildflowers. Close your eyes and listen. You may hear the melodious song of the canyon wren, the small *Pan* of western river canyons.

Fighting the river current, you round the bend of the canyon and find an eddy in which to rest. Looking upstream, you spot a small, mixed sand and gravel beach on river right. When the current is not too strong you can beach your boat on this gravel bar. This is as far as you can go. From the beach, explore up-river or stretch your legs and rest your shoulders after paddling against the current. Look up on the shady canyon walls to admire small ferns growing out of the crevices.

As the shadows begin to fall over the canyon's rim and the air begins to chill, it is time to leave this peaceful place and paddle home.

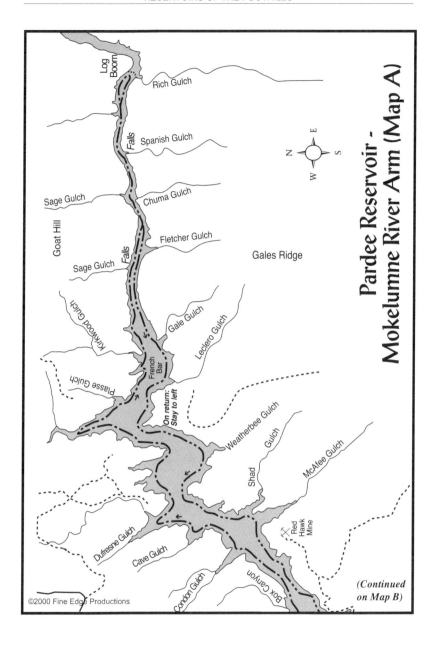

Pardee Reservoir -
Mokelumne River Arm (Map A)

Log Boom
Rich Gulch
Falls
Spanish Gulch
Sage Gulch
Chuma Gulch
Goat Hill
Fletcher Gulch
Gales Ridge
Sage Gulch
Falls
Kirkwood Gulch
Gale Gulch
Leclero Gulch
Plasse Gulch
French Bar
On return: Stay to left
Weatherbee Gulch
Shad Gulch
McAfee Gulch
Red Hawk Mine
Dufresne Gulch
Cave Gulch
Condon Gulch
Box Canyon

(Continued on Map B)

PADDLING AREA 2

Pardee Reservoir:
via Mokelumne River Arm (Map A)

Size: 2,200 acres; 43 miles of shoreline
Elevation: 568 feet
Counties: Amador, Calaveras

Trip Length: You can complete Pardee Marina to Black Gulch in one day, but at least two days gives you time to explore the many coves and gulches, hike the interesting knolls, and photograph the sights.
Paddling Distances:
Pardee Marina To Black Gulch Via Mokelumne River Arm
Day-use parking to Cypress Point: 2 mi. one way.
Cypress Point to French Bar: 3 mi. one way.
French Bar to logboom at Black Gulch: 1.3 mi.
Day-use parking to Black Gulch and return: 15 mi. (round trip).
North and South Arms (all one way)
Woodpile Gulch to Boom Line, South Arm: 2.5 mi.
Woodpile Gulch to waterfall, Lawrys Gulch: 2.5 mi.
Woodpile Gulch to South Gulch (far end South Arm): 3.5 mi.
South Arm Closed Area to Cypress Point (via South Arm): 3 mi.
Difficulty:
Pardee Reservoir is subject to wind which picks up at mid-morning and usually dies down by late afternoon. In the Mokelumne River Gorge arm, expect a strong headwind on your return paddle from the log boom above School Land Gulch.

Paddling close to shore, keep a lookout for submerged rocks just beneath the surface. Fortunately, the clarity of the water is superb allowing you to inspect the area you are approaching.
Season:
February through October; the best time is the spring and early summer. However, on a sunny day in February you'll share the reservoir with few boats and, as a bonus, see the waterfalls in full flow.
Maps:
USGS 7.5 minute series: *Jackson* quadrangle; *Valley Springs* quadrangle
Area/Road Maps:
Aqua Maps: *Pardee Lake* (official lake contour map)
De Lorme: *Northern California Atlas & Gazetteer*
Compass Maps Inc. *Alpine, Amador and Sacramento Counties*

Access: From Sacramento, take State Highway 99 South and, just past the town of Galt, exit onto Liberty Road heading east for approximately 12.5 miles until the road ends at Highway 88. Turn left (north) onto Highway 88 and follow it for 7 miles.

Turn right onto Jackson Valley Road and follow it to a four-way stop in the small historic community of Buena Vista. (The historic Buena Vista Store is located directly across the street and on your right at the intersection.) Make a right (south) onto Buena Vista Road and drive for approximately 2 miles; turn left at the Lake Pardee Recreation Area sign.

You are now on Stoney Creek Road which leads to the entrance of Pardee Lake Recreation Area and Marina. Drive for another mile, turn right at the nicely-designed entrance station. (Be sure to inform the entrance station personnel if you are not fishing.)

•There are two choices for put-in and take-out. The first site is the Day Use parking area next to the enclosed boat, trailer and RV storage compound. This site prevents having to compete with the launching or recovery of power boats.

The second choice is below the parking area for Mistletoe Fishing Access Area; advisable *only* when the reservoir is full. You can save 2 miles of paddling by eliminating the trip out and into the main marina recreation area.

You can launch at the marina with the other boats but, if you would rather have some solitude and not "mix it up with the power boat boys," take the small road on your right at the corner of the RV storage area and the entrance to the parking lot of the marina/boat launches. This narrow, winding road leads to the day-use area of Rainbow Point and Blue Heron picnic spots. Both have parking near the water and toilet facilities. If these two spots are taken, park in the small day-use parking lot directly across from the fenced RV compound that has a level, grassy launch area and an adjacent toilet.

Entrance and information center, Pardee Reservoir.

Highlights:

- The view from the heights of the Observation Point off Pardee Dam Road is worth the drive; for a bonus, complete the drive by crossing the dam via the one-way road. After crossing the dam, park in the first turnout on your right. To have a view of the lake, the inner gorge and the dam itself.
- To appreciate the beauty of the many wide and scenic bays, be sure to carry a topographic map.
- Many spectacular waterfalls.
- Pardee Reservoir is a public drinking water supply source. To prevent body contact with the water, all boats must have a definite enclosed cockpit area for the operator and passengers.
- Fee for day-use and use of a cartop boat; additional fishing fee.
- (Let the kiosk operator know that you are paddling only.)
- **Camping:** Camping with full facilities is available near the main entrance; showers and laundry facilities are available.

  Information or camping reservations can be obtained from the Pardee Recreation Area Office, open February-October, 9:00 AM to 4:30 PM every day. Phone (209) 772-1472.
- Poison oak is thick around the shoreline, so be careful whenever you take-out.
- A store and coffee shop (serving breakfast, lunch and dinner) is located just past the main entrance.

Description: For a scenic lake for paddling—not for swimming or hiking—you will find joy and contentment on the waters of Lake Pardee. When the reservoir—known for its fluctuations— is at maximum level, the many large bays, listed on the maps as gulches, are truly spectacular.

Prior to construction of the reservoir, this stretch of the Mokelumne River was famous for its many gold camps, mines, miners' cabins, and other historic sites. Many of the more important sites, where gold was found or a town once stood, are commemorated in the names of the gulches which are listed on the USGS topo for the area. As you paddle into one of these drowned stream beds, names such as Copper Mine Gulch, Grapevine Gulch, and School Land Gulch will enhance your appreciation of the area.

Pardee Recreation Area to Copper Mine Gulch

Your paddle begins at either the boat launch or one of the day sites within the developed area of the lake. Upon launching, paddle across the bay and head northeast for the point leading into Yagers Gulch. This entire bay is a "no-wake zone," so motorized craft leaving or arriving will not create any major wakes.

As you cross, notice the concrete structure that looks like a small dam behind you and to your left. This is the Jackson Creek Spillway that controls the flow of water between Pardee Reservoir and Lake Amador, whose Carson Creek Arm is less than a mile away. A jeep road that also acts as a hiking trail runs along the high-water line of the northeast arm of the lake. You can access it at Porcupine Point and follow it to its terminus at Tule Gulch, a distance of approximately 5 miles.

I avoid the official launch site, the boat ramp, and use the Day-Use Area facilities instead.

As you round the point into Yagers Gulch, the dense brush gives way to a view of gently rolling hills interspersed with stands of oak. This sudden transition from dense chaparral to grasslands, scraggly oaks, and an occasional manzanita, may indicate a change in soil type.

Scattered throughout California, are "islands" of weathered rock called *serpentine* or beds of ancient marine sands. As these rocks erode, they produce soil that is poor in nutrients. Plants and insects that attempt to survive on this soil (or any specific type of soil) are called *edaphic communities.* Plants that live on serpentine soils have short, curled, leathery leaves and long moisture-seeking roots and they tend to look dwarfed.

As you round the inlet, you enter a small gulch where a vault toilet secured to a barge is anchored to one side of the cove, one of many such *relief stations* anchored throughout the lake.

Paddle to the shady end of this small gulch and take a couple of minutes to listen for the sounds of the acorn woodpeckers vocalizing as they go about their feeding. Look down into the lake near your boat, to spot small groups of bass or trout nervously swimming about as they check out your presence.

Farther down the lake you pass a small logboom placed there to prevent the shore from clogging with debris. The boom sometimes serves as a resting spot for mergansers, other waterfowl, and turtles.

IN THE EDDY

Naming the Land II

Lake Pardee Dam is one of the oldest in California, completed in 1930. The Mokelumne River was always considered a source of pure, fresh water. After the gold mining claims played out, a consortium of eleven cities, calling themselves the East Bay Utility Company, began buying up the land. The president of the company was the former governor of California, George Pardee, for whom the dam and lake were named.

The Mokelumne originates high in the Sierras in Alpine County. It has three branches, the North, Middle, and South forks. Together, the branches drain an area 47 miles long and 16 miles wide. The main river is 130 miles long and drains 700 square miles before joining the Cosumnes River near the Delta Country of the Sacramento River. Both rivers eventually merge with the San Joaquin River and empty into the head of Suisun Bay.

The river is named after a Plains Miwok Village called Muk-kel; the suffix -*umne* means "people of" and *moke* may mean "fishnet." In 1817, Padre Narcisco Duran gave the name of the river as Moquelumnes. In 1848, John C. Fremont passed through the area; he used the present spelling.

The next unnamed inlet is a nice spot for a break. Paddle toward the large pine near the waterline where you can find a level spot to beach your boat. *Caution:* Poison oak is common and abundant near the shore. Be careful where you sit or place your clothing or other belongings. For a free brothure on this plant, send a business-sized SASE to UC Cooperative Extension, 4145 Branch Center Road, Sacramento, CA 95827. Request Pest Note # 32, *Poison Oak.*

The small, shallow spit of land that marks the entrance to Copper Mine Gulch and the Mokelumne River Channel is a good spot to remember when you return from exploring the inner channel. The leeward side of this spit can be used as a rest spot before you make your final paddle across the lake to the take-out.

Entering the channel, look across the water where you can see John Bull Peak (elevation 1,053'), named after "John Bull,"—the cartoon personification of the typical Englishman, similar to our "Uncle Sam."

Stay on the north side and paddle into Tule Gulch. This broad, open bay gives you a nice opportunity to take a break and view the different aspects of the lake. Across the main body of water toward the southwest, you can spot Pardee Dam.

The road paralleling the west side of the lake is Pardee Dam Road. This road, which becomes Sandretto Road south of the dam, leads to an intersection with Campo Seco Road, and from there to historic Valley Springs.

Directly across to the southeast Cypress Point marks the southern entrance into the channel. Jeep roads on the hills above lead to former mines and prospect sites.

Face your boat to the northeast looking up-channel. The only hint of channelization comes from the sight of the sheer rock walls farther up the lake. This first narrows is aptly called Box Canyon.

Looking past the narrow rock walls, the occasional rounding of the landscape at the water's edge gives you a hint of the many drowned valleys or gulches awaiting your exploration, so . . . let's get on with it!

Tule Gulch to French Bar (distance of 2.8 miles)

From Tule Gulch onward, the feel of paddling on a lake begins to change as you feel the first subtle tug of current. As you enter the narrow stretch of Box Canyon, paddle close to the shore and look for the subtly-colored lichen that cover the rock face. Clusters of yellow monkey flowers along with smaller bunches of paintbrush grow in the weathered ledges. The big, billowy shapes of California buckeye cover portions of the rock walls.

This conical knob is a landmark for the channel arm and the entrance of Condon Gulch.

Condon Gulch

Rounding the point and entering the waters of Condon Gulch, your eyes are immediately drawn to Chrome Mountain (elevation 1,207'), a prominent landmark for this part of the lake. The unnamed conical knoll in the foreground that rises steeply from the water's edge provides dramatic balance to the mass of Chrome Mountain. I have hiked to the top of the peak, and it is a hard, sweaty scramble; however, the view of the entire lake and countryside, is truly spectacular. I recommend beaching your boat to the right of the stream on the left (west) side of the mountain. There is no trail as such; the east side is less steep but has a dense cover of chaparral and poison oak. Use the eroded slope that faces the lake as your starting point and work your way to the top of the peak. *Caution:* The rocks are extremely loose, so wear adequate footwear and carry water.

McAfee and Shad Gulches

Directly across the water from Cave Gulch are two smaller gulches, McAfee and Shad. On the ridge bordering the southern entrance into McAfee Gulch, look for an overgrown trail that cuts down from the edge of the ridge and terminates in a bushy ravine midway between the top and the water's edge. Now, note the abrupt change in the vegetation and the pile of rock or *talus* forming a small *debris fan* that stands out from the brushy ground cover. The upper end of the debris fan marks the location of the old tunnel of the Red Hawk Mine (listed on the 7.5' Jackson quadrangle).

As you paddle on, you pass the small island that marks the entrance into Shad Gulch. In the late afternoon, I have sighted great blue herons sitting on the exposed tree stumps at the far end of the gulch. A small beach at the mouth of the stream makes a great break area. From here you have a good view of the surrounding hills and the bulk of Chrome Mountain.

Cave and Dufresne Gulches

Located on the opposite bank and up channel, are two small gulches, Cave Gulch and Dufresne Gulch identifiable by the trails and jeep roads that crisscross the expanse of the hillsides. These trails, enlarged versions of tracks made in earlier years, are kept clear by the feet of boaters who climb them for a view of the reservoir and surrounding valley.

Farther up Dufresne Gulch, you come to a small side-cove that harbors a small stream and waterfall in the rainy season.

The "Elbow" to French Bar

Immediately past Dufresne Gulch, the channel widens into an elbow. Stay to the left (north) shore. If you wish to take-out or take a break, now is the time to scout for a suitable beach; between Dufresne Gulch and French Bar, the banks are steep and rocky, with slim pickings for a take-out.

If you don't want to explore the two coves between Dufresne Gulch and Grapevine Gulch, I suggest landing on the small island adjacent to the tip of the finger of land that marks the left bend of the elbow. From the top of the island, you have an outstanding panorama of the surrounding hills, with their green grassy slopes and patches of oak.

Among the grasses, vines and poison oak is a small wooden marker for what may be a gravesite; the enigmatic marker reads: *John Jessup / 10-51 to 2-96 / 22-lb. catfish / I miss you John.*

If the wind is blowing or the sun is too hot for an island landing, the next best spot is just around the tip of the finger that extends behind the island. You can rest in the shade or be out of the wind and still have a grand view in both directions.

This small island lying between Dufresne and Grapevine gulches makes a beautiful spot for a break. The wildflowers are elegant brodiaea.

Grapevine Gulch

Grapevine Gulch is worth exploring. Not only is it fun to follow the twists and turns of this lengthy finger, but the open oak hills give way to a narrow brushy overhang of shady trees and vines. In late spring, when the rains have ceased and the streams have slowed to a gentle flow, the clarity of the water improves tremendously. Schools of large fish can be observed moving slowly beneath your boat.

On your return from the gulch, stay to the left (eastern) shoreline. You will pass over a shallow zone and near another small island as you round the point marking the drowned site of French Bar.

Small fish like to congregate in the reeds and brush growing in the water where they can feed without being eaten by larger fish. But it isn't the bigger fish that make meals of the smaller fry; this is efficiently handled by the small diving ducks, mergansers, or occasional grebe that bob on the surface or pop up suddenly from their underwater hunt.

French Bar to Black Gulch Logboom

Long before the Mokelumne River Channel was flooded, the sand and gravel bars were worked by French miners who used rockers and sluices to extract gold buried beneath the mounds of surface rock giving it the name French Bar. The adjacent slopes were covered with the miners' canvas shacks and their orchards and vineyards cultivated by the residents of French Bar. Today, the water lapping the shores and the wind brushing the tops of the oaks are the only sounds to be heard.

Within the area are four small gulches; two gulches on the north side of French Bar are Kirkwood Gulch and a smaller, unnamed gulch to the south of Kirkwood. On the south shore are two other gulches—Leclero and, to the north, another small unnamed gulch. On the same side, but up-channel from Leclero is Gale Gulch, whose stream flows down from Gales Ridge.

Up-channel past French Bar, the walls of the gorge begin to narrow and their sides steepen. As you approach the inner gorge, you hear the sound of falling water. Look to your left and up; you will be delighted by the sight of a thin ribbon of water, 20 to 30 feet high, cascading from the steep heights of a narrow Sage Gulch. For me, this ranks as the third-best waterfall in the reservoir.

The two dominant rock formations at the entrance are Goat Hill (elevation 1,518 feet) to the north, and Big Dome (elevation 1,436 feet) to the south.

Sage Gulch carves into the west flank of Goat Hill and Fletcher Gulch separates Big Dome from Gales Ridge (highest point, 1,324 feet), rising south of Fletcher Gulch.

The grassy slopes of Goat Hill hold a herd of Black Angus cattle. Their occasional bawling can be heard over the sound of the falling water. Small calves lie on level terraces dozing or sunning themselves.

On the opposite shore, Heather Gulch is the site of a relief barge.

Passing Fletcher Gulch, the wind picks up as it funnels into the gorge. The sides of the canyon rise rapidly. Deep fissures in the rock create shadows that delineate the exposed knobs and relief of the strata.

Fletcher Gulch marks the beginning of the Mokelumne River gorge. You enter through a stone "gate" whose left, upper layer contains a relief resembling a profile of a low-browed face staring across the canyon. A lone buoy marks the "no-wake zone."

Disk-like bands of color are the work of rock lichen and the color intensifies as the rains soak the rock. Varying shades of green fill the nooks and crannies of the rock walls. Tufts of grass, a thicket of brush, even a lone pine or buckeye cling to life, wherever a soil base has formed.

The last mile offers more dramatic scenery with walls of stone, plateaus lined with grass, or knobs covered by small groves of oak and pine. Three gulches, each with its own waterfall, add to the scenic drama taking place within the channel. Your first gulch, located on the south shore, is Chuma Gulch. On the opposite shore is School House Gulch, recognizable by the debris boom across its mouth. The last gulch encountered before reaching the logboom across Black Gulch is Spanish Gulch is the last gulch you can enter.

Inside the inner recess of Spanish Gulch, the sound of water tells you a prominent waterfall is nearby. As you round the bend, cascades of water slide down a wide opening of slick rock and splash into a

Journey's end, the log boom at Black Gulch.

pool at the base of the falls.

Overlooking the entrance to the gulch, a lone, manzanita grips the surface of a rounded slab of lichen-encrusted stone, its crimson bark adding color to the scene. Thickets of wild blackberry vines grow along the shore. In late spring, clusters of common monkey flowers and California honeysuckle add their hues to the scene.

Beyond Spanish Gulch lies the first of two debris booms that prevent further passage up the gorge. The inlet on the north shore, downstream from the boom, is Black Gulch.

Sometimes you find one or more boats tied to the boom, their owners fishing from their boats. They are often surprised by the appearance of a paddle craft this far up the channel. I have been offered a "ride back" many times; as yet, I have declined.

Take a long break, stretch your muscles, chug on the your water bottle, take a bite out of one of those "nourishment" bars and, start your paddle back.

IN THE EDDY

Chaparral!

Chaparral, a term that comes from the Basque word, *chabarra,* refers to scrub oak (a plant species within the chaparral community). The term became *El chaparro* ("evergreen scrub oak") in spanish and was later modified into *chaparajo,* the leather garment worn by the California *vaquero*—the first true cowboy—to protect his legs against dense stands of prickly chaparral. *Chaparajo* was later anglicized into "chaps." (For a detailed account of this word's linguistic progression, read Elna Bakker's *An Island called California.*)

As you gaze at the hills, the dense mat of chaparral stretches out and covers the entire area. Occasionally the vegetation is broken by small stands of oak and lone sentinels of the silvery-green Digger pine. Upon closer examination, you will see a variety of hues in this dense overlay of brush. After a spring rain or summer thundershower, the profusion of scents can captivate you—many of these plants are related to the sage family and give off a sharp, yet pleasing odor.

The primary plant in this chaparral community is *chemise*, a member of the rose family. With its tiny needle-like leaves, tiny, and delicate white flowers, it is well adapted to drought. Interspersed with similar plants is a bushy tree that is the California buckeye, a bushey plant that has long (4-6 inches), gorgeous clusters of white flowers. A member of the horse chestnut family,the buckeye is so abundant around Lake Pardee that the air is filled with its light, sweet scent.

Sometimes blending with the overall community, sometimes standing apart as a large shrub on a rocky knoll, is the venerable *manzanita.* This shrub is distinguished by smooth, reddish bark, and pale green leaves which have a waxy feel. Manzanita was used by many of the California tribes both as a food source and for its medicinal value. The sturdy limbs were used in construction of houses or for carrying heavy burdens.

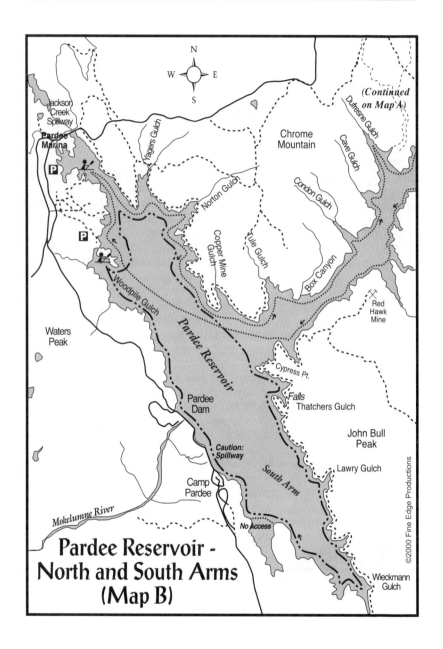

N
W E
S

Jackson Creek Spillway

Pardee Marina

Yagers Gulch

Chrome Mountain

Dufresne Gulch

(Continued on Map A)

Cave Gulch

Norton Gulch

Condon Gulch

Copper Mine Gulch

Tule Gulch

Box Canyon

Red Hawk Mine

Woodpile Gulch

Pardee Reservoir

Waters Peak

Cypress Pt.

Falls

Thatchers Gulch

Pardee Dam

John Bull Peak

Caution: Spillway

South Arm

Lawry Gulch

Camp Pardee

©2000 Fine Edge Productions

Mokelumne River

No Access

Wieckmann Gulch

Pardee Reservoir - North and South Arms (Map B)

The area around the lake is open and accessible, with a park-like feel.

PADDLING AREA 3

Pardee Reservoir, North and South Arms (Map B)

(For Highlights, Difficulty, Trip Length, Paddling Distances, Season to Paddle, Maps, and Access, see *Pardee Marina to Black Gulch Via Mokelumne River Arm*, above.)

Woodpile Gulch to Boom Line, South Arm

As you begin this 2.5-mile leg, note that the exposed shoreline of the reservoir is composed of rock layers tilted or folded into vertical planes. These layers of metamorphic—changed or altered—volcanic rock were part of a former sea floor that has been scraped and shoved against the edge of the continent by the forces of plate tectonics. When these same layers are exposed on the surrounding hillsides, their vertical position gives them an appearance of tombstones—the name given these exposed outcrops by the early miners.

The first part of this paddle follows a steep shoreline that has been scraped and cut; consequently, there are few take-out areas. (I try to take my first break at the grassy knoll before crossing the dam site where pines provide shade and you can hike to an overlook near the road for a view of the dam and gorge.

Woodpile, named after the piles of wood cut for campground use, is the first gulch you come to. Be sure to paddle over to the small stream lying below the outspread California buckeye growing at the lake's edge. The trail visible along shore is part of the Lake Pardee Shoreline Trail. You can hike around the lake following this trail system.

The weathered structure with the flag pole marks the access to the dam, built in the 1930s as part of the 1931 State Water Plan.

*There are many waterfalls along the shores of Pardee
Reservoir.*

The buildings and relay towers on the hill across the dam are part
of the East Bay Municipal Utility District (EBMUD) headquarters.
Immediately past the dam itself is the boom surrounding the gates of
the spillway where flocks of cormorants feed.

South of the boom that surrounds the spillway, another boom
prevents access to the channel containing the intake pipe of the Pardee
Tunnel where water from the reservoir is piped past Camanche
Reservoir and into the Mokelumne Aqueduct. The aqueduct carries
the water into Clifton Court Forebay, southwest of Stockton, where it
is eventually pumped into the concrete arm of the California Aqueduct.
Part of a pre-World War II development to provide fresh water to
Southern California and reduce flooding in the Central Valley, the entire
undertaking became known as the Central Valley Project.

South Arm: Closed Area To Cypress Point (distance 3 miles)

After you cross the boom line you near the shaded shore of a quiet cove—the entrance to Pardee Reservoir South Arm. The steep banks, common along the shores of the North Arm, have given way to gentle slopes that gradually descend into the water.

Not only are there beaches where you can take-out, but the vegetation changes as well. Instead of the monotonous blanket of chamise (the gray-green brush covering the hills on the east side), thin stands of oak mixed with Digger pine, and grassy meadows predominate and small bunches of reeds and cattails grow in the shallows near shore. In the exposed rock layers lining the shore, you can see the sparkle of quartz, more noticeable than the dark bands of schist.

The small stream flowing into the lake from the southwest at the end of the arm, marks the depression called Salt Gulch. Here, you can hear the croaking of frogs that live in a nearby spring-fed pond.

Crossing to the east shore, you will hear the sound of tumbling water, the first of several waterfalls located at this end of the reservoir whose is an intermittent creek that flows out of Wiedemann Gulch. At the entrance to the creek, you pass an outcrop of multi-banded rock. If the rains have been plentiful, take a close look at the variety of moss and lichen growing on the rock's surface. Hiding in a crevice you may spot a small tree frog. Flitting in and out of the brush are black-headed juncos and small groups of yellow-and-black goldfinches.

As you continue, you pass two small coves before entering a wider cove with a waterfall and a finger of land blocking the wind from the north. This sheltered cove is an excellent spot for a break or lunch. A small treeless hillock above provides an excellent view of the lake and the adjacent hillsides. As you enjoy lunch, turkey vultures pass overhead riding the thermals in search of their own meal. Sometimes the sound of brush parting and branches snapping betrays the presence of deer. . . and, somehimes, even a coyote. Be careful where you step; you can easily trample the emerging clusters of wild iris that bloom late in the spring. On a sunny day, rock lizards sun themselves on the nearby "tombstones." Caution: If you hike in the early warm days of spring, be watchful for rattlesnakes; the crevices and loose rock around weathered rock are especially suspect. If you sight a rattler, remain still and it usually moves away; if not, back away slowly. Please do not provoke it or kill it. Snakes are excellent hunters that help maintain the balance of nature by keeping the rodent population at normal levels.

Along the hills immediately north of the gulch, the oaks and pines give way to impenetrable carpets of chamise.

To spot Lawry Gulch, look for the floating relief barge usually crowded with a flock of cormorants sunning themselves on the foredeck—you'll want to pass by quickly to minimize your exposure to the odor.

Woodpile Gulch area: the put-in is to your right behind the tree.

In the protected cove flanked by chaparral-covered hills you will delight to the sight of a bridal veil fall that cascades over four pools from a height of about forty feet—one of the best within the reservoir.

Enjoy this splendid waterfall, then notice the rocky drop-off where the water tumbles into the reservoir. My hat is off to the work crew that stabilized this section of the road. Instead of piling up boulders or making a sterile concrete culvert to hold the water, they successfully, and artfully, allowed the water to fall against a backdrop similar to the natural channel on the hillside.

Gaze northeastward at the high knoll outlined against the sky. This is John Bull Peak, one of the prominent landmarks of the reservoir. Paddling around the peak's shoreline, you pass the entrance to Thatchers Gulch, a nice spot to break or enjoy the view before continuing. From here, your next landmark is Cypress Point, the entrance to the Channel Arm of Pardee Reservoir and the drowned valley of the Mokelumne River.

If the wind is blowing or you want to take a break before making the final paddle across the reservoir to your take-out, scoot into the sheltered cove along the eastern bluff of Cypress Point. From this cove you can take time to familiarize yourself with the landmarks that mark the entrance to Woodpile Gulch—your final take-out point.

If you paddle directly across the mouth of the channel, you come to Copper Mine Gulch. Use the windbreak of this low-lying finger of land to take a break before making your crossing. From here you can see the water tank on the northwest knoll across the reservoir; the entrance to Woodpile Gulch lies to the south of the water tank.

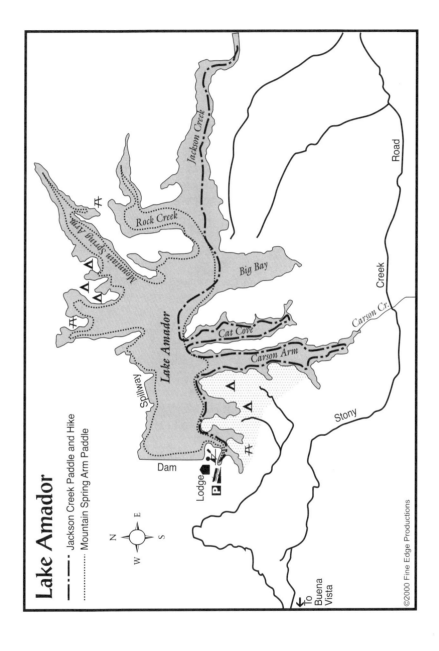

Lake Amador

- – · – Jackson Creek Paddle and Hike
- ········· Mountain Spring Arm Paddle

Jackson Creek

Rock Creek

Mountain Spring Arm

Big Bay

Cat Cove

Carson Arm

Carson Cr.

Carson Creek

Lake Amador

Spillway

Stony

Dam

Lodge

N
W E S

To Buena Vista

Road

PADDLING AREA 4

Lake Amador

Size: 400 surface acres; 13.5 miles of shoreline
Elevation: 485 feet
County: Amador (Both the lake and the county are named after Jose Maria Amador, a Spanish soldier who later became a wealthy Californio landowner.)

Trip Length: Lake Amador is a small intimate lake that can be paddled in its entirety within a day. However, to enjoy the many coves and lakeside trails you should plan an overnight stay at either the lake's primary campground or one of the boat-in camps.
Difficulty: A great family lake; afternoon winds may be a problem for beginning boaters. On weekends, motorized boat traffic becomes intense, so keep a wary lookout for motor-boaters.
Season: Throughout the year; the best season is spring through early summer.
Maps:
USGS 7.5 minute series: *Ione* quadrangle; *Jackson* quadrangle
Area/Road Maps:
Aqua Maps: *Lake Amador* (official lake contour map)
De Lorme: *Northern California Atlas and Gazetteer*
Compass Maps Inc.: *Alpine, Amador and Sacramento Counties*
Note: As of 1998, the USGS quads do not name the reservoir/lake.
Use the Aqua Map for area location.

Access: From Sacramento, take State Highway 99 South toward the town of Galt. Exit onto Liberty Road (just past the town of Galt);head east for approximately 12.5 miles until the road ends at the intersection with Highway 88. Turn left (north) onto Highway 88 and follow it for 7 miles, then turn right onto Jackson Valley Road. Continue on Jackson Valley Road for a short distance until you come to a four-way stop. Go directly through the intersection, past the historic Buena Vista Store on your right, and continue for another mile. Look for a weathered sign on your right marking the entrance to Lake Amador Drive. Unless the ticket booth is manned (if not, register and pay use fees at the lodge), continue across the dam and park in the gravel parking lot adjacent to Lake Amador Lodge. The entrance to the store/restaurant is on your right and to the back. After paying, take the road to the left of the restaurant to the boat launches located below the building. If you plan to camp, the access road to the campsites is across the boat launch parking lot, near the exit and to your left. *Note:* The lower parking area is deeply rutted, so watch your clearance as you drive through.

Highlights:
- Boat-in camping.
- Family atmosphere.
- The hike up Jackson Creek in the spring and early summer is well worth the effort.
- The fishing is great!

Description: Lake Amador exhibits a quiet charm that immediately makes you feel at home. Time seems to slow down and, from the moment you pay your use fee to the time you are under way, a quiet, pleasant rhythm begins to take hold.

Lake Amador is definitely a family lake. The campgrounds are nothing fancy, just level spots with table, fire pit and a view of the lake. The sounds of kids laughing and shouting come from everywhere.

But to think this is just another family vacation spot would be misleading—Lake Amador is a bass lake! (The world record for Florida bass was set here in 1981.) You will constantly see or hear fish jumping and feeding on the lake's surface and, in every nook and cranny, you'll find a fisherman attempting to catch that "ole' lunker" and make history. This doesn't mean a lack of peace, solitude and contentment on your paddle, but be forewarned; this is a fishing lake first and foremost; all else takes second place.

Lake Amador's boat ramp and put-in.

Even with that warning, I recommend the lake for its serenity and charm; try to paddle here in late spring or early fall when the lake is less crowded.

Boat Ramp to Cat Cove

The boat ramp is a busy place. To prepare your craft for the day's paddle without feeling rushed, use the level ground on the far right in the shade of the oaks lining the bank. If you park your vehicle just behind those oaks, you have just a short walk as you load or unload your boat.

Take a moment to study the water and you'll understand why this is a fishing lake. Every once in a while the lake looks as if a gust of wind were kicking up the water, an effect created by hundreds of small fry as they dart in schools from one spot to another.

As you begin your paddle, head for the entrance to the main body of the lake, but stay close to the point with the RVs on it. Round the point and paddle past the first small cove on your right. Before you enter the entrance to the Carson Arm, take a moment to stop and soak

Beaver are common here; watch for signs of their handiwork.

in the beauty. To the west, you can spot the earthen dam and the road you drove across. Directly across from you to the north is a roped-off area; this is the entrance to the spillway used to dump water from the lake back into Jackson Creek. On a typical spring or summer day, you will probably need to dodge the many fishing boats trolling near the dam.

Approximately 800 yards into the arm, look for a small cluster of Digger pines on the west (right) side. In mid-morning, turkey vultures like to perch and sun themselves on the top-most tree limbs. Glide slowly under the trees, where you may be able to watch them without startling them.

Paddle past the camp dock located on your right (west), past the campers and, when you reach the split in the arm, take the cove to the left (south). This is the lower end of Carson Creek.

On a late spring or summer morning, take a moment as you enter a cove to spot the back-lit silken canopies of the parachute spiders. In calm conditions, you may spot a spider skimming along the surface of the water. Attached to the spider is a long thread of silken webbing that acts as a kite or parachute, keeping the spider aloft as the breeze carries it to a new home.

Darting among the webs are dragonflies, darners and the smaller damselflies. (Dragonflies and darners, in addition to being larger then damselflies, hold their four wings horizontally at right angles to the body when at rest. Damselflies have four netted wings that, at rest, fold vertically over their bodies.) Occasionally, one of the dragonflies will skim across the lake's surface and appear to take a drink.

As you make your way deeper into the arm, look carefully into the shady niches created by the overgrowth of trees and shrubs. I have often been startled by the "squawk" and flapping of wings as a great blue heron noisily opposes my intrusion.

Swimming in the sunlit shallows along the shore are varieties of fish. The well-known bluegill dart around the boat as you come to a halt. After a few moments, larger bass and trout make their appearance. As long as you make no sudden movements or sounds, you can study these interesting fish for long minutes before moving on.

Eventually you will arrive at the end of the arm. At low water you can spot a barbed-wire fence running across the edge of the arm, separating the lake from Carson Creek. At high water, you might not spot the wire until you pass over it. This fence marks the boundary between Lake Amador and the wildlife preserve that borders much of the lake. The lake, up to the high water mark where the fence stands, is open to the public but the wildlife preserve is closed.

Where the vegetation along the water's edge has not taken hold or the rock strata is visible, you will be able to see the folding that has occurred in the rocks. Intense heat and pressure forced the rock to

The only whitewater on the lake, Jackson Creek is the end of the line.

soften and bend into lithic lines, not unlike the folds of a cloth napkin pushed away from the dinner table after a satisfying meal.

Cat Cove

The first bay on your left in Cat Cove contains a nice level area under the shade of a small oak, great for taking a break. A short hike through the clearing surrounded by a dense growth of chamise will take you to high ground where you have a nice view of the lower lake and dam.

If you paddle close to the shore in Cat Cove, it's not uncommon to come across a deer bent low over the water satisfying its thirst. The dense chaparral along the shores provides good cover for wildlife. I have even come upon deer swimming across the cove.

Note: Prior to crossing Big Bay from Cat Cove, take time to orient yourself on the map; the upper coves of the lake can become confusing due to the narrow approaches separating Mountain Spring Arm from Jackson Creek Arm.

Big Bay to Jackson Creek

To reach Jackson Creek Arm, cross the mouth of Big Bay keeping to the south shore. You will enter the narrow channel with the unlikely name of Devils Gate. (The name refers to the features of the landscape before the dam was built; two streams, Rock Creek and Jackson Creek, merged here).

Continue straight ahead as the channel narrows. The hillsides become steeper and good landing beaches disappear. In spring just around the right bend, the entire southwest rock wall is covered with the flowering California buckeye. Hidden among the trees are small caves and lichen-encrusted rocky niches. The sweet, descending notes of the tiny canyon wren may greet your arrival into the bird's territory. Small mud turtles and bull frogs drop into the water from their resting spots. Be quiet and listen for the echo of the frogs' croak.

Look down onto the water and note that its clarity is improving. The sight and feel of a current should be another clue that the lake is ending and the stream starts just ahead.

When you reach the beginning of Jackson Creek, beach your boat and follow the small footpath that runs along the left side of the creek. It will take you to a short, picturesque gorge of the creek. From the upper ledge, you will be able to view the rushing waters of the creek and admire the many wildflowers in bloom.

By the time you return to your boat, the lengthening shadows on the steep walls of the drowned creek channel provide welcome shade as you begin your paddle back to the main body of the reservoir and your take-out.

Sauntering along the sandbar, this handsome tarantula eventually disappeared into the brush.

IN THE EDDY

A Drive to Clinton Bridge

As you paddle over these inundated gulches, do you ever wonder how they looked before the waters of the reservoir covered them? To appreciate these narrow stream valleys, drive down Gwin Mine or Middle Bar roads.

Gwin Mine Road is accessible from the small community of Paloma. Heading east from Pardee Reservoir, the exit is visible from Paloma Road. To access Paloma Road, cross over Pardee Dam onto Campo Seco Road which merges into Paloma Road at Campo Seco. Continue on Paloma Road for approximately four miles. At the top of the ridge are clusters of houses and several adjoining streets. The turnoff for Gwin Mine Road is just before the Paloma State Historical Landmark.

The distance from the top of the ridge to the dead end at Clinton Bridge is three miles along a paved, but narrow, one-lane road converted for two-way traffic. Many of the former mine sites are visible just a few yards off the roadway. Pull in at the turnouts and explore the foundations and ruins. At one of the larger mining areas, the gulch widens onto a clearing. Tucked into the smaller side streams are extensive foundations where the stamp mills and mine shafts of Gwin Mine sit silent.

The mine was owned and operated by Senator Gwin who, in 1851, became California's first senator. Gwin Mine operated from the beginning of the Gold Rush era in 1849 until 1908. Much gold was extracted from the Gwin and the other "lodes." You see remnants of these lode mines as you continue down the road.

Eventually you cross a small stream and parallel the upper portion of Pardee Reservoir Channel Arm. The channel begins to lose its appearance as a lake and slowly takes on the personality of a river. At a clear break among the trees, you will sight the burnished sheen of Clinton Bridge. Soon the road leaves the trees and is squeezed between the rock wall of the ridge on your right and the Mokelumne River flowing below.

On a sunny weekend afternoon, chances are you'll encounter several families fishing off the bridge with dogs and children chasing each other up, down and around the bridge. Before walking onto the bridge, look up at the crosspiece where the bridge name and date of construction is visible.

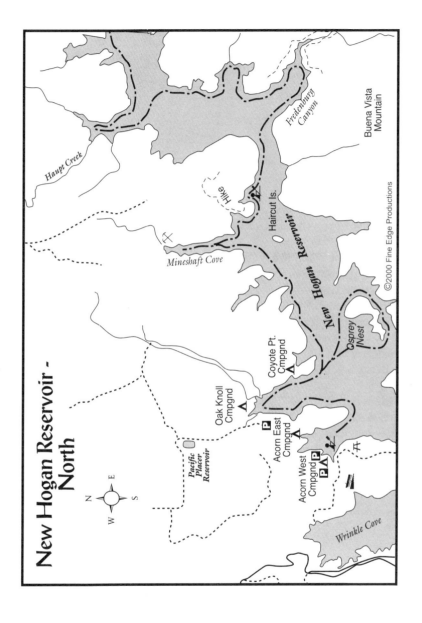

New Hogan Reservoir - North

PADDLING AREA 5

New Hogan Reservoir
(North Fiddleneck to Haupt Creek)

Size: 4,400 acres; approximately 8 miles long with 50 miles of shoreline.
Elevation: 713 feet
County: Calaveras

Calaveras is Spanish for "skulls." The name was used wherever human skeletal remains were found. Sometime between 1836 and 1837, John Marsh and his party came across a great many skulls near the site of the present day river; as a result, they always referred to the area as Calaveras. The original Spanish name for the Calaveras River was Rio San Juan.

Fiddleneck to Mine Shaft Gulch
(including Calaveras River Arm to Haupt Creek)
Trip Length: A weekend allows you to paddle the lake comfortably and fully enjoy its charm.
Paddling Distances (one way):
Fiddleneck to island off Fiddleneck Day-Use Area: 0.5 mi.
Fiddleneck to Deer Flat Boat-in Campground: 1.5 mi.
Fiddleneck to take-out, Mine Shaft Cove: 2.5 mi.
Fiddleneck to take-out, Fredenburg Canyon below Deer Peak: 3.2 mi.
Fiddleneck to Haupt Creek: 3.5 mi.
Fiddleneck to North Fork Fishing Access, Latimer Gulch: 5.0 mi.
Fiddleneck Day Use to North Fork Arm, Calaveras River: 6.5 mi.
Season: Spring through early summer; fall when the crowds are gone and migrating cranes or geese can be seen and heard. (I have paddled the lake as early as February, but it takes an exceptionally warm day to do so.) By late March, the days begin to lengthen and the afternoons are warm enough to take the edge off the afternoon breeze.

Maps:
> USGS 7.5 minute series: *Valley Springs, Jenny Lind, San Andreas* quadrangles
> Aqua Maps: *New Hogan Reservoir*
> U. S. Army Corps of Engineers: *New Hogan Reservoir* (free at Visitor's Center)
> Area/Road Maps:
>> Compass Maps Inc.: *Calaveras and Tuolumne Counties* or *Alpine, Amador and Sacramento Counties*
>> Thomas Bros.: *California Road Atlas & Driver's Guide*

New Hogan Reservoir: "There's a lot of water to paddle."

Difficulty: The paddle from Fiddleneck to the coves of North Arm is long and suited for intermediate to advanced boaters. Novices and beginners will find the Whiskey Creek Recreation Area better suited for their paddling experience. Lake Hogan presents the same kinds of difficulties as paddling on any large, exposed body of water. Unless you are comfortable with long distances, explore one of the many smaller coves.

Be aware of the weather when planning a long trip on the lake. In the spring and early summer, thundershowers with wind and possible lightning strikes are a hazard if you are caught crossing one of the large open bays.

Strong wind gusts can unexpectedly blow over the lake at midday; plan your crossings accordingly. Once you pass the open main channel and reach the coves bordering "haircut isle" or the upper north arm, you are protected from wind and fast boats.

Partially-submerged rocky outcrops that extend from shore are the primary obstacles encountered on the lake. The majority of these rocky reefs occur near a point.

Access: Take State Highway 99 South to Lodi and exit onto State Highway 12 East. Continue on Highway 12 (it merges with State Highway 88 outside Victor) until you reach the town of Valley Springs. Turn right (south) onto State Highway 26 and go approximately 1000 yards, then merge left onto Hogan Dam Road. Hogan Dam Road takes you to park headquarters and Observation Point, a good spot for viewing the lake and your paddle area.

If you are planning on using Acorn Campgrounds as your launch point, backtrack on Hogan Dam Road for approximately 2 miles and make a right turn onto New Hogan Parkway at the sign for the marina. Make a left turn just before the gate and kiosk (ticket booth) and follow it to Acorn West or East campground entrance.

Fiddleneck Day-Use and Picnic Area is located on the same road, before you reach the entrance stations to the Acorn campgrounds.

Note: At the time of this writing, parking in the newly paved parking lot located to the left (northeast) of Acorn West Campground and launching a car-top craft was free of charge until the official opening in April. Otherwise day-use parking at this site is up to the discretion of the kiosk operator. This area is used as overflow parking for campers only; if you camp at one of these campgrounds, you may hand-launch free of charge at any shoreline site adjacent to your campsite.

Highlights:
- New Hogan Dam, built and administered by the U. S. Army Corps of Engineers, primarily impounds water from the Calaveras River and several major streams. Because the reservoir does not monitor snow melt for flood control, the levels of the lake are usually higher than nearby reservoirs.
- Lake volumes of 199,800 or higher are ideal for put-in and take-out. At those levels, the "bathtub" effect is minimal.
- Put-in and take-out from a day-use area without the use of a boat ramp is free, otherwise a day fee is charged. (The rangers encourage people with hand-launched boats to use areas other then the launch ramp to minimize congestion.) Combined fee for day-use and launching from a boat ramp.
- Part of the pleasure of boating on Hogan Lake is the opportunity to hike along the miles of shoreline. Bring appropriate footwear.
- The River of Skulls Interpretive Trail (0.75 mile) is located below the dam on the way to Whiskey Creek Day-Use Access.
- Poison oak is prevalent around the lake. Be especially careful in the early spring before the leaves bud.
- **Camping:** There are three standard drive-in campgrounds, one group campground and one boat-in campground. Two campgrounds—Acorn West and Acorn East—have showers.
- The lake headquarters staff is polite and courteous, willing to answer questions on paddling conditions or other information. If you want to make a hit, bring some popcorn—a guaranteed staff pleaser!

Description: Your first impression of the lake may cause you to gasp, "That's a lot of water to paddle!" That's certainly what I thought!

However, I quickly developed a mantra to cope with all that water-filled shoreline: "One section at a time; one bay only!" I repeated this phrase every time I felt overwhelmed, or when the research deadline began to creep closer on my calendar.

Repeating this phrase in my head, I settled down and began to enjoy the lake—one section at a time. I purposely stayed out from the main body of the lake because it is extremely exposed, allowing strong gusty winds to blow unchecked into the coves and bays of that portion of the lake.

Fiddleneck to Coyote Point Group Campground

Start your paddle from any shoreline site at the Fiddleneck picnic area. If you camping at the Acorn East campground, use the small cove located directly below the overflow lot near the campground kiosk. If you paddle into the channel any time before April, use the overflow parking areas adjacent to Acorn East Campground for parking and to walk your boat to the water. The use of this adjacent cove shaves some distance off the mileage. (Mileage is figured from the Fiddleneck Day-Use Area.)

Note: The wind blows steadily from the west up the narrow channel. Following the southeast shore on the outward leg of the paddle keeps you on the leeward side, away from the majority of gusts. On your return leg, stay along the northwest shore to avoid a headwind.

Upon launching, head for the large island visible from the shore. As soon as you round this island, continue across the channel to the

Looking east from Mine Shaft Cove.

rounded island with the osprey nest silhouetted against the skyline. *Caution:* If the nest is occupied, please do not land—you will stress the parent birds. Instead, allow your boat to drift with the wind and observe the activities in the nest from a distance.

On many of the round-topped hills, grazing cattle graze can be heard bawling as you paddle by.

Along the green hillsides, groves of oaks provide limited shade. These trees—an important source of food and nesting sites for birds—are predominately blue oak whose abundant acorns fed the Miwok, early hunter-gatherers of California. Evidence of their having lived here can be found in the bedrock mortar sites where outcrops of flat rocks lie close to oak groves and streams.

The fruit of the abundant California buckeye—a large oval nut—was another source of food for local Native Americans. Like the acorn, the buckeye nut was first leached in running water for several hours to eliminate its bitter tannin. Then, crushed into a flour and served as a thick mush, it was known as *pinole;* served as a soup, it was called *atole.*

Two predominant species of plants that growing in the chaparral throughout this area are chamise and *ceanothus*, commonly called buck brush. Closer to the water, on north-facing slopes, the infamous poison oak and California buckeye are common. Manzanita (Spanish for "little apple"), a large shrub that can be mistaken for a small tree, is also a member of the chaparral community which grows apart; some specimens reach the height of smaller blue oaks that grow next to the manzanita.

Interspersed with oaks and chaparral are stands of Digger pine (gray pine), known for their tenacity to survive in harsh soils and conditions of drought. Their pine nuts are sweet and nutritious.

Paddling along the Fiddleneck Day-Use shoreline, you will spot a massive, angular outcropping of "tombstone rock," its sharp angles outlined against the sky. Smaller versions of these rocks are evident along the roadsides as you climb into the foothills from Central Valley. (These are primarily metamorphosed volcanic rock from ancient undersea volcanoes that has been changed by the heat and pressure of mountain-building forces. These same forces upended the layers, forming these slabs of dramatic shape and size.)[1]

Heading up-channel, you pass a large unnamed island mid-way between Fiddle Neck, Acorn campgrounds, and the southeastern shoreline; the largest and most prominent of the islands that dot the lake, it has many spots to explore and picnic.

Paralleling the southern shoreline is a fire road that provides access around the lake; it makes a good starting point if you beach your craft at some cove and wish to hike.

Hidden from view, but definitely worth visiting, are the coves hidden by out-thrust points of land. These sheltered bodies of water protect waterfowl, hawks, the American bald eagle, and other wildlife from the cold wind and openness of the main bay. To catch a glimpse of these creatures, enter the cove quietly, approaching from a shaded side that masks your entry.

As you pass Coyote Point, notice the picnic tables and campground sites. Plan to stop for a break here; the view is great and the site peaceful during the off-season.

Coyote Point to Mine Shaft Cove

If you stay on the northern shoreline before entering Mine Shaft Cove, you will pass four shallow coves whose surrounding slopes are densely covered by a mat of chaparral. A hiking trail follows the contours of the scrape zone and may be seen from your boat. The last cove

To see this abandoned homesite, take a short hike up the streambed from Mine Shaft Cove.

bifurcates into a short, narrow inlet entering from the west, and a longer finger cove with a channel entry to the north.

Located mid-channel are two islands (at high water only one island is visible). The smaller island glistens with a white sheen from the silt covering its surface. The second and much larger island is topped with brush and trees. The island has no name but I call it "Haircut Isle," because it reminds me of the style favored by kids today—bushy on top and shaved around the ears. Unfortunately, at low water the steep banks make landings difficult.

The approach to Mine Shaft Cove is directly across from the north side of the island.

For the best lighting conditions enter Mine Shaft Cove in early morning or late afternoons.

Once you have entered the cove, follow the shore past the buoy and look for an outcrop of orange-yellow rock on the northeastern horizon below the the larger hills. The area to explore is located below this outcrop with the take-out adjacent to an outcropping eroded by a small stream.

If the run-off is not too strong, you may hear the deep bass of frogs hiding in grass-covered pools adjacent to the stream. You can hike the trail on the south (left) shore or walk in the meadow on your north (right). Note the depth of the small cleft of rock and the colors of the exposed surface. This rock probably captured the interest of early miners as they searched the surrounding ravines for minerals. Look above and to the left of the cleft whre you can see the depression that marks the now filled entrance to the former mine.

Follow the stream as it meanders up to the first bend above the exposed rock. Hidden among the oaks on the north (right) bank are remains of a stone foundation possibly that of an early miner's home.

The view of the surrounding hills and lake makes this a wonderful spot for a picnic or a lunch break.

Don't leave without hiking the stream to the end of the lake's boundary just a few hundred yards upstream. As you follow the stream past the oak grove, you come upon a lovely view of the stream flowing past a sunlit meadow. The exposed slabs of rock bordering the banks of the stream are covered by abstract patterns of almost fluorescent-orange lichen. High above the stream-cut valley past the fence line of the lake are yellow-orange rocky slabs visible from the entrance to the cove. To view the entire meadow, with the stream and cove below, follow the fence line to the rock pile visible above the north bank of the stream—be careful of the poison oak!

To Fredenburg Canyon (Below Deer Peak)

By now you have noticed that New Hogan Reservoir has a tendency to narrow, then widen into large, open bays before tapering into a slot or channel. It is this feature that gives the impression of vast distances of open water between shorelines.

As you paddle out of Mine Shaft Cove toward Deer Peak and the take-out at the stream that flows out of Fredenburg Canyon, that impression is reinforced. From the mouth of Mine Shaft Cove, the distance to the opposite shore looks rather intimidating. However, if you paddle along the northern shoreline, the bay narrows as you round the flank of the dominant hill and it is a short crossing into the mouth of Fredenburg Canyon.

Back at the small cove where you began the hike and in your boat once again, follow the southern shore into the narrow mouth of Fredenburg Canyon. Notice the piles of driftwood that accumulate along the high-water line. Previous boaters have built elaborate, whimsical structures from these bleached wood piles; everything from a common windbreak or sunshade to complex towers with pennants "a-flappen." Many of these architectural "delights" recall San Francisco Bay Area structures of the 1960s and 70s erected on Interstate 80/50 between Berkeley and Emeryville.

Be wary of partially-submerged, jagged rocks near the outlet to the stream. Beach your boat on the shallow beach located on the north shore; the southern shore has cobbles and other debris.

To stretch your legs, take the jeep trail south, ford the stream, and follow a smaller, yet distinct trail that parallels the right bank of the creek. In early spring or soon after a rainy day, listen for the sound of water tumbling down a series of short, steep drops and enter the main creek.

The trail you are following is the former flood plain of the creek on your left. The soil is rich in nutrients, giving rise to the thick and varied vegetation that grows here. Eventually, you pass a massive old valley oak that continues to survive and dominate the area.

Valley oaks which require large amounts of water to sustain themselves, are usually found near a river or perennial stream. Another fallen valley oak that lies nearby provides an excellent seat from which to view the green grassy slopes of the meadow across the stream. Deer

Fredenburg Canyon is a delightful place to visit; Deer Peak rises in the background.

Peak (elevation 1,921 feet), rising beyond the meadow, is part of a larger ridge known as Hogback Mountain (highest point is 2,812 feet).

Don't be surprised to meet a herd of cows on your return hike; they use this same trail to reach the grasses growing near the water.

Haupt Creek

Haupt Creek is identifiable by the lone dead trees whose tops rise above the waterline of the cove. Some of these sentinels in bold contrast against the sky   are quite photogenic. Paddle close to some of these dead trees and look for the cavities pecked into the trunks by woodpeckers; some of the holes have been enlarged to serve as nesting cavities for birds.

Three streams empty into Haupt Creek Cove. The first stream is to the left as you enter; the second to the northwest is Haupt Creek.

At the end of the channel, there is a narrow canyon whose rocky walls bear evidence of scouring by years of flood waters: witness the piles of varied cobbles and other debris carried down in spring runoff.

After exploring Haupt Creek, return to the knoll that separates Haupt Creek channel from the other, unnamed stream inlet. Look for the glitter of quartz in the surrounding terrain; this outcrop of quartz extends around the entire bend of the knoll following the contour of the cove. Beach your boat and take a closer look at the outcrop so you can study the numerous small, perfectly-shaped crystals within the matrix of the quartz.

Paddling farther into this pocket cove, you pass through a skeleton forest of dead oaks that grew here before the reservoir was created. Beyond this stand of deadwood lie the gentle banks of a small stream. Beach your boat here, enjoy a lunch, and explore the surrounding area.

Calaveras River Arm

Past the conical knoll north of Haupt Creek Cove, the channel begins to narrow and the beginnings of a current is felt. Pass the entrance to the last cove, on your left, round the left bend, and enter the narrow channel of the former Calaveras River.

The diagonal slash visible across the upper side of the knoll to your left was a spur line of the Southern Pacific Railroad. This line ran from Lockeford (Stockton), paralleled Highway 12 and terminated at the cement plant near the Kentucky House south of San Andreas. The tracks are long gone but the grade remains, providing a nice path through the gorge.

Past the first bend you enter the channel proper and encounter a pile of huge rock slabs that slid down during the construction of the railroad grade. The railroad grade is easily visible up-channel on your left where it parallels the former bed of the Calaveras River. The effects of the current grow as you paddle deeper into the gorge. Mergansers and other ducks explode from hiding spots among the boulders that

Haupt Creek invites your explorations.

dot the channel. Angry squawks from Great Blue herons that take flight as you enter their fishing grounds. High above, slow, circular patterns are flown by the ever-present turkey vultures.

Eventually you reach the former train trestle at the South Fork Arm of the Calaveras, the turnaround point of your paddle.

[1] Oakeshott, Gordon B., *California's Changing Landscapes: A Guide to the Geology of the State.*

There is nothing which impresses me more strangely than the fluming operations. The idea of a mighty river being taken up in a wooden trough, turned from the old channel, along which it has foamed for centuries, perhaps, its bed excavated many feet in depth, and itself restored to its old home in the fall, these things strike me as almost a blasphemy against Nature . . .

–Louise Amelia Knapp Smith Clapp, *The Shirley Letters from the California Mines,* 1851-1852

IN THE EDDY

Take a Side Trip

*An eddy short of the entrance
to the South Fork Arm of the
Calaveras.*

For an excellent side venture, paddle into the cove located north (left) of the entrance to the narrow main channel past Haircut Isle. Beach your boat on the left (south) bank and walk to the end of the cove. From here, hike to the saddle above and left of the cove and look for the stream channel running downhill. Before starting the hike along the streambed, listen for the sounds of the mourning doves calling to each other from the trees in the grove.

Instead of following the creekbed itself, hike along the oak groves bordering the grassy slopes. In these sunlit fields you come across several varieties of wild flowers, including colorful brodiaea and carpets of orange fiddlenecks.

Flying from oak to oak are male Western bluebirds defending their nest sites from rival males. Soaring above the common fray are the turkey vultures and sometimes a hawk or two. If you suddenly catch the unmistakable scent of a skunk, don't be too surprised. These nocturnal foragers like to spend their daylight hours in downed trees and there are many such deadfalls.

When you reach the top of the hill, congratulate yourself on making the climb and enjoy the views. The lake spreads out in front of you and you can study the many coves and miles of shore to plan future explorations.

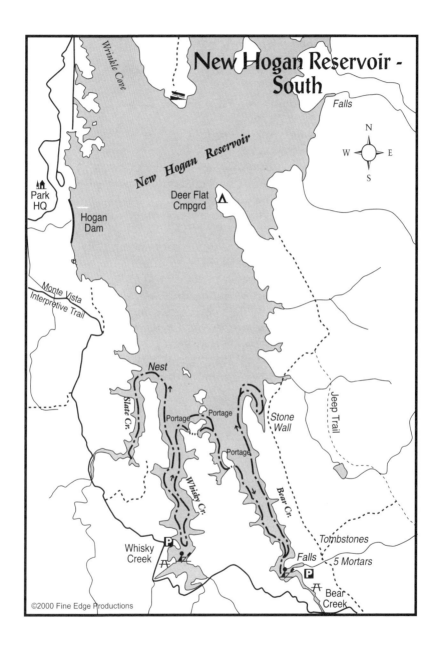

New Hogan Reservoir - South

Wrinkle Cove

Falls

New Hogan Reservoir

Park HQ

Hogan Dam

Deer Flat Cmpgrd

Monte Vista Interpretive Trail

Nest

Slate Cr.

Portage

Portage

Stone Wall

Jeep Trail

Portage

Whisky Cr.

Bear Cr.

Whisky Creek

Tombstones

Falls

5 Mortars

Bear Creek

©2000 Fine Edge Productions

PADDLING AREA 6

New Hogan Reservoir South:
Whiskey, Slate and Bear Creeks

(For additional information on New Hogan Reservoir, see Paddling Area 5.)

Trip Length: A perfect, full-day paddle.

Paddling Distances (one way):

Whiskey Creek to finger cove at Bear Creek (no portages): 1.5 mi.

Whiskey Creek put-in to Bear Creek take-out (no portages): 2.5 mi.

Whiskey Creek put-in to 1st portage: 0.6 mi.

From portage into Bear Creek channel entrance to finger cove, west shore: 0.2 mi.

Mouth of first cove, Bear Creek, to finger cove and break spot: 0.5 mi.

From finger cove to take-out at Bear Creek: 0.5 mi.

Whiskey Creek put-in to entrance of Slate Creek: 1.5 mi.

Slate Creek channel entrance to trailhead: 0.5 mi.

Difficulty: The greatest problem can be crossing the exposed open stretch between Whiskey and Bear creeks. On your return leg, the wind is up and may make for a choppy crossing.

Two short portages and a third optional portage are described to shorten the paddling distances. None of the portages are difficult or extreme.

Season : Spring or early summer before the heat begins and crowds arrive; early fall if the water levels are high.

Maps:

USGS 7.5 minute series: *Valley Springs* quadrangle; *Jenny Lind* quadrangle

Aqua Maps: *New Hogan Reservoir*

U. S. Army Corps of Engineers Brochure: *New Hogan Lake* (free at Visitor's Center)

Area/Road Maps:

Compass Maps Inc.: *Calaveras & Tuolumne Counties* or *Alpine, Amador & South Sacramento Counties*

Thomas Bros.: *California Road Atlas & Driver's Guide*

Note: The spelling of Whiskey Creek is confusing. On newer maps, and handouts printed by the Corps of Engineers, the name is spelled "Whiskey." On the USGS 7.5 minute map, the spelling is "Whisky."

Access:

[See New Hogan (Fiddleneck) Paddle above for directions to the Observation Point, Visitor's Center and lake headquarters.]

To reach the Whiskey Creek Day-Use Area, take Hogan Dam Road below the dam and make a left turn at the intersection with Silver Rapids Road. Drive past the Monte Vista Fishing Access and Trailhead parking area (this is the start of the River of Skulls Interpretive Trail) and continue for 3.4 miles. The entrance to Whiskey Creek Day-Use Area is on your left off a gravel road. (To reach the parking lot for Bear Creek, continue on Hogan Dam Road for another 1.9 miles. The entrance is on your left just after crossing the Bear Creek Bridge.)

Upon entering Whiskey Creek Day-Use Area, I drive to the water's edge near the information center and toilet area and park close to the water. The vehicle acts as a landmark easily spotted on my return paddle.

Highlights:
- Day-use access is free for hand-launched car-top boats.
- You may drive down to the water's edge to launch your boat.
- There are portable toilets and garbage cans.
- Put-in/take-out is in a sheltered cove with a 5-mph speed zone.
- The paddle to Bear Creek is worth every stroke.
- A low-profile shoreline allows easy access to break areas and places of interest.

The cove at Whiskey Creek; Bear Mountains are in the background.

- Allow time to hike the area of Bear Creek, especially above the falls.
- The hike to the ridge top from Slate Creek for wildflower displays.

Description:

For a lake the size of Hogan, it may seem strange that a full-day, ready-made paddle exists. Well, it does, with all the ingredients necessary for enjoyable paddling, hiking, photography, fishing, picnicking, and even swimming. The route can be paddled as described or customized to fit each paddler's agenda.

What makes this area so unique is the accessibility of the shore, the coves protected from strong winds, and even a speed zone throughout the paddling area. Add to the above list interesting scenery that begs exploration, abundant varieties of animals, birds and plants, and this section of New Hogan Reservoir becomes a truly enjoyable place to paddle.

Whiskey Creek

Upon casting off from shore, a big decision poses itself; in which direction do I want to paddle first? If you paddle due south, farther up the channel, the narrow finger of the cove twists and turns through a shoreline of oaks, manzanita and pine. Eventually, the channel crosses under the roadway and disappears into the narrow stream bed of Whiskey Creek.

Smaller side channels that lead into the remainder of the day-use area harbor delightful shadows and low-hanging, moss-covered branches of the ever-present live oak.

If you choose to go north, the channel widens yet conceals many openings into smaller side channels that call for a reconnoiter. If you have a time constraint, forego the coves in the south and indulge your curiosity at Bear Creek. Otherwise, take your time and enter the coves slowly; you will be rewarded by the sight of mergansers fishing in the shallow waters or by deer browsing near shore. In some of the coves, great blue herons stand sentinel, waiting for a small fish, frog, or other prey. Keep a watch over the treetops for hawks, osprey or even a bald eagle. When perched, these predators blend into the leafy branches, so scan the trees slowly as you enter a cove. Ospreys seem to favor bare branches or standing deadwood, but eagles and hawks often perch on the smaller branches.

As you head north, you leave the narrow channel of Whiskey Creek and cross the buoy line. Before you enter the main body of the lake, look to your right (southeast) for a shallow saddle separating a string of low knolls. This area, as shown on your topo sheet or on the AQUA Map, shows these knolls as islands. However, the lake level seldom rises enough to cover this stretch of low ground.

Mule Ears

Paddle into the shallow cove and beach your boat. Walk up and over the gentle rise, where you will see the entrance to the mouth of Bear Creek Channel. The distance between Whiskey Creek and Bear Creek is approximately 80 feet. Make a short portage and you can save yourself 20 minutes of paddling. But before you depart, take time to enjoy the view and walk through the small grove of blue oak and Digger pine to the top of the knoll. The dominant hills to the east are the Bear Mountains. Buena Vista Mountain, at 2,240 feet, dominates the northern end of the range.

As you walk around the area, notice the many burrows dug into the ground. Sit still and the small head of a nervous California ground squirrel will make its way slowly out of the burrow, carefully observing the surroundings before venturing from the safety of its home. It is the presence of these ground squirrels, their burrows excavated in the scrape zone along the shoreline, that attracts the many raptors and other predators to the area.

As you walk toward the brush, you may notice a sudden, pungent odor, from the emerging leaves of a mullein plant. This member of the figwort family which is easily recognizable by its pale green, velvety leaves and its sharp scent was used by Native Americans as an herbal medicine. By summer, its tall green stalk rises with a bloom of small yellow flowers. By fall or winter, the stalk reaches a height of several feet; as it begins to dry, it changes color to a deep golden brown. The early Greeks and Romans dipped the stalks into tallow and used them as funeral torches.

The sight of oddly-tilted rocks thrusting at an angle into the sky hints at the more dramatic strata you will see when exploring Bear Creek. These "tombstone rocks" are a common feature in parts of the Gold Country; unfortunately many of them are disappearing with the increased development around the low-lying foothills. Here, within the protected boundaries of the lake, you can hike among these natural wonders and appreciate their dramatic appearance.

As you portage across the narrow saddle separating the two channels, note the sparkle of white rock along the shore. Much of Lake Hogan's shoreline contains broad bands of this quartz which adds to the sheen of the soil and creates the airy light for much of the scenery. Iron oxide in the soil base may account for the reddish-orange tint to the surface.

This narrow saddle acts as a natural throughway for many of the birds that fly between the ridges. By sitting quietly beside an oak, you may spot a raptor cruising low and slow through here. You may even sight a bald eagle that frequents the lake. Bands of quail fly down from the cover of the oaks for their late afternoon drink, then retreat into the safety of the brush. Seasonal visitors such as swallows and the colorful Western bluebird fly about and occasionally land on the oak branches near your resting spot, and across the channel you may spot a small herd of deer browsing, drinking or quietly resting beneath the oaks.

Slate Creek

If time constraints prevent your making the longer paddle to Bear Creek, a viable alternative is to paddle into Slate Creek. Upon launching from Whiskey Creek, paddle up the channel and follow the northwest shoreline. Skirt the islands separating Bear Creek Channel from Whiskey Creek and round the point of the small peninsula shown as Siberia on the Valley Springs quadrangle.

Note: As you round the point, look for a hawk's nest hidden in an oak tree near the water's edge. One of the parent birds may be sitting on the eggs or feeding the young, so please do not stress the birds by approaching. Let your boat drift with the wind and current past the nesting tree.

As you enter the narrow mouth of Slate Creek, look at the rocky walls of the ridge to your left covered with patches of orange monkey flowers. These bushy plants are a source of nectar for humming birds in early spring.

In the late afternoon light, the slabs of rock that jut out from the side walls of the channel exhibit hues and textures not visible during the bright midday-light. Examine the surface of this rock composed of small angular fragments cemented together. These conglomerates, deposited after traveling just a short distance, retain their sharp

Paddling along Slate Creek.

features; fragments that traveled longer distances were subject to more abrasion and are more rounded. (The weathering conglomerates at the mouth of Slate Creek are called *breccia* from the Italian for "breaking.")

Note that the western shoreline of Slate Creek Channel has a shallow slope dominated by chaparral, whereas the eastern shoreline is steep and dominated by a cover of oak, Digger pine and shrubs. The more-accessible west shore contains several small coves that invite inspection.

Farther down-channel, you bend to the right. Just after this there is a small inlet to the left where you can beach your boat. Take the trail that leads uphill to the ridge-top where you will be rewarded with a shady oak grove and the sight of dozens of elegant brodiaea. Farther upslope near a large mossy oak, grow bunches of bright yellow mule ears. Be wary of poison oak that grows in abundance along the trail. Look for the small blue flowers of blue-eyed grass that grow in clear areas near the trail.

When you reach the top of the ridge, your reward is a clear view into the cove of Whiskey Creek to the left side and the green slopes of Gopher Ridge running north to your right.

Back at your boat, follow the main channel around the bend to the terminus of the high-water area. Hike the creek for a short distance, to reach the crossing site of Hogan Dam Road.

Channel Mouth of Bear Creek
Launching from the protected cove of the portage site, you enter the wide mouth of Bear Creek Channel. Stay on the west side, parallel to shore to

avoid any wind blowing across the channel. Take note of the buoy line position as you cross it; it acts as a guideline to the portage site.

A short distance from the buoy line is the entrance to a small finger cove that bends to the left and is enclosed by oaks and pines that grow along the hillsides. Paddle slowly and quietly along right bank where you may approach a family of deer that routinely used a shaded, grassy drainage for their rest area.

As you continue your paddle in the main channel, it's difficult not to avoid the urge to stop every hundred yards or so and beach your boat—the whide expanses, the green hills with their mantle of oaks, and accessibility of the shoreline are tempting.

Bear Creek Channel

Bear Creek Channel is dominated by the Bear Mountais that trend north-south to your left and the lower hills of Gopher Ridge.

The smooth water and its clarity allows you to spot large carp swimming near the surface. A 5-mph speed limit within the channel eliminates whining noise and wakes from motorized craft.

Small ravines often give way to deeper, accessible coves that pique your interest. The northern shore is densely covered by chamise, buck brush, and California buckeye. The south shore is more open with groves of oack and manzanita.

The high-water line is easily identifiable by a zone scraped free of vegetation. Driftwood lies scattered along this shoreline.

The coyote is more apt to be visible in the late afternoon or early morning, I have spotted the wily trickster numerous times during midday. Once I was fortunate enough to watch one stalking and running down ground squirrels in the middle of the afternoon.

Pick a prominent point with a good view of the channel, beach your boat, and take out your binoculars. In time, you'll pick out the pattern of a hawk on the hunt. You may even spot a coyote running down a ground squirrel in, or in the fall, wild turkeys feeding on acorns.

Approximately 0.5 mile from the entrance to the first finger cove, you will spot a V-shaped entrance to a short gulch. In season, look for purple lupine that stretches between a small grove of trees and a strata of tombstone rocks. At the end of the cove where you can take-out, a small stream flows down from a grove of oaks.

Upon exiting your boat, look to your right (north). You may see a large patch of blue at ground level; walking to the spot, you'll be pleasantly surprised by beautiful baby blue eyes surrounded by clusters of milk maids whose small white flowers provide a contrasting background to this spring display.

Looking out from shore you see shadows and light glancing off the blue-green water. Across the channel, the horizontal slash of the shoreline marks a distinct separation of the dark, opaque water from

A 40-foot portage and you put in at Bear Creek Cove.

the equally-dark, dense stand of oak. Acting as a frame around this natural composition and rising above it are the uplifted rocks of the Bear Mountains.

As the shadows become deeper, a chill sets in and it is time to pack up and paddle on.

Bear Creek

Continuing on through the former bed of Bear Creek the channel narrows. You pass solitary dead trees where a feisty belted kingfisher may be seen perched on one of the bleached limbs. Your presence will no doubt annoy him and he will launch himself off the branch with scolding cries.

Past the zone of dead trees, you round the first bend and spot a gently-sloping island, its surface glistening in the sun.

You reach the island, cast your eyes to the left, and are immediately presented with a broad view of a stream-filled valley bordered by groves of oaks. In the foreground, the glare from the exposed cobbles hurts your eyes as they reflect the sun's rays. Sloping banks covered with grass and an occasional patch of colorful wild flowers provide a buffer between the stream and the line of oaks. Framed dead center, a waterfall cascades down a shelf of rust-colored boulders.

After paddling down a narrow channel with banks muted by increasing shadows, this unexpected, wide-open and airy valley will cause you to sit up and take notice. The rock-bound stream is a side creek that flows into Bear Creek, visible around the small knoll to your right.

The snake-like curves of Bear Creek.

Beach your boat on the level, grassy bank and follow the stream toward the waterfall. One of the flat boulders close to the falls contains a bedrock mortar, evidence of early Native Americans.

The waterfall descends from pool to pool before splashing into the lowest hole whose deep water acts as a mirror to the sky.

Examining the slick, water-smoothed stone near the falls provides a hint of the rocks' geologic past. This melange of metamorphic strata are actually schist, cherts and greenstones, whose fractures were injected with minerals that eventually became quartz. These veins of quartz may be seen in almost all of the rock throughout the New Hogan Reservoir shoreline.

A trail leads up from the base of the falls to the top. From there, look out toward the lake where you are rewarded with another great view of the stream coursing into the main channel of Bear Creek. The slopes bordering Bear Creek are part of the peninsula that separates Bear Creek from Whiskey Creek.

Don't leave without taking a short hike along the stream above the falls. In an oak grove nearby, you'll be delighted by a carpet of the elegant brodiaea and small yellow buttercups.

Beyond the tree line a dirt road that crosses the stream. Follow it south to where it crosses Bear Creek, look for a patch of smooth, level rock on the north bank where the road fords the creek. You will find five "cups" ground into the rock surface—bedrock mortars similar to the one below the falls, again evidence of the Miwok, the valley's former inhabitants.

Continuing on the road, you intersect Hogan Lake Dam Road approximately 0.5 mile ahead. By following the stream, you can trace your steps back to the waterfall and your boat beached below. Then it's time to head back to your take-out site.

APPENDIX I
Maps

The most commonly-used maps for paddlers and backpackers are the topographic (contour) maps put out by the United States Geological Survey (USGS). The 7.5 minute series quandrangles show the most detail and are easiest to use.

Unfortunately, many of the topographic maps for places that paddlers, hikers and other users of the backcountry visit are out of date. (USGS is updating their map series based on budgetary availability and area priorities.)

Private companies also put out maps that cover many of the popular paddling areas.

Note: The higher the map's scale ratio, the smaller the detail available. One inch on a scale of 1: 250,000 represents about 4 miles; this is a small-scale chart. One inch on a map scale of 1: 24,000 represents 2,000 feet; this is a large-scale chart.The terminology is often misunderstood.

SOURCES FOR MAPS AND MAP PRODUCTS

You can order California Index to Topographic and other map coverage from:

USGS Earth Science Information Center (local office)
345 Middlefield Road, Mail Stop 532
Menlo Park, CA 94025-4309
Hours: (M-F) 7:45- 4:15
Phone: (650) 329-4309
Fax:(650) 329-5130

USGS (Western Regional Office)
USGS Map Sales
Federal Center
Box 25286
Denver, CO 80225
Phone: (888) ASK-USGS or (303)202-4700
Fax: (303) 202-4693
[For a sheet showing all public phones and world-wide web sites, request their fact sheets: *USGS Sources of Information* and *USGS World Wide Web Information]*
website: http://edcwww.cr.usgs.gov/content_products.html

Maps of all National Forests and Wilderness Areas may be obtained from:

USFS
Attention: Map Sales
1323 Club Drive
Vallejo, CA 94592
Phone: (707) 562-USFS (8737)

Eldorado National Forest Visitor's Center
[Desolation Wilderness Area]
3070 Camino Heights Drive
Camino, CA 95709
Phone: (530) 644-6048

Georgetown Ranger District (Eldorado Nat'l Forest)
Georgetown, CA 95634
Phone: (530) 333-4312

Placerville Ranger District (Eldorado Nat'l Forest)
4060 Eight Mile Road
Camino, CA 95709
Phone: (530)644-2324

Lake Tahoe Basin Management Unit
[also Desolation Wilderness Area]
870 Emerald Bay Road, Ste. 1
South Lake Tahoe, CA 96150
Phone: (530) 573-2600

Tahoe National Forest (Supervisor's Office)
[Granite Chief Wilderness Area]
631 Coyote Street
PO Box 6003
Nevada City, CA 95959-6003
Phone: (530) 265-4531

Tahoe National Forest District Offices

Foresthill Ranger District, Tahoe NF District
22830 Foresthill Road
Foresthill, CA 95631
Phone: (530) 367-2224

Truckee Ranger Station, Tahoe NF District
10342 Highway 89 North
Truckee, CA 96161
Phone: (530) 587-3558

California Division of Mines and Geology

(DM&G provides a variety of maps and publications on California's geology, mineral resources and seismic hazards; subscription to *California Geology* or information on maps and publications)

California Division of Mines and Geology
Geological Information & Publications
801 K Street, MS 14-33
Sacramento, CA 95814-3532
Phone: (916) 445-5716
Fax: (916) 327-1853
email: dmglib@consrv.ca.gov

U.S. National Oceanic and Atmospheric Administration (USNOAA)
(For a free Index Catalog to navigation charts and publications for the US Pacific Coast : Chart # 2; and Lake Tahoe Navigation Chart D-18665.)

NOAA Distribution Division, N/ACC3
National Ocean Service
Riverdale, MD 20737-1199
Phone: (800) 638-8972

Corps of Engineers
New Hogan Lake
2713 Hogan Lake Dam Road
Valley Springs, CA 95252
Phone: (209) 772-1343
(For a free brochure/map request CESPK 360-1-3/92 edition, entitled *New Hogan Lake* map.)

Pacific Gas & Electric Company
(To obtain a copy of *PG&E Recreation Areas* booklet with maps of all PG&E reservoirs and campgrounds.)

PG&E Group Reservations Center
2730 Gateway Oaks Drive
Sacramento, CA 95833
Phone: (916) 923-7142/(415) 973-5552

Sacramento Municipal Utility District
(For a copy of SMUD's free foldout map/campground list: *Crystal Basin Recreation Area*, 1995 edition.)

Sacramento Municipal Utility District
6201 S Street
Sacramento, CA 95817-1818
Phone: (916) 452-7811

Private Map Companies

AquaMaps
PO Box 162961
Sacramento, CA 95816
Phone: (916) 456-4137
(Maps depict the layout of many California reservoirs and lakes.)

Compass Maps Inc.
1172 Kansas Ave.
Modesto, CA 95351
Phone: (209) 529-5017
(Excellent road maps of California and the counties.)

FHS Maps (Fishing Hot Spots, Inc.
PO Box 1167
2389 Air Park Rd
Rhinelander, WI 54501
Phone: (800) 500-MAPS (6277)
(Designed for the fisherman, but very handy for the paddle boater, too. Printed on a slick water-resistant paper.)

Fish-N-Map Company, Inc.
8536 West 79th Avenue
Arvada, CO 8005
Phone: (303) 421-5994
Fax: (303) 420-0843
(Similar to FHS maps; on water-resistant paper)

Thomas Bros. Maps
Irvine, CA: (714) 863-1984
Los Angeles, CA: (213) 627-4018
San Francisco, CA: (415) 981-7520
(A well-established map company, makers of excellent maps. I particularly like their *California Road Atlas & Driver's Guide*. Emphasis is on the road networks, depicting many small secondary roads; no reliefs shown on maps.)

CD-ROM maps

MAPTECH
Digital Mapping Technology
655 Portsmouth Avenue
Greenland, NH 03840
Phone: (800) 627-7236
Fax: (603) 433-8505
www.maptech.com/topo
(Uses the USGS quadrangles as its base; covers the entire state on CD-ROM.)

TOPO!
Interactive Maps on CD-ROM
Wildflower Productions
375 Alabama Street, Ste. 230
San Francisco, CA 94110
Phone: (415)558-8700
info@topo.com
www.topo.com
(An excellent map series that allows you to customize your maps. The drawback is that they use the dated USGS quads as their base maps.)

Retail Map Sales

California Surveying & Drafting Supply
4733 Auburn Blvd.
Sacramento, (Carmichael) CA 95841
Phone: (800) 350-6277/(916) 344-0232
Fax: (916) 344-2998
(They sell USGS topo sheets, BLM maps, road maps—Compass Maps and others—and maps on CD-ROM.)

Ogden Surveying Equipment Co.
5520 Elvas Ave.
Sacramento, CA 95819
Phone: (800) 350-6277/(916) 451-7523
Fax: (91) 451-2865
(An established HQ for all sorts of maps, guidebooks and assorted navigational stuff. . . a great place to browse.)

Recreational Equipment Incorporated (REI)
1790 Exposition Parkway
Sacramento, CA 95815
Phone: (916) 924-8900
Fax: (916) 924-9070
(In addition to standard map sales, REI maintains their own on-line service related to map needs. A very popular store for outdoor enthusiasts of many different sports.)

Sierra Outdoor Center (SOC)
440 Lincoln Way
Auburn, CA 95603
Phone: (530) 885-1844
Fax: (530) 885-0451
-sierraoc@jps.net
(In addition to a retail and rental store and kayaking/rafting school, SOC also carries a full line of USGS topos, guide books and paddle-related literature.)

Stockdale Marine & Navigation Center
4730 Myrtle Ave
Sacramento, CA 95841-3610
Phone: (916) 332-0775
Fax: (916) 332-2500
(An established center for sailboating, they are the primary agents for the sale of NOAA navigation charts.)

 # APPENDIX II

Paddling Clubs & Organizations

American Canoe Association
7432 Alban Station Boulevard
Ste, B-232
Springfield, VA 22150
Phone: (703) 451-0141
Fax: 703-451-2245
E-mail: ACADirect@aol.com
("Big Dog" of canoeing organizations.)

American Red Cross
(Sacramento Chapter)
PO Box 160167
Sacramento, CA 95816
Phone: (916) 368-3167
Fax: (916) 368-3224
*(Still a leader in First Aid,
CPR training & canoeing classes)*

Becoming an Outdoors Woman
Sponsored by:
Calif. Dept. of Fish & Game and
Univ. of Wisconsin-Stevens Point,
College of Natural Resources
PO Box 1945
Sacramento, CA 95812
Phone: (916) 657-4333
(A program of workshops focused on outdoor skills; canoeing is one of the courses taught. Sign up early; the canoeing class is extremely popular.)

Chico Paddle Heads
Attn.: John Alden
12428 Centerville Rd.
Chico, CA 95928-8320
Phone: (530) 345-2453
E-mail: paddlenet@aol.com
(Touring & white water enthusiasts sponsored in part, by North Rim Adventure Sports in Chico, CA.)

APPENDIX III

Retailers, Outfitters & Map Sales

Adventure Sports
1609 Watt Avenue
Sacramento, CA 95864-2963
Phone: (916) 971-1850
Fax: (916) 971-1942
Web: sierragear.com
(Sales, rentals on canoes, kayaks, inflatables & outdoor gear. Demos, classes & trips offered.)

California Canoe & Kayak
Nimbus Winery
12401 Folsom Blvd., Ste. 205
Rancho Cordova, CA. 95742
Phone: (916) 353-1880
Fax: (916) 353-5171
E-mail: CalKayak@aol.com
Web: www.calkayak.com
Classes & trips: (800) 366-9804
(Retail sales, rentals & guided trips; carries the largest selection of name brand canoes in Northern California.)

California Canoe & Kayak
Jack London Square
409 Water Street
Oakland, CA 94607
Phone: (510) 893-7833
Fax: (510) 893-2617
E-mail: Calkayak @aol.com
Web: www.calkayak.com
Classes & trips: 1-800-366-9804
(Retail sales, rentals & trips; specializes in sales, repair and outfitting of sea kayaks as well as recreational, touring kayaks & canoes.)

Current Adventures
Kayak School & Trips
PO Box 828
Lotus, CA 95651
Phone: (530) 642-9755
Fax: (530) 642-9725
Web: www.kayaking.com
For reservations or information:
Toll Free: 1(888) 4-kayaking

(ACA Instruction/Certification programs available; kayak classes from beginner through advanced; summer kids program in kayaking.)

Klepper West
Western Folding Kayak Center
6155 Mt. Aukum Rd.
Somerset, CA 95684-0130
Phone: (530) 626-8647 (local)
Toll Free: (888) 692-8092
Web: www.klepperwest.com
(Sales & repair on new and used folding kayaks. Exclusive dealer in folding kayaks in Sacramento & Bay Area.)

North Rim Adventure Sports
346 Broadway
Chico, CA 95928
Phone: (530) 345-2453
Fax: (530) 345-0369
(Retail sales of paddle craft, bike & climbing gear. Classes in kayaking are also offered.)

Recreational Equipment
Incorporated (REI Inc.)
1790 Exposition Parkway
Sacramento, CA 95815
Phone: (916) 924-8900
Fax: (916) 924-9070
(Specializes in quality outdoor gear & accessories. In addition, has a rental program, provides classes & trips)

The River Store
Box 472/1032 Lotus Rd.
Lotus, CA 95651
Phone: (530) 626-3435
Fax: (530) 626-7036
Web: www.coloma.com/riverstore
(Retail sales, demos, & guided trips. Specializes in white water & touring kayaks.)

(SOC)
440 Lincoln Way
Auburn, CA 95603
Phone: (530) 885-1844
Fax: (530) 626-7036
E-mail: sierraoc@jps.net
(Retail, rental, school, and trips; carries full line of local USGS topo quads. Knowledgeable staff on raft sales & repair; offers both white water kayak & raft guided trips.)

Sports Fever
Ski ' N ' Sport
682-C Freeman Lane
Grass Valley, CA 95949

Phone: (530) 477-8006
Fax: (530) 477-8318
(Retail sales of canoes, kayaks & other sports)

Wolf Creek Wilderness
595 E. Main Street
Grass Valley, CA 95945
Phone: (530) 477-2722
Fax: (530) 477-6038
Web: www.wolfcreekwilderness.com
(Retail sales rentals & guided trips. The owners specialize in trips on the lakes & rivers of Northern Calf. in addition to other areas.)

Bibliography & References

Adney, Edwin, Tappan and Howard I. Chappelle. *The Bark Canoes and Skin Boats of North America.* Washington D. C.: Smithsonian Institution Press, 1983 reprint.

Brinck, Wolfgang. *The Aleutian Kayak Origins, Construction, and Use of the Traditional Seagoing Baidarka.* Camden, MA: Ragged Mountain Press, 1995.

Dowd, John. *Sea Kayaking: A Manual for Long-Distance Touring,* revised ed. Vancouver, BC: Greystone Books, 1997.

Dyson, George. *Baidarka, The Kayak.* Anchorage, AK: Alaska Northwest Books, 1997.

Getchell, Annie. *The Essential Outdoor Gear Manual.* McGraw Hill, International Marine: Blacklick, OH: 1987.

Hutchinson, Derek C. *The Complete Book of Sea Kayaking,* 4th Ed. Globe Pequot Press, Inc Old Saybrook, CT, 1998.

Jacobson, Cliff. *Canoeing Wild Rivers: A Primer to North American Expedition Canoeing.* Merrillville, IN: ICS Books, Inc., 1984.

———. *Canoeing and Camping Beyond the Basics.* Merrillville, IN: ICS Books Inc., 1992.

Mason, Bill. *Path of the Paddle: An Illustrated Guide to the Art of Canoeing,* Revised Ed. Minocqua, WI: Northwood Press, Inc., 1997.

———. *Song of the Paddle: An Illustrated Guide to Wilderness Camping.* Minocqua, WI: Northwood Press, Inc., 1988.

Ray, Slim. *The Canoe Handbook: Techniques for Mastering the Sport of Canoeing.* Harrisburg: Stackpole Books, 1992.

Riviere, Bill. *Pole, Paddle and Portage A Complete Guide to Canoeing.* Boston: Little, Brown and Company, 1969.

———— and the L. L. Bean staff. *The L. L. Bean Guide to the Outdoors.* New York: Random House, Inc., 1981.

Stienstra, Tom. *California Boating and Water Sports.* San Francisco: Foghorn Press, 1996.
————. California Fishing. San Francisco: Foghorn Press, 1995.

Warren, Graham. *Making Canoe Paddles in Wood.* United Kingdom: Raven Rock Books, 1997.

Guide Books
(Cultural, Natural History and Reference)

Alden, Peter and Fred Heath. *National Audubon Society Field Guide to California.* New York: Alfred A. Knopf, Inc., 1998.

American River Natural History Association. *A History of the Lower American River.* Sacramento: 1991.

Arno, Stephen F. and Ramona P. Hammerly. *Timberline Mountain and Arctic Forest Frontiers.* Seattle: The Mountaineers, 1993.

————. *Discovering Sierra Trees.* Yosemite National Park, CA: Yosemite Association, 1973.

Bakker, Elna. *An Island Called California.* Berkeley: University of California Press, 1972.

Bright, William. *1500 California Place Names: Their Origin and Meaning.* Berkeley: University of California Press, 1998.

Browning, Peter. *Place Names of the Sierra Nevada: From Abbot to Zumwalt.* Berkeley: Wilderness Press, 2nd ed, August 1992.

Castle, Ken. *Tahoe: The Complete Guide*, 2nd ed. San Francisco: Foghorn Press, 1997.

Clark, William B., ed. *Gold Districts of California,* Bulletin 193. San Francisco: California Division of Mines and Geology, Rev. 1998.

Gudde, Erwin G. *California Place Names: The Origin and Etymology of Current Geographical Names,* 4th ed., revised. Berkeley: University of California Press, 1998.

Hart, John. *Walking Softly in the Wilderness: The Sierra Club Guide to Backpacking*, 3rd ed. San Francisco: Sierra Club Books, 1998.

Hill, Mary. *Geology of the Sierra Nevada*. Berkeley: University of California Press, 1975.

Hoover, Mildred Brooke, Hero Eugene Rensch and Ethel Grace Rensch. *Historic Spots in California*. Berkeley, CA: University of California Press, 1962.

Hutchinson, Judy L. and G. Ledyard Stebbins. *A Flora of the Wright's Lake Area*. Pollock Pines, CA. 1986.

Guyton, Bill. *Glaciers of California*. Berkeley: University of California Press, 1994.

Johnston, Verna, R. *California Forests and Woodlands: A Natural History*. Berkeley: University of California Press, 1994.

Lekisch, Barbara. *Tahoe Place Names: The Origin and History of Names in the Lake Tahoe Basin*. Lafayette, CA: Great West Books, 1988.

National Audubon Society. *Western Forests*. New York: Borzoi Books, published by Alfred A Knopf, Inc., 9th printing, March, 1997.

National Geographic Society. *Field Guide to the Birds of North America*, 2nd ed. Washington D. C.: National Geographic Society, 1996.

Office of Historic Preservation California State Parks. *California Historical Landmarks*. Sacramento: State of California, The Resources Agency, 1996.

Pavlik, Bruce M. et al. *Oaks of California*. Los Olivios, CA: Cachuma Press and The California Oak Foundation, 1995.

Peattie, Donald Culross. *A Natural History of Western Trees*. Boston: Houghton Mifflin Company, 1991.

Powell, Jerry A. and Charles L. Hogue. *California Insects*. Berkeley: University of California Press, 1979.

Schaffer, Jeffrey, P. *Desolation Wilderness and the South Lake Tahoe Basin*, 3rd ed. Berkeley, CA: Wilderness Press, 1996.
———. *The Tahoe Sierra: A Natural History Guide to 106 Hikes in the Northern Sierra*, 3rd. Ed. Berkeley, CA: Wilderness Press, 1990.

Schoenherr, Allan A. *A Natural History of California*. Berkeley: University of California Press, 1st paperback printing, 1995.

Spellenberg, Richard. *The Audubon Society Field Guide to North American Wildflowers*, The Western Region. New York: Alfred A. Knopf, Inc., 1979.

Stratton, George. *Camping California's National Forests.* (Formerly The Recreation Guide to California's National Forests.) Helena: Falcon Press, 1991.

Storer, Tracy I. and Robert L. Usinger. *Sierra Nevada Natural History.* Berkeley: University of California Press, 1963, 13th printing.

Whitney, Stephen. *The Sierra Nevada*, 6th ed. San Francisco: Sierra Club Books, 1979.

————. Western Forests, *National Audubon Society Nature Guides.* New York: Alfred A. Knopf, Inc., 1997.

Technical Sources
(Cultural, Geology and Natural History)

Gilluly, James, A. C. Waters, and A. O. Woodford. *Principles of Geology* 3rd ed. San Francisco: W. H. Freeman and Company, 1968.

The Historical Committee of the Wrights Lake Summer Home Association. *The Wrights Lake Story: A Historical Sketch of the Wrights Lake - Dark Lake Area, Eldorado National Forest, El Dorado County, California,* Pollock Pines, CA: 1994.

Hundley, Norris, Jr. *The Great Thirst: Californians and Water, 1770s-1990s.* Berkeley: University of California Press, 1992.

McPhee, John. *Assembling California.* New York: Farrar, Straus and Giroux, 1993.

Mora, Jo. *Californios.* Garden City, NY: Doubleday and Company, Inc., 1949.

Parker, Marilyn. *The Pollock Pines Epic.* Placerville, CA: Placerville Press, 1995.

Scott, Edward B. *The Saga of Lake Tahoe.* Crystal Bay, NV: Sierra-Tahoe Publishing Co. 1957.

Secondary Sources: Boats, Paddles and Gear

Aiken, Zora and David. *Simple Tent Camping: Basics of Camping from Car or Canoe.* Camden, ME: Ragged Mountain Press.

Burch, David. *Fundamentals of Kayak Navigation,* revised ed. Old Saybrook: Globe Pequot Press, 1999.

Coale, John. *Canoeing the California Highlands: A Quiet Water Guide to Paddler's Paradise.* Cedar Ridge, CA: Changing Sky Publications, 1998.

Daniel, Linda: *Kayak Cookery: A Handbook of Provisions and Recipes,* 2nd ed. Birmingham: Menasha Ridge Press.

Hill, Rick. *"11 Family Tripping Canoes."* Paddler, September/October 1999.

Jeneid, Michael. *Adventure Kayaking Trips from the Russian River to Monterey.* Berkeley: Wilderness Press, 1998.

Jones, Lowell. *"Focus On Photography: Photographic Tips and Techniques for Paddlers."* Sea Kayaker, June 1998.

Kesselheim, Alan S. *"Outfitting Family Trips."* Canoe and Kayak, May 1997.

Mckowan, Doug. *Canoeing Safety and Rescue: A Handbook of Safety and Rescue Procedures for Lake and River Canoeists.* Calgary: Rocky Mountain Books, 1999.

Roberts, Harry. *The Basic Essentials of Canoe Paddling.* Merrillville, IN: ICS Books, Inc.

Schumann, Roger and Jan Shriner. *Guide to Sea Kayaking in Central and Northern California: The Best Day Trips and Tours from the Lost Coast to Morro Bay.* Old Saybrook: Globe Pequot Press, 1999.

"The Trials and Tribulations of Paddling Double," Sea Kayaker, February, 1997.

Van Dyke, Elizabeth. *"Paddling with Deaf and Hard of Hearing Kayakers,"* Sea Kayaker, December, 1997.

Whilden, Kevin. *"Overboard with Electronics: Trip Planning with a Computer: A review of four new GPS units."* Sea Kayaker, December 1999.

Wyatt, Mike. *The Basic Essentials of Sea Kayaking,* 2nd ed. Merrillville, IN: ICS Books, Inc., 1996

Videos

Holman, Larry. "Sea Kayaking: Getting Started." Moving Pictures, 1995. 83 minutes. *[A comprehensive reference with examples and demonstrations on correct paddling and boat-handling techniques.]*

Holt, Joe and Bob Beazley. "From Here to There Canoe Basics." Joe Holt Productions, 1997. *[An excellent choice for beginners; sound advice on boats and gear, as well as proper strokes.]*

Mason, Bill. "Path of the Paddle Quiet Water." Northwood Press, Inc. 1997. 54 minutes. *[Follows the format of his book with stunning visuals and clear, concise instruction on paddling a canoe tandem or solo.]*

"Performance Sea Kayaking." Performance Video and Instruction, Inc., 550 Riverbend, Durango, CO 81301. *[An excellent guide for the beginner; includes a multitude of solid information. Kent Ford acts as host.]*

About the Author

Born in Pau, France, and raised in Santa Cruz, California, Bill has enjoyed surfing and snorkeling since he was a teenager. After completing his Air Force commitment with a tour in Vietnam as an aerial reconnaissance photographer, he graduated from San Francisco State University with a Bachelor of Arts degree in Anthropology and a teaching credential.

Bill worked as a caretaker at the Calico Early Man Site under the tutelage of Ruth DeEtte Simpson. He also participated in several projects and field surveys conducted by the Paleontology and Geology Department of the Museum of Northern Arizona with William J. Breed as curator. In the early 1980s, Bill volunteered as a docent, then became a paid staff member at the Ano Nuevo State Reserve in San Mateo County, California.

Bill's love of nature, archaeology and geology, plus his skill as a photographer, brought excitement to the classroom where he taught social studies and science classes for over 10 years. In 1984, he moved to Sacramento where he worked for California Canoe and Kayak.

Recently, he has joined the staff of Current Adventures as a naturalist/guide and writes full time.

Bill is married, the father of one 13-year-old boy who loves to fish, kayak, and skateboard, and stepfather to a 22-year-old young man who is currently in the Army.

Mountain Biking Guidebooks
from FineEdge.com

Mountain Biking Northern California's Best 100 Trails, by Fragnoli & Stuart, ISBN 0-938665-73-1 (classic routes, 80 detailed maps, 300 pages), $18.95

Mountain Biking Reno & Carson City Best Trails, by R.W. Miskimins, ISBN 0-938665-66-9, $15.95

Mountain Biking Southern California's Best 100 Trails, 2nd Ed., Fragnoli & Douglass, Eds., ISBN 0-938665-53-7 (classic routes, 80 detailed maps, 352 pages), $16.95

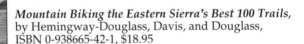

Mountain Biking the Eastern Sierra's Best 100 Trails, by Hemingway-Douglass, Davis, and Douglass, ISBN 0-938665-42-1, $18.95

Mountain Biking South Lake Tahoe's Best Trails, by Bonser & Miskimins, ISBN 0-938665-52-9, $14.95

Mountain Biking North America's Best 100 Ski Resorts, by Fragnoli, ISBN 0-938665-46-4, $16.95

Mountain Biking North Lake Tahoe's Best Trails, by Bonser & Miskimins, ISBN 0-938665-40-5, $14.95

Mountain Biking California's Central Coast Best 100 Trails, by Fragnoli, ISBN 0-938665-59-6 (classic routes, 90 maps, 272 pages), $18.95

Mountain Biking Santa Monica Mountains' Best Trails, by Hasenauer & Langton, ISBN 0-938665-55-3, $14.95

For trail information check www.MountainBikingPress.com

Lake Tahoe's Top 20 Bike Rides on Pavement & Dirt,
by Miskimins, ISBN 0-938665-36-7, $5.95

Mountain Biking the San Bernardino Mountains,
by Shipley & Thibault, ISBN 0-938665-16-2, $10.95

Mountain Biking the San Gabriel Mountains' Best Trails,
with Angeles National Forest and Mt. Pinos, by Troy & Woten,
ISBN 0-938665-43-X, $14.95

Paddling Guidebooks

Up the Lake with a Paddle, Canoe & Kayak Guide, Vol. 1,
Sierra Foothills, Sacramento Region, by Van der Ven,
ISBN 0-938665-54-5, $18.95

Recreation Topo Maps

The Great Flume Ride, ISBN 0-938665-75-8 - NEW!	$3.95
Eastern High Sierra- 2nd Ed., ISBN 0-938665-77-4 - NEW!	$8.95
Santa Monica Mountains, ISBN 0-938665-69-3 - NEW!	$8.95
San Bernardino Mountains, ISBN 0-938665-78-2 - NEW!	$8.95
San Gabriel Mountains, ISBN 0-938665-13-8	$8.95
North Lake Tahoe Basin, ISBN 0-938665-34-0	$8.95
South Lake Tahoe Basin, ISBN 0-938665-68-5 - NEW!	$8.95

Prices are subject to change. ©2000 Fine Edge Productions

FineEdge.com
13589 Clayton Lane
Anacortes, WA 98221
Phone: (360) 299-8500
Fax: (360) 299-0535

For trail information check www.MountainBikingPress.com

UP THE LAKE WITH A PADDLE VOLUME 2

Chapter List